PITTSBURGH THEOLOGICAL MONOGRAPH SERIES

General Editor

Dikran Y. Hadidian

23

Signs and Parables

Semiotics and Gospel Texts

The Entrevernes Group

SIGNS AND PARABLES
Semiotics and Gospel Texts

With a study by
JACQUES GENINASCA

Postface by
A. J. GREIMAS

Translated by
GARY PHILLIPS

The Pickwick Press
Pittsburgh, Pennsylvania

1978

Originally published as *Signes et Paraboles; sémiotique et texte évangélique* by Éditions du Seuil, 1977.

Library of Congress Cataloging in Publication Data
Main entry under title:

Signs and parables.

(Pittsburgh theological monograph series ; 23)
Translation of Signes et paraboles.
Includes bibliographical references and index.
1. Jesus Christ--Parables. 2. Jesus Christ--
Miracles. 3. Bible. N. T. Gospels--Criticism, inter-
pretation, etc. I. Geninasca, Jacques. II. Series.
BT375.2.S5313   226'.7'06   78-12840
ISBN 0-915138-35-2

The Entrevernes Group

Entrevernes is a village in the mountains of Haut-Savoy where this project began to take form. The implementation and editing of the book was entrusted to the biblical scholars and semioticians who work together in the Centre pour l'analyse du discours religieux:

> Jean Calloud
> Georges Combet
> Jean Delorme
> Corina Galland-Combet
> Francois Génuyt
> Jean-Claude Giroud
> Louis Panier
> Annie Perrin

Jacques Geninasca, Assistant Professor at the University of Zurich and member of the supervisory committee of l'Association internationale de Sémiotique and of the journal *Semiotica,* has published *Analyse structurale des "Chimères" de Nerval* (Neuchâtel: La Baconnière, 1971) and *Les Chimères de Nerval. Discours critique et discours poetique* (Paris: Larousse, 1973).

Algirdas Julien Greimas, Director of Research at the Ecole des Hautes Etudes en Sciences sociales in Paris, is the author of *Sémantique structurale* (Paris: Larousse, 1966), *Du Sens. Essais sémiotiques* (Paris: Seuil, 1970), *Essais de sémiotique poétique* (Paris: Larousse, 1972), *Sémiotique et sciences sociales*, et *Maupassant. La sémiotique du texte: exercices pratiques* (Paris: Seuil, 1976).

v

TABLE OF CONTENTS

viii

PREFACE TO THE AMERICAN EDITION

Despite the excellent English translation provided
by Gary Phillips, this collective book nonetheless remains
deeply French because of its distinctive reading of miracle
stories and parables. For the American and British scholar
everything about its approach will have a foreign flavor:
the type of questions addressed to the text; the kind of
textual features regarded as particularly significant; the
goal of the studies of specific Gospel texts; the pre-under-
standing with regard to the nature of meaning in general and
of the meaning of a text in particular; and, of course, the
technical vocabulary which is, in effect, a foreign meta-
language.

In brief, this book offers a new vision of the meaningfulness of the Gospel texts which calls exegetes out of their
old visions. Consequently we as exegetes feel deeply threatened, and rightly so, by this work despite the numerous statements emphasizing that the approach taken here neither invali-
dates nor is a substitute for exegesis and its various goals.
As exegetes we have committed ourselves to the task of elucidating *what* the biblical text meant and means. We assume
that this elucidation is the condition for a proper understanding of the biblical text by our contemporaries; and we
place the blame for our eventual failure to reach this ultimate goal on the various methodological flaws which prevent
adequate elucidation of one or the other aspects of the meaning of the text. The type of study presented in this book,
one which the authors refuse to consider as a form of exegesis, quietly challenges the preceding assumption by bracketing
out any consideration of *what* the text meant and means in

order to elucidate *how* the text meant and means. Of course, we, as exegetes, often study *how* the text meant and means but this research has as its goal to establish some aspect of the meaning of the text (the *what*). By contrast, the authors aim at studying *how* the text is meaningful for its own sake. Indeed, they presuppose that the condition for a proper understanding of the biblical text by the modern reader is an understanding of how it is meaningful through a deconstruction of the text's meaning effect. The results of exegesis are valid and useful indeed; it would be impossible to understand the mechanism which produces the meaning effect without understanding the "meaning" of words, symbols, sentences, and other larger textual units. However, these exegetical concerns are no longer an end in themselves but are a means toward another end. In fact, reading a text is not appropriating its meaning (viewed implicitly or explicitly as an object) but rather "constructing our relationship to the text" (cf. Epilogue: 2. "Another Relation to the Text"). Deconstructing the text as to how it is meaningful through the analysis of the relational network of its textual features has as an effect the construction of our relationship to the text by leading us to see our own experience through a similar relational network.

We can appreciate the value of such a view expressed in a related way by the so-called "New Hermeneutic School." Yet in most instances this view does not affect our way of studying the text because we maintain a distinction between the exegetical and hermeneutical tasks to such a degree that the main goal of our exegeses remains that of elucidating certain aspects of the textual meaning. For us, "constructing our relationship to the text" is the task of hermeneutics. In their approach the authors imply that the primary study of the text—the analysis—should itself reflect the relational nature of the text's meaning effect.

In this fashion the authors challenge us to see the text in another way and thus to have "another relation to the text." We immediately resist their approach because, in challenging our view of the meaning of the text, they challenge our very *raison d'être*.

It is quite possible that we may eventually wish to reject their approach and its presuppositions concerning the nature of "meaning" and the phenomenon of interpretation (hermeneutics) but in this moment their book deserves a fair hearing. Whether we ultimately accept or reject their view of the text, we shall be enriched by a true dialogue with them. For this purpose we must take the risk of overcoming our initial resistance and its manifestation through superficial objections and artificial appropriations.

One such superficial objection to a semiotic approach of the text has to do with the technical vocabulary employed. It is easy to brand it "incomprehensible jargon," and thus to have an excuse for not taking semiotics seriously into account. The authors have striven for a minimal use of technical vocabulary. Yet, they have had to make use of a new meta-language precisely because their approach involves a new vision of the text. Far from being superfluous or gratuitous, such a meta-language is necessary. Just as it is crucial to study Greek in order to gain a better understanding of the Greek vision of reality, in the same way learning the semiotic meta-language gives us access to the semiotic vision of the text. It is in fact a rather limited vocabulary which can be relatively easily appropriated as it is progressively introduced in the unfolding of the book (note that the collection of essays has been organized so as to provide a pedagogical progression).

A second type of superficial objection concerns the kind of questions the authors raise and the results they obtain. It is true that most of their research can be brushed aside

as not providing answers to our exegetical questions. We
would like for them to reach some conclusion concerning what
a given text means or what characterizes the genres "miracle
story" and "parable." We grow impatient because of their way
of "skirting" these issues especially when, at times, they
seem so close to providing very "interesting" conclusions.
But once again it must be said that their sole aim is to show
how it is that the text is meaningful.

A third way of avoiding true dialogue with our authors
is by way of an artificial appropriation of their research--
by using results from their research without adopting their
vision of the meaningfulness of the text. For example, we may
want to learn how the text is meaningful so as to use this
knowledge (for instance, by means of a structural exegesis) to
elucidate one or another aspect of the meaning of the text
(the *what* of the text conceived as an entity rather than as a
meaning effect). My own research aimed at developing a method
of structural exegesis as a practical application of theoretical semiotic research could easily be misinterpreted in this
way. My exegetical goal, however, is to elucidate a specific
level of the meaning of a text: the "system of deep values"
it presupposes (cf. Daniel Patte and Aline Patte, *Structural
Exegesis. From Theory to Practice,* Philadelphia: Fortress
Press, 1978). This level of meaning could be construed as a
dimension of the *what* of the textual meaning, despite the fact
that in my view it is a network of semantic relations which
contributes significantly to the way in which (the *how*) the
text offers a diversity of potential meaning effects. In
turning away from theoretical semiotic research, I do not do
so at the expense of its vision of the meaningfulness of the
text. The book by the Group Entrevernes provides a necessary
complement to my own research at the theoretical level as well
as to structuralist practical research, as it is taking place

within the Society of Biblical Literature. This will help
us in keeping our specific exegetical goal and the vision of
the text that it presupposes in view.

The fact that I in my own work have chosen to walk the
thin edge between semiotics and exegesis as contrasted with
the authors' resolute pursuit of a semiotic theoretical quest
is a matter of emphasis. Both the Group Entrevernes and I
have the same vision of the meaning of the text. Rightly or
wrongly, and I am not the one to judge this, my research focuses on certain types of relations which, in my view, are
the most helpful ones in elucidating primary characteristics
of the meaning effect of a particular text, *i. e.*, how a
given text produces meaning in its own specific way. By contrast, the authors' research here is much broader to the extent that they are concerned with many other kinds of relations; they constantly aim at elucidating both the significant
characteristics of a given text and how texts *in general* are
meaningful. Their book contributes significantly to the development of semiotic research as A. J. Greimas notes in his
Postface. For this reason, the book offered here addresses
the reader at two levels: it can be read both by those who
want to introduce themselves to a semiotic or theoretical
approach (owing to its pedagogical character) and by those
already involved in semiotic and structuralism research of
biblical texts (owing to the progress and advancement in
extending semiotic research).

The reader should be aware of the composite nature of
the book. As a consequence of the diversity of interests on
the part of different contributors there is a diversity of
methodological approaches. Jacques Geninasca's specialization
in semiotics of poetry leads him to focus his analysis on
"symbolic" (my term) relations. By contrast, both A. J.
Greimas and the Group Entrevernes, who have devoted much time

to narrative semiotic research, emphasize, as the first step of their analyses, the narrative organization of the text. Greimas' concern to establish a general literary semiotics can be perceived in his *Postface*, while the Group Entrevernes' interest in the semiotics of religious discourses appears most clearly in their two concluding chapters. These complementary approaches woven together in this book offer the reader a multifold entrance into the semiotic vision of the text.

Daniel Patte
Vanderbilt University
June 1978

TRANSLATOR'S PREFACE

The emergence of semiotic methods bodes a new and ex-
citing era in the analysis and interpretation of biblical
texts. The more traditional historico-critical methods with
their paradigms of knowledge and truth have now to make room
for different methods whose views of text and meaning are
heavily dependent upon an understanding of communication
theory, linguistics and semiosis. The more often semiotic
methods (and here the stress is upon the *plurality* of methods)
are employed in the reading of biblical texts, are refined
and thus made available to the scholarly community, the more
likely the possibility that those persons unfamiliar with
semiotic approaches can benefit from their contribution.
Equally as important, however, is the critique that will be
brought reflexively back upon such methods. The reader's
rightful demand for clarity of thought, precision of word
and pertinence of application are crucial for the development
of any method and in particular semiotic ones whose structural
linguistic and communication presuppositions frequently appear
confusing if not contradictory. Only in the arena of public
inspection and debate will semiotic methods develop their full
potential as analytic tools.

   It is with the hope of such greater familiarity and
thorough-going critique that this translation of *Signes et
Paraboles* is made available to the English reading public.
Despite its composite methodological character the attempt
has been made to employ a common terminology. This seems
justified given the common dependence upon the semiotic approach fashioned by A. J. Greimas. Furthermore, in opting

for a series of exegetical essays the authors have chosen
not to enter into methodological definition or debate. For
that type of discussion the reader must look to the excellent
introduction by Joseph Courtès, *Introduction à la sémiotique
narrative et discursive* (Paris: Hachette, 1976) and the journal *Semiotique et Bible* published by Le Centre pour l'analyse
du discours religieux under the section entitled "Rudiments
d'analyse" (vols. 1-9). We shall all be aided in this regard
by the publication and proposed translation of Greimas' *Sémiotique: dictionnaire raisonné et comparé* (Hachette, 1978).

Finally, I would like to express my gratitude to those
persons who have aided me throughout the course of this project. To professors Calloud and Delorme and my other friends
of the Groupe d'Entrevernes; to Professor Greimas who gra-
ciously included me within his seminar in Paris; to Pickwick
Press and the patient General Editor, Dikran Hadidian; but
most especially to Professor Daniel Patte who was instrumen-
tal in involving me in the translation project and who has
spent long hours in proofing the translation, I express my
deep appreciation.

Gary A. Phillips
Vanderbilt University
June 1978

PREFACE

This book is a collective work. A. J. Greimas, whose
research has been a constant source of inspiration for us,
kindly agreed to offer his comments on our work in a Postface. J. Geninasca has repeatedly enlightened and stimulated
us in our undertaking; the study with which he has entrusted
us and which we publish here is a witness to that fact.

Our workshop, in collaboration with many persons, has
labored over the past several years: through late evenings,
on weekends and in summer sessions. When it came time to
implement and edit this work, the communication among us was
such that any question of individual copyright was out of
place. In the midst of a common methodology we have all
benefited from the exchange which comes from a variety of
competencies. The exchange has encouraged rather than dis-
couraged the differences existing among us. The diversity
of writings from one chapter to the next bears witness to
that fact.

We are guided by a two-fold interest: on the one hand
in the Gospels and on the other hand in the way in which
texts signify. We turn to the Gospels for reasons other than
that of pure knowledge. Yet as soon as we begin to be interested by their meaning, the questions which arise call for
a reflection which is controlled and which guarantees its
own coherence. The most common question is known to all:
what does this text wish to say? Exegesis is equipped with
certain principles and procedures in order to answer this
question. Its results are used largely today even in the
most popular editions of the Bible. Another question comes

1

to mind: how does it happen that there is meaning? As with
any text, the Gospels appear as a series of signs to be de-
ciphered. What is it that organizes them into a readable and
sensible discourse? That is the question which interests us
here.

It is out of the latter question that a new discipline,
semiotics, which strives for the elucidation of signifying
systems wherever meaning is produced, sprang forth.[1] We
wanted to test its hypotheses and its procedures upon the
Gospels. It was necessary for us to serve our apprenticeship
with patience. Others have taken an interest in our progress.
However, semiotics still remains for many either a domain en-
shrouded in mystery or a desirable path to follow, but a path
sown with pitfalls. Some suspect it of concealing sinister
goals. It is for this reason that we risk writing this book.

Let us be more specific about our intentions.

1. WHY?

We have often been asked: if it is the operation of
meaning in texts which intrigues you, why do you choose to
study the Gospels? Are you not afraid of robbing them of
their persuasive force, of their sacred character? We prefer
to say: if it is proper to question texts about the way in
which they signify, why not the Gospels? Are they not writings? This would not be the first time that they offered a
favorable ground for research upon language. By scrutinizing
them, grammarians of ancient Greek, philologists and specialists in oral tradition have tested and oftentimes perfected
methods of analysis which had not been conceived particularly
for the Gospels. The history of exegesis shows us that

present-day questions about the text--its relationship to
the reading, the plurality of meanings in the Scriptures--
are older, more convoluted and more stubborn than oftentimes
imagined. The semiotics of discourse of the text[2] enables
us to take up these questions again from a new angle and with
controllable instruments. Why not do this with writings
which continue to stimulate research? Indeed, we think that
the believing community and the use that it makes of its
Scriptures invite this sort of approach to the text.

From Reading to Semiotics

The Gospels were not transmitted for the purpose of
being preserved in a shrine. If we allow a theological,
exegetical, literary or historical discourse about the Gospels to become repetitive, they thereby become imprisoned.
In that case we want to transmit *a* meaning, *a* reading; an
ideology is established, the speech is closed off, the book
is shut.

Fortunately, experience teaches us that one cannot read
the Gospels without risk. Perhaps here more than in any
other place, the reader can say to himself that this reading
could take place in another way. The meaning is never acquired once and for all. It must always be reinvented; the
book opens itself, offers the word and invites speaking. It
loses its taboo value and becomes the instrument of a quest.

Readings of the Gospels today take many tracks. Often
they are left to themselves. It also happens that they would
like to be controlled. Then the "spontaneous" readings reveal a greater conformist attitude than one would like. It
appears that it is not enough to attempt to vary the points

of view taken toward the text in order for the text to
change its tone. Whatever may be the "reading perspective"
adopted, we can make it speak just as easily as we can render it silent. We are faced with an inevitable problem:
what relationship does a writing hold with its readers?

This problem cannot be resolved by experience alone.
Experience would provide nothing other than another reading
even if it aspired to a super-reading. A theoretical reflection about the conditions without which there could be
neither text nor reading is necessary. And in order for us
to make these conditions apparent we cannot do without
"models." Every reader recognizes the necessity for grammatical models in order to understand sentences, especially
if he happens to read an old book or one in a foreign language. But the problem is much broader than this. The discourse and the text, which integrate several sentences without being their sum total, call for other models which semiotics seeks to construct and to test.

A theory of meaning cannot be replaced by the discourse
and the text. Is this not a new tyranny by a third party
protected by intimidating concepts, which inserts itself in-
between the readers and the object of their pleasure or concern? On the contrary. Bringing to light the mechanisms of
meaning production liberates the power-to-read. It stimulates the creative faculty which functions through and upon
the text. We have only to think of the theories in physics:
by inserting themselves as a third party in-between man and
nature they have liberated man's power over nature.

Concerning Meaning

It has been repeatedly written that semiotics is not a technique for establishing the meaning of an oral or written discourse. This is quite true. By refusing to be such a technique, semiotics is free to be more concerned with meaning but in a more fundamental way than in any exegesis. And when it verifies its hypotheses upon a particular discourse it is indeed the meaning of *this* discourse which is questioned.

However, we think that there is an advantage in scrutinizing a text, not as if the meaning were already there and as if it were enough to extricate the meaning in order to repeat it, but as if the meaning were produced by an internal mechanism. It is a matter of locating this mechanism, or rather of simulating it, for it cannot be observed. By virtue of what relations between what elements does a text produce meaning? By means of what interplay of rules of combination and transformation? Semiotics constructs a representation of this signifying process using for this purpose an unambiguous language (a "metalanguage") which is ultimately capable of describing how any text becomes meaningful without taking up the text's terms again or paraphrasing them.

Thus to consider meaning from the standpoint of its internal conditions of production is not to avoid it nor to reduce it but to expose it at its very roots. It is possible in this way to appreciate what is at stake (with respect to the meaning) in the ambiguities of the letter which have often made the exegete waver. It is possible to evaluate the divergence between a text, its variants, the commentaries upon it and the discourses through which its readers prolong it.

Yet, semiotics does not have an answer for everything.
It explores the *how* of the meaning, not the *why*. It does
not steal its task and its criteria for evaluating meaning
away from the philosopher, the hermeneut or the theologian.
However, it offers them the occasion for putting their tasks
and criteria into operation, perhaps for redefining them in
function of a reasoned explanation and no longer in function
of an experience of meaning which is immediately sought.

2. HOW?

The Selection of the Pericopes to be Examined

We have singled out four pericopes from the Gospels
for the purpose of analyzing them. The operation is not
without its risks especially when the semiotic point of
view is adopted. For this point of view, the relations
predominate over the elements that they articulate and the
overall organization of a text over its component parts.
This provisional decision was imposed upon us as a matter
of convenience and for pedagogical reasons: relatively
short texts lend themselves to practical examination where
the procedures for analysis can be better observed and the
tools more easily presented whenever their use is required.

The pericopes were not chosen haphazardly. We have
taken up parables and miracle stories because they raise
acutely the problem of signification. Within the Gospels
the parables and the miracles of Jesus call for an interpretation; both of these ways of signaling—both in words
and in deeds—are built upon a system of signs, namely
that of the text which fashions the narrative out of them.
The terrain is particularly suited for a semiotic exploration.

Consequently, we shall attempt to consider in the same way both types of narrative. When reading, no one confuses these types of narratives which the experts characterize as distinct "literary forms." For the sake of differentiating parables from miracle stories, numerous studies have organized them into separate categories in order to compare them either with rabbinic parables or with the miracles attributed to Jewish and Hellenistic miracle workers. We shall not follow this track. It is quite clear that the parabolic narratives attributed to Jesus and the stories told about his miracles demand different treatments if we are concerned with their origin, their history and literary pre-history. Their differences do not carry the same weight if we question the immanent conditions of their signification. And since the Gospels integrate elements which are of so dissimilar a nature into their narratives, it becomes crucial for us to determine just what this difference *signifies*.

The Proposed Trajectory

The four analyses deal alternately with two pericopes taken to be parables (Chapters I and III) and two others considered to be miracle stories (Chapters II and IV). These analyses will open the way for a more comprehensive study of parables and miracles and of their function within the Gospel narrative (Chapter V).

The first four chapters can be viewed as practical exercises from which the readers will be able to familiarize themselves with the analytical tools. It happens that people find the language of semiotics to be tedious. Is it not enough to observe the text carefully in order

for it to deliver up its secrets? Certainly the observations made about a text are always of interest, but how
can we determine their importance when it comes to explaining the meaning produced? In this instance, as in others,
observation leads to explanation only if we can lay out
some hypotheses and the models that they generate in such
a way that the abstract terms will be defined and illustrated by the analysis as it progresses. We have provided
many terminological footnotes, especially in Chapter I.
With the aid of the index, the reader will easily locate
the definition of the technical words that we employ.

In moving on to Chapter IV, the reader will sense that
a change has taken place. The first three chapters bear witness in their diversity to a common labor undertaken by our
research group: the reader is immediately struck by their
common source of inspiration. Several of us have attended
the seminar of A. J. Greimas at l'École des Hautes Études
en Sciences Sociales. We owe our procedures and models to
Greimas. Chapter IV comes from J. Geninasca, Professor at
the University of Zurich, who took an active part in our
working sessions. His approach to the pericope of the "Abundant Catch" in Luke owes much to the experience he has gained
from the analysis of poetic texts, in particular the *Chimères*
of Nerval. Jacques Geninasca tries to test the operational
character of his hypotheses according to which Luke's narrative, like a poem which is articulated in strophes and groups
of strophes, is constituted by the relations that are maintained between the unities (which he calls discursive unities).
These unities are definable first and foremost by a relation
of semantic equivalence with respect to which the parallelisms
observable at the surface level of the Greek text function as

an index. This accounts for the priority that Geninasca
gives to the textual articulations which precede the establishment of narrative connections. As much from the point of
view of analytic procedures as in the form of the semantic
representations, the differences separating his approach from
ours do not, however, cast doubt upon our basic agreement on
a common theory of signification.

Chapter V will perhaps appear ambitious, but we could not
restrict ourselves to the semiotic description of just certain
passages from the Gospels. It was necessary to compare them
one with the other and to consider their function within the
Gospel text which incorporates them. And since we are dealing
here with short pieces classified into different literary
genres, we were led to consider all of the parabolic narratives and the miracle stories in order to formulate certain
hypotheses. The analyses which are presented here do not
sufficiently ground these hypotheses and we were unable in
this book to give a detailed verification of them by presenting the analysis of each Gospel pericope involved. We wanted
to illustrate rather than to prove the fruitfulness of the
semiotic point of view for the study of larger segments of the
Gospel literature. The historical preoccupation found in most
exegetical studies dealing with these texts did not permit
exegetes to examine how, in different ways, two types of texts
produce meaning in a much larger text which sustains them,
affects them, and is affected by them. With any new point of
view there are new questions.

At the conclusion of this trajectory we will go back
over the path we have traveled. Some clarification will be
given to the choices made and the steps taken. We will compare them with other ways of approaching and questioning a

text (regardless of what it may be). Some important questions will be considered so as to open the way to a new approach to the Gospel or biblical text. Some readers will no doubt hurry on to these concluding pages. Let them realize that they are not intended to be conclusive and they cannot be separated from a specific way of reading and of analysis which must be carried further.

Since the route that we have tried to follow has been opened up and marked out by the theoretical reflection and the analytic efforts of A. J. Greimas, we have submitted our essays to him. For the kind and critical attention that we have received from him and for his interest in our work as manifested in the Postface written for this book, we offer him at this time our deepest thanks.

The mode of communication which has governed the collective implementation of our effort would be deceiving were it to be taken as an authoritative discourse now that it has been fixed in written form. On several occasions the text has been reworked; whenever anything is said there is always something to say (critically) about it. We have found pleasure and benefit in the exchange. We hope that others will have the same experience even if it involves challenging our work.

NOTES

1. F. de Saussure called *semiology* the "general science
of signs." By the term *semiotic* Charles S. Pierce designated
a "quasi-necessary or formal doctrine of signs." Both terms
are often used as synonyms for one another or as complementary terms for designating the study of systems of signs.
Hjelmslev proposed reserving *semiotics* for particular domains
(literary, gestural, pictoral) and *semiology* for the general
theory of semiotics. The international usage ("Association
Internationale de Sémiotique," which publishes the journal
Semiotica) tends to downplay "semiology" in favor of "semiotics." We ourselves refer in this text to the semiotics of
discourse or of *text*, studied as a meaning-producing organization.

2. The *semiotics of discourse* benefits from the work in
linguistics while posing problems in a totally different way.
Linguistics views them as emerging from within the framework
of the sentence; discursive semiotics views them in the dimension of a discourse which is ordinarily made up of several
sentences. The *analysis of the narrative* as a signifying
organization has been decisive for the passage from a linguistics of the sentence to a semiotics of discourse. We
speak rather indifferently and in an approximate way of *discourse* and *text*. Quite pragmatically, in the studies which
are to follow the discursive organization presents itself in
the form of written texts. It will be apparent at once that
the text is distinguished from purely oral discourse by certain important characteristics and that it offers certain
advantages to the analysis.

I.

"Go and Do Likewise"

Narrative and Dialogue (Luke 10:25-37)

Luke 10:25-37

25*And behold, a lawyer stood up to put him to the test saying: "Teacher, what shall I do to inherit eternal life?"* 26*He said to him, "What is written in the Law? How do you read it?"* 27*He responded, "You shall love the Lord your God with all your heart, with all your soul and with all your mind, and your neighbor as yourself."* 28*And he said to him, "You have responded rightly. Do this and you will live."* 29*But wanting to justify himself, he said to Jesus, "And who is my neighbor?"* 30*Jesus replied:*

"A man was going down from Jerusalem to Jericho and fell into the hands of robbers who having stripped him and beat him departed leaving him half-dead. 31*By chance, a priest was going down that road; he saw him and passed by on the other side.* 32*Likewise, a levite when coming to this place saw him and passed by on the other side.* 33*But a samaritan while journeying came where he was; he saw him and was filled with compassion,* 34*and he went to him, bound up his wounds, pouring on oil and wine; then he placed him on his own beast and led him to an inn and took care of him.* 35*The next day he took out two denari and gave them to the innkeeper saying: 'Take care of him and whatever more you spend I will repay you on my return.'* 36*Which of these three do you think proved neighbor to the one who fell into the robbers' hands?"* 37*He said, "The*

13

*one who showed mercy to him." Jesus responded to him: "Go
and do likewise."*

"And behold a lawyer stood up and said to him ..." The
entry onto the stage and then the exit of this new character
in the Gospel of Luke marks the boundary of a narrative which
can quite readily be lifted out of the book. In a more or
less intuitive, specific way every reader finds it to be
meaningful. This suffices to stimulate our curiosity: how,
namely, is meaning produced? By what internal mechanism?
It is clear that the place and function of this narrative in
the book contribute to its meaning. But within its boundaries
it offers sufficient material for analysis. In order to
familiarize ourselves with the problems and the instruments
of the semiotic analysis of the text, a short passage will
serve better to focus our attention.

First of all, let us see how the text is presented.

Without any difficulty two sections can be distinguished.
Each begins with a question from the lawyer: "What shall I
do to inherit eternal life?" (v. 25)[1] and "Who is my neighbor?" (v. 29). Each section is concluded by a command from
Jesus: "Do this and you will live" (v. 28) and "Go and do
likewise" (v. 37). These elements parallel one another but
nevertheless present certain points of difference. Each of
the lawyer's two questions has its own particular function.
With the first he "tests" Jesus; with the second he wishes
"to justify himself." The first of Jesus' two commands refers to the words of the Law which were just quoted ("this"),
while the second refers to the behavior of one of the characters in the story told by Jesus ("Do likewise"). These
points of difference signal the presence of *transformations*
within each section and from one section to the other.

Within the discourse of both sections we can also note

the movement of elements which will have to be examined.
Jesus does not answer the two questions addressed to him by
the lawyer but counters both with a question. Jesus' first
counter-question ("What is written in the Law?"), however,
leads the lawyer to quote his reference, while the second
brings to a close the narrative of a man who had fallen
into the hands of robbers and transforms the lawyer's previous question. The latter question--"Who is my neighbor?--
becomes "Which of these three do you think proved himself
neighbor to the man who fell among robbers?" These shifts
thus signal a *progression* in the debate. Do the Law which
is quoted and the story which is told have comparable functions here? We will have to ask the same question about
another substitution, namely that of the actors and roles.
Indeed, Jesus' commands follow upon an evaluation: in the
first instance it is Jesus' assessment of the Law quoted by
the lawyer--"You have answered rightly"; in the second it is
the lawyer's assessment solicited by Jesus with regard to
the story--"Which of these three do you think proved himself
neighbor ...?"

These indices suffice to manifest the presence of transformations and so of a narrative progression. All of the
text is geared toward the production of meaning. It is a
matter then of describing and explaining this process with
the aid of models which have been developed for the purpose
of analyzing narratives. Since this text tells of a debate
within which a character in turn tells a story, we shall
carry out the analytical procedure twice. The meaning emerges
from a totality of organized elements; thus it would be preferable to move from the text as a whole to the narrative
incorporated within it. But for pedagogical reasons we will
follow the reverse route: the shorter story requires a
simpler set of tools than does the debate.

A. THE NARRATIVE:
"A MAN WENT DOWN FROM JERUSALEM TO JERICHO"

In the debate between Jesus and a lawyer, the story
which is told by Jesus introduces new characters.[2] The in-
terrupted debate then picks up again with the question posed
by Jesus to his interlocutor: "Which of these three proved
himself to be neighbor to the one who fell among robbers?"
This question clearly indicates that the story is used for
the purpose of the debate, but it nevertheless constitutes
a meaningful unit which can be analyzed in and of itself.

At first glance we quickly discover an interplay of similarities and differences; certain contrasts, underscored by
repetitions, appear clearly. For instance, the samaritan's
acts are the opposite of the robbers' acts. The priest, the
levite and the samaritan all see the half-dead man, but the
first two "passed by on the other side" whereas the third
"was filled with compassion and went to him." But behind
these initial, obvious oppositions there lies a more subtle
interplay of relations among the characters; other relations
are taking shape. For example, the encounter between the
man and the robbers ("He fell among robbers") as well as the
arrival of the priest and levite ("by chance," "likewise")
are characterized as being unexpected. Again, the robbers
as well as the priest and levite when leaving the scene
separate themselves from the half-dead man. But whereas
the priest and levite go down from Jerusalem to Jericho,
the robbers and the samaritan move off in no specific direction. Finally, one character stands out in contrast to
all of the others: "a certain man" is the only one who
does not fall into a precise social category.

This interplay of relationships goes against the

impression of a fortuitous succession of events and characters. The only one who remains on stage from the story's beginning to its end--the man--manifests a narrative progression
through his successive states. But he is not the only one to
change. The other actors are also transformed through the
course of the action. Taken together they represent a global
transformation of the meaning on front-stage. We must now
search for a way to describe and to evaluate this transformation.

The analysis of the narrative has two primary points of
view. Each point of view enables us to consider but a single
aspect of the text and leaves aside a remainder for consideration from another vantage point. There are two types of internal organization which contribute to the production of
meaning. The one has to do with the *narrative* component common to every narrative, whether it be a story in picture or
in film, or an oral or written narrative discourse. The other
type of organization is characteristic of linguistic discourse
as such and concerns what we shall call the story's *discursive*
component. This distinction will be made more specific as
it is put to use.

1. THE NARRATIVE ORGANIZATION

The narrative organization assures the coherence of the
succession of the narrative elements. It regulates the passage from an ititial state to a final state by way of a
transformation. In the case of our pericope, for example,
the man's state changes first as a result of the intervention
of the robbers and then of the samaritan. States and transformations may be transcribed in the form of a relation between the two posts of *subject* and *object*. In stripping the
man, the robbers assume the position of subject with respect

to an object which they acquire and the man loses. We will say that they pass from a state of disjunction to a state of conjunction with the object, whereas the man submits to just the opposite transformation. In fact, the half-dead man represents a *subject of state* disjoined from certain values related to life (valeurs de vie); the samaritan as the *operating subject* undertakes to transform the man into a subject of state conjoined with the object-life. The states and transformations are linked together in a chain-like fashion into a *narrative program* which lies behind the unfolding, narrated actions. We shall try to show this.[3] Our attention will be directed to the characters, their projects and their quests, and the goods and values that they either receive or lose. We will attempt to identify the subject-object relations which underly the narrative and the manner in which they intersect either by being opposed to or being integrated with one another.

The Characters' Quests

Four out of the six characters are in motion at the moment they enter on stage. Movement in and of itself has no significance; it exists only for the sake of an action which is to be performed somewhere or following an action which has taken place somewhere. Therefore, it is inserted within a quest and manifests the desire of a subject for an object.[4] What is the man in search of, or what has he just acquired when he goes down from Jerusalem to Jericho? That we do not know; but we do recognize his position as subject in relation to an object. The same thing holds for the priest, the levite and the samaritan.

The text organizes all of the quests about the man's quest.

The robbers' quest succeeds and interrupts the man's. Not only can he not continue on his voyage nor acquire the object he desires, but also by being left half-dead he is deprived of a value-life that he had at the outset. In order to recover it he is subjected to the possibility of a transformation which he himself is incapable of realizing and which calls for the intervention of another actor as operating subject.

The three characters who next appear show us that the narrative is in search of just such an actor. The priest and levite refuse this role; the samaritan assumes it. The first two characters follow their own quests; the third, without abandoning his own quest--namely that of traveling-- takes up the quest which consists in caring for the wounded man.

However, before tossing the characters into action the text shows us how they are prepared for it.[5]

a. *By knowledge*. All three see the half-dead man. They acquire knowledge about the man's state. In the first two instances, the man is perceived to be an obstacle to be avoided in order to continue traveling; in the third instance, he is perceived as a subject who is deprived of a good which is to be recovered for him. The man's state is interpreted differently: the samaritan's interpretation is characterized by "compassion."

b. *By want*. The knowledge which is acquired and inter- preted prepared the way for the wanting-to-do: for both the priest and levite it is a wanting-to-go-around the man; for the samaritan who "had compassion" it is a wanting-to-give- assistance. What is the source of this wanting? Does it come by way of a command, or as advice, or as an obligation

as in other stories? It is nothing of the sort in this
case. There is no pre-established plan of action for the
priest and levite; they happen onto the scene by chance.
The samaritan finds in himself the source for his wanting
as he does for his knowledge about the man's state (his
compassion). This compassion brings him to choose the
half-dead man's life over his own traveling and thereby
to function as a sender of the wanting which leads him to
action.[6]

c. *By power.* The transformation of the wounded man,
which is undertaken by the samaritan and carried on by the
innkeeper, unfolds within space (alongside the road and at
the inn) and time (one day and the day following). The
power of the operating subject is represented by the oil,
the wine and the mount; they are as much the helpers[7] for
his traveling quest as his money which the samaritan uses
to delegate the innkeeper to continue caring for the man.
The two quests--that of the object sought for by traveling
and that of the restoration of the goods to the man--are
not mutually exclusive. The helpers in the first quest
serve in the second. The expected return of the samaritan
plays a part in both quests as well: it is a part of the
traveling quest and it allows the samaritan to exercise
the power that his money gives him on behalf of the man
up until the end. Likewise, if the innkeeper proceeds
with his quest for an object represented by the money that
he earns, this object is not exclusive of the object that
he can enable the man to obtain.

The Overall Narrative Organization

a. *The Narrative Programs*

The narrative introduces successively onto the stage:

-- A process of degradation: an initial state of con-junction (presupposed by the man's movement) is negated by an anti-subject who appropriates the object (the goods) for himself at the man's expense. A state of disjunction from another object (life) opens up the possibility of a potential program of conjunction for the purpose of recovering this object.

-- The establishment of an operating subject for the conjunction. Of the three actors who are already established in a subject-object relation as indicated by their movement, only the third character acquires the knowledge and the want necessary for the program of conjoining the man to his object.

-- The realization in process of this program of con-junction owing to the power provided by the helpers from a previous program, namely that of his traveling program, which for its part continues to be realized.

The narrative draws to a close with the announced return of the samaritan as if it had to do not so much with the restoration of the man as with the establishment of and per-formance by an operating subject for that restoration. The anticipated conclusion with the samaritan's return is not the return of the man to life nor the taking up again of his tra-vels, but rather the fulfilling of the role which the samari-tan assumes on his behalf. There is a narrative selection here. It points to an act of narration, Jesus' speech act, which is introduced into the debate of which our story is a part.[8]

b. *Programs and anti-programs*

Several narrative programs intersect with the man's program: they either exclude or become compatible with his. The robbers, as operators of a disjunction, represent an anti-subject[9] with respect to the man. We are forced to say the same thing for the priest and levite. We could imagine that they in fact leave the man in the state in which they find him, that they are there to emphasize the samaritan's conduct by means of two deceptive episodes. Popular narration likes to triple the performances: two failures or semi-failures forecast success. However, according to the text the priest and levite do not merely continue on their way; they pass by on the other side. The man is left aside and deprived of one additional value. The lack is aggravated (we will return to this point in the discursive analysis). However, from now on we must register the priest and levite as disjunctive operators. Although they belong to another order of values, they, along with the robbers, represent an anti-subject, whereas the samaritan with the aid of the innkeeper is opposed to them all as a conjunctive operating subject.

This narrative organization of the text equips us to recognize the organization of the meaning content as represented by the words and the linguistic phrases which make this story a discourse.

2. THE DISCURSIVE ORGANIZATION

The narrative structures provide the text with a type of skeleton which could compare with another story having other actors in other places. It is important for the meaning that the roles defined by the narrative analysis (operating subject, subject of state, object, helper, anti-subject) be held by "a man," "some robbers," or "a priest," that the lack be expressed by "half-dead," that the transformation be brought about through bodily care, paid with money, etc. These linguistic elements of the discourse are themselves organized. They are meaningful because they are articulated at a level other than that of the narrative structures.

In order to describe this organization we must do away with the illusion which takes the words of a text to be entities endowed with meaning in and of themselves. If that were the case, it would be enough to draw out of the language stock these words with a fixed meaning and to toss them onto the tracks traced out by the narrative structures. In the production of meaning by the discourse the words have a value which is more than themselves in the sense that we do not draw them from out of the lexicon as if it were a sack of marbles; they appear with the traces of their use in previous discourses which have drawn them together and associated them within larger wholes. They are less than themselves to the extent that within the language (la langue) each word already conceals a plurality of potential meanings with each discourse realizing only one or another of them.

The Characters

Let us take the characters as an example. We could narrate many events connected with the robbers. Our story pictures them in an attack upon a traveler, but this is only one of the possible representations of robbers within a discourse. We shall say that this is one of the *figurative trajectories* of a larger set which forms a *discursive configuration* within the language of a given society.[10] We can

say the same thing for the "priest," the "levite," and the
"samaritan," but with this difference: our story introduces
them within a figurative trajectory ("going down" or "traveling") which is in no way specific since it applies as well
to "a man." They assume the same role as traveler, a *role*
which we will call a *thematic role* (in order to distinguish
it from the *actantial roles* defined by the narrative structures).[11] A priest, a levite and a samaritan could be inscribed within other thematic roles in discursive configurations aside from that of traveling. These other roles remain
virtual. Yet they are not at all blotted out; the discourse
produces meaning in its differentiation from other discourses,
that is from the different possibilities presented by the
language. Our text thus introduces a difference between the
priest, the levite and the samaritan, with the latter being
the only one of the three who takes on a new thematic role,
namely that of providing assistance; he is the one who appears in a new configuration. The innkeeper may belong to
the traveling configuration, but he shares as well in the
role of providing assistance.

Through the actions of the characters several discursive
configurations are blended together. Several figurative
trajectories interact with each other so that this "priest,"
this "levite" and this "samaritan" receive a new semantic
definition within this text. In order to analyze this definition we must step down from the figurative trajectories and
thematic roles (which extend beyond and encompass the words)
to the semantic features or *semes* which are units smaller
than the words. Given the fact of the polyvalence of words
how does this text select the simpler features which it re-
peats and combines in order to build a homogeneous meaning?[12]

In the case of our pericope the characters may be
grouped by the contrast in their denominations between those

features approximating or opposing one another: a socio-professional feature, we might say, for the robbers and the innkeeper; a geographico-religious feature for the priest, the levite and the samaritan.[13] These characters, on the other hand, are brought together in opposition to another character who carries no social definition: "a man." The opposition of the features /overdetermined/ and /determined/ can account for this contrast:[14] /overdetermined/ encompasses the differences (that is, the social particularities); /determined/ is here quite simply the fact of being human.

This initial identification of semic features is not very satisfactory. We must now consider the actions of the characters so characterized in terms of their denominations.

States and Transformations of the Characters

By means of the narrative analysis we have distinguished between the subjects who effect a transformation and the only transformed subject, "a man." The former either deprive the latter of values or bestow them upon him. The values are organized along two semantic axes (deux lignes de sens) which are shaped by the repetition of opposing semic features. The operators of lack deprive the man of two types of values: some deprive him of a concrete value (robbers) and others of a more abstract value (priest, levite). Similarly, the transformation of the half-dead man is brought about in a concrete way as a result of the samaritan's and the innkeeper's actions. But even prior to that moment the man received a value from the samaritan which was similar to the one which the priest and levite had disjoined from him: a value belonging to the domain of regard for a person, or better, in accordance with the compassion which distinguishes the samaritan's vision from that of the priest and levite, a value which belongs to the domain of affection.

The concept of *isotopy* accounts for what we have just described as the two semantic axes.[15] Beneath the words of a text elementary features are repeated and create planes of signifieds upon which differences emerge. We found this already to be the case with the denominations of the characters. Two isotopies intersect within these denominations: a socio-professional one and a geographico-religious one. And in each case two posts emerge in contrast to one another. The robbers and the innkeeper in the first instance and the priest, the levite and the samaritan in the second. The same characters are opposed by their very actions which we label, respectively, as the isotopies of the concrete and of affection. There is, however, one difference: the samaritan acts in both isotopies. To appreciate the importance of this fact we must examine the successive states of the man.

Stripped, beaten, and left half-dead: these phrases can be defined in terms of several isotopies. The same applies to the man's forthcoming states. The appeal to the two isotopies—of the concrete and of affection—permits the opposition of two terms in a more precise way. A traveling man and a half-dead man differ with respect to the concrete sphere in the same way as /human/ does to /sub-human/, /living/ to /non-living/. (This last term does not in this case refer to biological death but rather to the negation of bodily wholesomeness and of the capacity to move about and to engage in one's own affairs.) The samaritan is intent upon restoring the values /human/ and /living/ to the man. With respect to the sphere of affection, the half-dead man who is avoided by the priest and the levite and the pitiful being who attracts the samaritan's attention differ in the same way as /rejected/ does to /accepted/.[16] Moreover, the man's states are expressed by means of the spatial and

bodily relations which the various characters establish with
him. On the one hand, he is successively /left/ and /put at
a distance/ or /approached/ and /contacted/ in the spatial
order, and on the other hand /attacked/ and /shunned/ or
/come to/ and /cared for/ in the bodily sphere.

With little difficulty we observe that the man's states
are paired off either dysphorically (non-living and rejected;
left and put at a distance; attacked and shunned) or euphori-
cally (adopted and living; approached and contacted; come to
and cared for). The dysphoric states are the result of
/excluding/ behavior and the euphoric states of /including/
behavior. In fact, the robbers', the priest's and the
levite's quests exclude the man's quest, whereas those of the
samaritan and innkeeper are compatible with his. Exclusion
is expressed in spatial terms by disjunction and inclusion
by conjunction: robbers, priest and levite leave the man
alongside the road and go on their own way; the samaritan
approaches him, takes the man along with him and entrusts
him to the innkeeper's care.

We pointed out above that "a man" differs in denomination
from other characters in the same way that /determined/ differs with respect to /overdetermined/. /Determined/ may be
considered a more fundamental feature which is further specified by the features /human/ and /living/. The trait
/overdetermined/ breaks down into certain opposed characteristics: robbers *vs.* innkeeper; priest and levite *vs.* samaritan. The same feature appears in the priest's and levite's
conduct: their manner of ignoring what is human, of avoiding the half-dead man, of keeping their distance with respect
to him affirms the feature /overdetermined/ under the banner
of /excluding/. By contrast, the samaritan by his compassion
comes into contact with what is human in the man left alongside of the road from Jerusalem to Jericho: he denies what

is /overdetermined/ (the Judean overdeterminism of the man
and his own foreign overdetermination) and affirms the feature /determined/ by concretely restoring the wounded man
to his status as /human/ and /living/ under the banner of
/including/.

The Logico-Semantic Model of the Narrative

The states and transformations of the characters manifest upon the story's stage the manipulation of elementary
units of signification which we have attempted to identify.
We may venture an overall representation of these elements,
their relations and the operations that the text realizes
upon them. Following A. J. Greimas, we have recourse to
the model of the elementary structure of signification:
the semiotic square.[17] It is this model which has guided
our analysis up to this point. Once invested with the
semantic categories that we have constructed on the basis
of this text, it permits us to simulate the functioning
of its signification in the following form:

/EXCLUDING/   /INCLUDING/

/overdetermined/   B   A   /determined/
/rejected/   /human/
/placed at a distance/   /living/
/shunned/   /contacted/
                                          /cared for/

/non-determined/   non-A   non-B /non-overdetermined/
/sub-human/   /adopted/
/non-living/   /approached/
/left/   /come to/
/attacked/

          where A <-> non-A = axis of the concrete
                B <-> non-B = axis of affection

In theory we posit that the narrative transformations represented at the discursive level (the robbers attacking a traveler, etc.) correspond to logical operations upon the elementary contents, A and B, which maintain logical relations between them. We might state these relations as follows: A and non-A, B and non-B are contradictories; A and non-B, B and non-A are in a relation of implication; A and B are contraries; non-A and non-B are subcontraries. These relations make possible two operations: negation, which enables the passage from one term to its contradictory; assertion, which enables the passage from non-A to B or from non-B to A. The succession of both of these operations enables the passage from one term to its contrary (negation of one, then affirmation of the other).

We have placed the fundamental features of our narrative--/determined/ and /overdetermined/--in A and B. The relation of contrariety between the two is not obvious in itself. It is the nature of the narrative to create it.[18] The two contradictory lines correspond to the isotopies of the concrete (A <—> non-A) and of affection (B <—> non-B). The features located beneath /determined/, /overdetermined/ and their contradictories define the textual figures, mainly including the man's states (attacked, avoided, approached, cared for).

Because of the shortness of our text it has the advantage (for the analysis) of creating a double trajectory from A to B and then from B to A. And its originality rests to a large extent in the choice of isotopies (the two contradictory axes). In the isotopy of the concrete the robbers deny A. From there the priest and the levite assert B in the isotopy of affection. Upon becoming sub-human in a concrete state as a result of the robbers' attack, they place the seal of disregard and of distance

upon the relations of the heart and the body. These two
operations fall under the heading of exclusion. The following two operations realize inclusion. In fact, the samaritan contradicts B in the affection isotopy by denying any
separation in the name of some overdetermination either of
one's self or of the other. And this negation makes possible the passage to the isotopy of the concrete by restoring
the wounded man to his worth as a living man. It is this
intersection of the concrete and affection which explains
the way in which this text defines the axis of contraries
as illustrated by the figures of priest and levite (B) and
samaritan (A).

The concrete manifestation of human determination
takes place by the affectionate negation of all overdetermination which would be capable of engendering exclusion. This could be the message suggested by the structure
of our story.

From the Model to Other Figures in the Narrative

From the states and transformations of the characters
we can return to other figures in the text[19]--those of
place and time, for example--to see if the proposed model
integrates them as well.

Up until the samaritan comes onto the stage the
characters are clearly localized: a man falls into the
hands of robbers *between Jerusalem and Jericho;* a priest
comes down by *this* road; a levite happens upon *this* place.
Then from the samaritan's appearance onward, coming as he
does from an unknown place, the spatial movements are reported not in terms of particular places but in terms of
the man: the samaritan happens by close to him; he comes
to him; he leads him to an inn. The latter is not

topographically situated; it is there in order to provide
care for the wounded man's needs, hence it is because the
inn shelters the man that it becomes one pole of the
samaritan's movements. Everything takes place as if the
affirmation of the feature /including/ corresponded to the
wiping away of local characteristics marked as belonging
to the /excluding/ side. Paradoxically, the priest and
the levite exclude the man in-between Jerusalem and Jericho,
that is in the Judean space, which they both have in common
with him and leave to the samaritan, a foreigner, the task
of including him within a space which is not marked by the
text.

The temporal references begin with the samaritan's
arrival: his action involves a "next day" and he anticipates what will happen in the future up to the moment of
his return. A continuity over time corresponds to inclusion, whereas the excluding activities follow upon one
another in a discontinuous fashion lacking any connection
other than that of the unexpected (the man *falls* among
robbers) or chance (which marks the arrival of the priest
and levite).

It is clear that the priest and levite on the one
hand and the samaritan on the other are not opposed to
one another here as the language would lead us to expect.[20]
"By chance" signifies that the priest and the levite in
this text are introduced outside of the figurative trajectory anticipated for "priests" and "levites" by a
dictionary of the culture. Precisely as in the case of
the samaritan, they are both redefined by their relationship with the half-dead man. Instead of opposing them as
called for by the culture upon the geographico-religious
isotopy, this text substitutes the opposition of /includ-
ing/ and /excluding/ which they represent in this case,

upon other isotopies. "Chance" indicates that this priest
and levite are not bound to represent exclusive overdetermination. If their title brands them (as it does the samaritan) with the feature /overdetermined/ in the geographico-
religious domain, chance leaves them in the presence of the
wounded man with the possibility of either affirming or
denying this overdetermination. By affirming it they reverse the order of values associated with their titles
according to the language, for the language situates them
on the positive side of the geographico-religious normality.[21]
In this instance, the positive values which are defined in
relation to the man are manifested by the samaritan. This
divergence between this discourse and the language can in-
tensify the meaning effect produced by the intertextuality.
This way of attributing the negative sign to the two official cultic leaders and the positive sign to a samaritan
who has compassion for a wounded man evokes the classical
antithesis in the Prophets and the Gospels between ritual
sacrifice and mercy.

The robbers and the innkeeper are themselves redefined
in isotopies other than that of the language, but in a less
provocative way. They perform their jobs, as it were,
according to the expectations of the language: the robbers
at the voyager's expense; the innkeeper for the sake of his
clientele and for his own sake. And they realize here the
possibility which is offered by the language of opposing
one another in the same way that stolen money is opposed
to earned money without reversing the order of values which
situates them respectively on the negative and positive
poles of the socio-professional normality.[22]

However, the story does not introduce two different
ways of obtaining money for oneself. It underscores the
economic aspect of the robbers' misdeed less than it does

their violence.[23] Even if the man were robbed, it is not
the lost goods which are considered as the lack to be recti-
fied but rather his half-dead state. It is a matter of restoring him to his status as a living and not as a rich
human being. The samaritan's money will not be given to him;
it will be spent for the sake of his health and the innkeeper
is there to make certain that this is the intended goal for
the money he receives. Thus, the /economic/ feature which
according to the language is common to both the robbers and
the innkeeper also characterizes the samaritan. This trait
is accounted for on the isotopy of the concrete: the economic goods acquired in and of themselves by the robbers illustrate the concrete and exclusive character of the negation
of the /determined/, /human/, and /living/ values. The assertion of these values, which is itself also concrete but
inclusive, is illustrated by the money spent on behalf of
others.

We see that the opposition of the contraries /over-
determined/ and /determined/ as constructed by this text
does not reproduce that which could make a difference at
the level of the language between several characters overdetermined by an official title or social affiliation and
a character simply determined as a man. The contrast that
their denomination establishes between them is a way of
calling attention to a semantic axis; the discourse re-
serves for itself the definition of the isotopy by having
the actors act and react to the presence of "a man."

3. PROVISIONAL RESULTS

There is quite a distance, the reader might say, from
the narrative as it is read in the Gospel of Luke to the
narrative skeleton, and then to the semic model that we
have abstracted from it. In order to represent the semic

values[24] and their interrelation, would not other characters,
actions and places do? Rather than a priest and levite, why
not a lawyer and a pharisee? Why not a sinner instead of a
samaritan? Moreover, we are speaking only of characters who
are typical of the Gospel literature and of the cultural
milieu to which it belongs. In another society of discourse,
could not the structure set forward here be invested with
other individual or collective actors? Without any doubt
we must answer yes.

By drawing attention to several levels in the interplay
of meaning the analysis leads to a description which comes
closer and closer to the individual text. However, what is
unique about it always manages to escape the description in
some way. At the very least we can establish varying degrees
of kinship between a text and other texts, whether realized
or virtual, on the basis of a matrix which is common to them
all. This type of analysis is demanded in particular for
narratives which are ordinarily considered to be parables,
which are able to be rewritten for different applications and
are capable of being perceived in a number of variant forms.

One additional remark. Our narrative has been analyzed
as if it had no narrator. In the form in which it has been
taken from out of its context it is spoken in the third person without any indication of some "I" who speaks it or a
"you" to whom it would be directed. However, the organization
of its elements betrays a choice: the underlying structure
presupposes a structuration. The abbreviated conclusion of
the narrative and its focus upon the operating subject and
not upon the restoration of the man reflects a narrative
strategy. It is precisely the context which situates the
enunciation of this narrative. It is Jesus, a character in
Luke's Gospel, who recounts the narrative in response to a
lawyer's question. This fact gives rise to the effect and

transformation of meaning that we must now examine. We can already anticipate that the subversive power of this short narrative will not be neutralized.

B. THE DEBATE:
"BEHOLD, A LAWYER STOOD UP TO PUT HIM TO THE TEST"

As in the case of the story we will make a distinction between the narrative and discursive structures. In other words, we will treat the debate as a story. Can the analytic procedures established for the study of narrative be applied to a dialogue? The answer is yes. But this dialogue will force us to present our tools with more precision. At the same time we will try to progress in our understanding both of these tools and of the text.

1. THE NARRATIVE ORGANIZATION

The Lawyer's Two Questions

The lawyer asks two questions one right after the other. In each instance the text distinguishes between what he says (the stated question) and what he does when saying it (by the act of enunciation). The first time he "puts Jesus to the test"; the second time he wants "to justify himself." In both cases the object at stake is knowledge. In the first instance the lawyer attempts to find out what Jesus knows with the intention of evaluating and thereby of acquiring a knowledge about him. In the second he wants to be recognized: by wanting to justify himself he still aims for knowledge, but this time about himself, a knowledge which Jesus must acquire.[25] This reversal of the situation marks a progress in the narrative.

After stating his questions the lawyer is placed in a narrative program in which his concern is to obtain eternal life, but he lacks the knowledge to do this. "What shall I do to inherit eternal life?"[26] Once he has been informed of what he must do ("You will love the Lord ... and your neighbor ..."), he shows further ignorance about one of the receivers of the "Love" performance: "Who is my neighbor?" In both instances he lacks a competence in knowledge to accomplish the doing upon which the object, the inheritance of eternal life, depends. No other competence features are manifested; we do not know if he wants and is able to realize this performance. The debate focuses exclusively upon knowledge.[27]

The text leads us then to distinguish between two types of knowledge: the one which has to do with a quality, let us say, of *being*, of either Jesus or the lawyer; the other which is a condition for a *doing*, constitutes a competence for the performance.[28] The one is sought after as an object, a value which brings the quest to an end; the other is also acquired but as a modality, that is as a modal object which is necessary for the obtaining of the value.[29] These two types of knowledge characterize two narrative programs whose relationship to one another has need of unraveling.

The First Stage of the Debate: To Test or to Love

The lawyer realizes an initial program ("to test" Jesus) by searching for knowledge about the second program (a doing which leads to an inheritance of eternal life). He asks Jesus to give him information about the second program in order to obtain by interpretative means knowledge about Jesus' being. He pretends not to look for eternal life but for a prior knowledge; and he searches for it as necessary

information not in order to obtain eternal life but in order
to acquire knowledge about Jesus for its own sake. The second
program is inserted within the first. In the first program
the lawyer assumes in practice a role within which he provides
for himself, in the second program, a role in word.[30]

We have just established a new distinction with respect
to the knowledge: there is on the one hand an *informative*
knowledge, an object communicated by a sender to a receiver,
and on the other hand an *interpretative* knowledge, an object
which is acquired by the receiver about the information.[31]

Jesus does not take on the role proposed for him by the
lawyer; he does not provide the answer asked of him. He indicated the place where it is to be sought--in the written
Law. When Jesus in turn asks the question: "How do you read
it?", he is not aiming merely at the content of the reading
(what do you read?), that is the informative knowledge drawn
out of the writings. This question takes for granted that
the reading required a competence, an ability to read, which
leaves the reader in a position to acquire the sought-after
response in the Law for himself. Thus, the lawyer is directed
back to the Law and to himself in order to find out what it is
he has asked of Jesus. In so doing Jesus avoids the test
which the lawyer tries to make him undergo.

The scripture which is cited introduces a speaker who
addresses a "you" in order to tell him what to do in the form
of a commandment--a proposal of wanting--to love God and his
neighbor.[32] "You have responded rightly": Jesus affirms the
fact that the lawyer possesses the informative knowledge
that he has asked of him. He also approved of the lawyer's
reading and recognizes his competence to read correctly:
Jesus performs an act of interpretative knowledge. Thus, it
seems that Jesus turns around and tests the lawyer. We could
imagine the text ending here. Each character would have

acquired or would be in a position to acquire knowledge about the other's competence. In the program of testing, the contest would be scored an even match. But the text is not interested in that, for Jesus adds: "Do this and you will live."

If, in fact, Jesus approves of the lawyer's knowledge, it is for the purpose of introducing him into the program of "loving." Since the lawyer knows how to read and knows what to do, it is up to him to want to and to do so. "Do this": this imperative relays the commandment of the Law. He does not claim any special ability-to-command. Neither the command nor the promise which corresponds to it ("You will live") are dependent upon Jesus' authority.[33]

But this does not mean that Jesus does not assume a specific role in a well defined program. He wants to make the lawyer—who is a competent subject with respect to knowl-edge—into a willing and performing subject. And this implies that instead of looking for knowledge about Jesus' being (as a value-object) the lawyer uses his knowledge as a modal ob-ject for the performance of "love." Jesus removes himself from his questioner's testing program and places himself in the service of a "loving" program so that it might be realized.

The Second Stage of the Debate: To Justify Oneself or to Become Neighbor?

"But wanting to justify himself ..." In relation to the first "testing" program the roles here are reversed: the law-yer wants to make Jesus acquire knowledge about himself. This confirms the failure of his first attempt, but it does not signal a success on Jesus' part. The lawyer puts off the wanting-to-do which Jesus proposes and searches once again for an informative knowledge which is prior to the doing: "And

who is my neighbor?" This search, moreover, is not demanded
by a wanting "to love" but by a wanting "to justify himself."
The knowledge about being remains the sought-after value
object.[34] At that point Jesus tries anew to establish the
lawyer as subject in a program of "loving" which has now
become "loving the neighbor." The competence in terms of
knowledge will be acquired through the interpretation of a
story and no longer of the Law, from which point it will remain for him to pass to a stage of wanting and of doing.

a. *Knowledge*

There are many differences between the story told by
Jesus and the text cited from the Law by the lawyer. In both
instances the knowledge to be acquired requires an act of interpretation: to the question "How do you read it?" there
corresponds the question "Which of these three *do you think*
proved himself neighbor ...?" However the interpretation of
the Law leads to the recognition of a having-to-do which is
in direct response to the question: "What do I do?" The
interpretation of the story leads to knowledge about its
characters which does not directly resolve the problem, "Who
is *my* neighbor?" In order to appreciate the story's function,
it is worth the trouble to compare the question that follows
with the one that precedes it.

"Who is my neighbor?" is transformed into "Who became
neighbor to such a one?" Neighbor: the close relationship
holds in both senses of the term: "My neighbor" may be just
as much the one who is neighbor to me as the one for whom I
am neighbor. But the roles of both characters change in
accordance with their close relationship either preceding or
following a narrative transformation.

Who is the neighbor whom I am to love? In this instance

closeness precedes "loving" and defines the receiver, that
is, the one who is to be loved.[35] Recognition plays a part
in the competence of the operating subject of the program
"to love" (the neighbor is the one who *is*). But if a character becomes neighbor to another, as the counter-question implies, the closeness is a result of a performance the enact-
ment of which is presented by the narrative (the neighbor is
the one who *does*).[36] The receiver is the one who has fallen
into the robbers' hands; the operating subject is to be singled out from among three characters to whom the story lends
this role for the purpose of transforming the man: a priest,
a levite and a samaritan. And it is the latter who is recognized as having become neighbor. He makes himself such by
showing mercy to the man.

The act of interpretation which leads to this recognition comes after the story at the moment of reflection upon
the events. In other texts this is the moment of the hero's
recognition and sometimes even of his glorification. In our
case the actors are entrusted with the recognition not of the
narrative but of its narration: Jesus who tells and the
lawyer who listens. That does not alter the nature of the
operation. On the basis of the completed performance it is
a matter of acquiring a knowledge about the being of the
operating subject. The difference between the story which
is told and the story which is interpreted is appreciable:
the first speaks of aid either given or not given to a half-
dead man; the other of "becoming neighbor" and of "showing
mercy." The passage from one level to another is assured
first of all by Jesus' interpretation and then by the lawyer's
interpretation. In the light of Jesus' question, a narrative
about the providing or not providing of assistance to another
becomes a narrative about becoming or not becoming neighbor.
Jesus depersonalizes the lawyer's question about his neighbor

and projects it upon the actors in the story. In the
telling he shifts and changes the proposed question. By
his questioning he interprets the story and fixes the point
of view for interpreting it. Thus he proposes an ability
to interpret. The lawyer adopts this point of view and may
then read the story and recognize the "neighbor" in "the
one who showed mercy" to the man.

b. Want

If this text were a riddle it could come to a stop
right here. But what was just acquired--an interpretative
knowledge about the doing and being of a subject--is not
enough. Jesus makes way for something else: "Go and do
likewise."

"Go": the imperative puts an end to the debate. It
suggests a movement representing a quest to be realized somewhere else with the competence that was just acquired. The
knowledge about the story's characters is not to be possessed
as if it were some value object, as a thing which is good to
know, but rather as a modal object, as a capacity to be put
to use. "Do likewise" proposes the wanting by bringing the
lawyer around to the program of "justifying himself." Jesus
attempts once again to make a knowing subject into a wanting
and doing subject.

"Do that" takes us back to the text of the Law. With
"do likewise" the action to be realized is no longer in a
relationship of identity with the commandment in the Law but
is in a relationship of similarity with the performance of
one of the characters in the narrative as over against the
two others. If a power-to-command is manifested here it is
no longer sheltered behind the authority of the Law. In
order to come to the point of "doing likewise," it was

necessary to make a detour by way of the story and a new
interpretation of "neighbor." The story does not include an
actor endowed with some power-to-command. The priest and
levite pass by by chance without orders that they must carry
out. By contrast, the samaritan alone discovered, through
his compassion, what he had to do. In concluding the debate
with an explicit order does Jesus perform an authoritative
act comparable to the Law?

It is not in this direction that we must look in order
to identify the role and competence of Jesus. "Do likewise"
in narrative terms means: assume the samaritan's and not the
priest's or levite's role. These three characters in the
story have seen the man lying half-dead alongside the road,
interpreted his state and had to decide upon a program of
action and accomplished it. However, the samaritan has acted
in order to transform the man from being half-dead into being
alive while the other two acted in function of their programs
of exclusion. "Do likewise" covers not only the doing but
also the acquisition of knowledge and wanting: open your
eyes; see the other's needs; conceive a program of action,
decide upon it and realize it. Jesus does not say what must
be done nor does he give the order to do it. He persuades
the lawyer who has just demonstrated his interpretative
ability in a fictional situation to put it to use in reality
by finding out what is to be done in order for him to become
neighbor to another man and by his wanting to do it. Jesus
does not impose knowledge and wanting upon him; he renders
the lawyer capable of acquiring them for himself.[37] Jesus
puts his competence in the service of the lawyer's competence.

The text comes to a close without specifying the lawyer's reaction. Does he in fact take up the program of
"loving the neighbor"? Does he remain in his original program, judging for example that from here on out he has the

means to evaluate Jesus or to justify himself? We do not
know. But we do know how Jesus has tried to establish a new
subject, what competence he has tested him for and what new
competence he attempted to have him acquire. The text stops
here as if Jesus' role were ended. This closing off of the
debate is reminiscent of the narrative's conclusion. We do
not know if the man has recovered his health and taken up
his travels again, but in any case an operating subject was
found to restore him. And as this conclusion to the narrative points back to its enunciator and to his function
within the debate, so also this conclusion to the debate
points to an instance of enunciation and a function of the
text. We shall return to this point later on.

Overall Narrative Organization

In the narration of a debate between Jesus and a lawyer
the text interrelates two narrative programs: the one in
which the lawyer wants to know one of the qualities of Jesus
or to make known one of his own; the other that he states
verbally and which Jesus endeavors to have him adopt in practical terms.

Jesus' program aims at making the lawyer pass from the
first to the second program through a process of persuasion.
This operation consists in having him acquire a knowing and
a wanting competence on his own. The text as a whole manifests Jesus' program. It is the story of the construction of
a competent subject in view of doing ("loving"). This operation presupposes an adequate competence on Jesus' part and
this text shows its being put to use though not its acquisition. It is within this second part of the debate that a
persuasive competence is manifested both in terms of narrative
competence (capacity to interrelate narrative programs) and

interpretative competence (capacity to interrelate two levels of knowledge). This persuasive competence is successfully put to use when making the lawyer acquire knowledge about "loving the neighbor." We do not know if it succeeds in having him acquire the wanting.

The text's dramatic effect consists in the fact that the lawyer is at first engaged in a program and that we do not know in the final analysis if he wants to realize the contrary program for which he has acquired the necessary "know-how."

2. THE DISCURSIVE ORGANIZATION

The text forces us to distinguish clearly between the narrative and the discursive points of view in the analysis: the same words from both text and analysis--for example, the words "knowledge" and "doing"--may express narrative relations or involve more specific semic content. The verb "doing" is repeated several times in the text and the questions and answers exchanged between both interlocutors are equally as well requests for and declarations of knowledge. However, this "doing" is "to love God and the neighbor," "to become neighbor," "to show mercy," "to do like" an actor in the narrative. And the knowledge in this text has to do not only with this "doing" but first of all with a capacity of two of the actors--the one defined as "lawyer," the other called "teacher." In both instances this capacity belongs to the order of competence, or better, of scholarly competence in the sphere of religious morality: one scholar questions another in order to know what he knows and to evaluate his degree of learning. Then he wishes to justify himself as a scholar by posing a question that is asked among persons who value knowledge.[38]

In narrative terms, the text opposes knowledge about

being (sought after as a value object) to knowledge about
doing (proposed as a modal object). This knowledge is opposed in the final analysis to the doing itself. In discursive terms this being and doing are defined by their respec-
tive contents which are opposed to one another in the form
of "being knowledgeable" versus "loving."

Thematic Roles and General Isotopies

A lawyer addresses a "teacher" and "puts him to the
test." These words point to the world and to the language
of didactic discussions upon problems of ethical and religious knowledge. To question and to counter-question, to
read Scripture, to evaluate or to ask the opinion of another,
to try to prove oneself right--all of these figurative trajectories point to a common discursive configuration.[39]
The lawyer acts as a scholar and treats Jesus as if he were
the same.

Jesus appears to behave in just the same way. He
demonstrates a know-how in avoiding the test, in altering
the question and in persuading; this know-how might well
define a "teacher." But only the lawyer calls him such and
Jesus does not reciprocate with this title. He does not
speak for the purpose of evaluating the other's knowledge
nor to display his own. The knowledge that he wants him
first of all to display by quoting the Scripture and then to
acquire by interpreting the story does not play a part in a
program of scholarly investigation; rather it is an aptitude
for "loving." Without claiming this title for himself Jesus
acts like a "teacher," but this term is redefined by means
of its use in the service of "loving" and not of "knowing."
He attempts to make a man of knowledge into a man of practice.

At first sight an organization stands out. The opposed

contents are articulated in two isotopies: that of knowledge
and of practice.[40] We propose to organize them in this way:

/sufficiency/   C 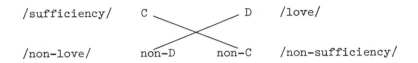 D   /love/

/non-love/   non-D   non-C   /non-sufficiency/

where $C \longleftrightarrow$ non-C = axis of knowledge

$D \longleftrightarrow$ non-D = axis of practice

In the isotopy of knowledge ($C \longleftrightarrow$ non-C), it is not the
knowledge as such which is the pertinent trait but its self-
sufficiency. In C, knowledge is sought after for its own
sake; non-C is neither ignorance nor the refusal of knowledge
but its negation in so far as it would be sufficient to complete a quest. In narrative terms this negation corresponds
to the passage from one position of knowledge about being
(in this case being a scholar) to a position of knowledge
about the "doing" (in this instance, "loving"). This is the
transformation of the lawyer which Jesus strives for in order
that he might bring him to practice /love/. This implies the
renunciation of the sufficiency of religious knowledge.

In the isotopy of practice ($D \longleftrightarrow$ non-D), /non-love/ is
not the abhorrence of but rather the non-practice of love.
Non-D corresponds to the way in which the lawyer places the
parentheses around the "do this" and through his wanting to
justify himself comes back to the sufficient value of knowledge (about being, that is his own scholarly being). Already
at the beginning of the dialogue his entirely verbal declaration of a program ("to inherit eternal life") in function of
a quest for knowledge about Jesus corresponded (in C) to the
negation of this program in the practice isotopy (in non-D).

The first stage of the debate represents an initial

trajectory, C——>non-C——>D, in which the doing proposed
for the lawyer's practice is defined according to Scripture
as "to love God" with all of one's might and "to love the
neighbor as one's self." With the lawyer's return to C
("wanting to justify himself") Jesus offers him a new trajectory, C——>non-C——>D, which forces him to redefine
"the neighbor" and "love."

What is Loving the Neighbor?

To ask the question, "Who is my neighbor?" before loving
him is to define him by means of features which render him
in advance "like myself." According to the traits which specify another as similar to or dissimilar to me there either
will be or will not be an obligation to love him. To pose
the question, "Who becomes neighbor to such a one?" after the
action is to define him not by the features common to both
persons at the beginning but by those common features which
have been acquired by means of the transformation. In this
instance, the neighbor is "the one who showed mercy" to the
other in contrast to those who did not do it. The opposition
is a binary one: one character is distinguished as over
against two others ("which of these three ...?"). The opposition is expressed in four parts in the narrative: the samaritan is opposed to the priest and levite on one isotopy and
to the robbers on another. The samaritan showed mercy in one
way, but in the narrative there are two ways in which it is
not practiced. These distinctions may be represented system-
atically:

48

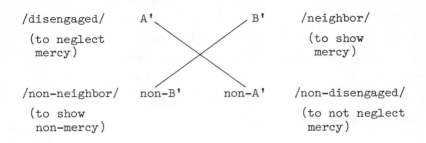

/disengaged/   A'   B'   /neighbor/
 (to neglect   (to show
  mercy)   mercy)

/non-neighbor/ non-B'   non-A'   /non-disengaged/
 (to show   (to not neglect
  non-mercy)   mercy)

An actor in B' became neighbor to another. The two characters, the priest and levite, against whom he is set over,
represent the contrary value which we designate with /disen-
gaged/. Their difference with respect to the robbers enables
us to distinguish in the non-showing of mercy between the
practice of non-mercy and the non-practice or neglect of mercy.
As for the showing of mercy in B', it presupposes in the narrative a position which is contradictory to that of the priest
and the levite. We shall designate it by non-A': to not
neglect mercy.

This system of values which is represented in the interpretation of the narrative within the debate may be contrasted
with the system of values of the narrative itself. Let us
place them alongside one another:

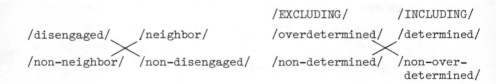

                                /EXCLUDING/   /INCLUDING/
/disengaged/   /neighbor/   /overdetermined/ /determined/
/non-neighbor/ /non-disengaged/ /non-determined/ /non-over-
                                                    determined/

If we superimpose the two squares, the definition of the
neighbor is stated specifically: the neighbor assumes an including, determined, value in the concrete isotopy. An excluding, overdetermined, value in the affection isotopy marks the
contrary figure to the one who is disengaged. "To show mercy"

and its contrary may be defined in the same way. This semic
organization of the story and its interpretation also enables
us to describe what the lawyer does when he interprets the
story and what Jesus asks him to do that is similar to the
samaritan.

A Lawyer, A Priest and A Samaritan

To the question "Who became neighbor?" the lawyer does
not respond by saying: the samaritan. Rather, he says "The
one who showed mercy." The geographico-religious overdetermination of the character is removed for the sake of the
thematic role which is actually taken up and which defined
the neighbor. Similarly, Jesus does not address his questioner as "teacher" (a socio-professional overdetermination):
this title makes way for the role which is actually to be
filled. We have something here which is comparable to the
samaritan's behavior. The samaritan denies any particularity,
either of himself or the other which could keep him away from
the wounded man. In coming to the wounded man he affirms the
including and determined values, thus making them neighbors.
Let us examine this more closely.

The question "Who is my neighbor?" presupposes that the
men are overdetermined by the features which either bring
them together or keep them apart from one another. In raising
the question, one poses the feature /overdetermined/; one acts
upon the isotopy of knowledge in the same way that the priest
and levite act upon the isotopy of affection. On the contrary,
when the lawyer interprets the story he passes from an overdetermined definition to a determined definition of the neighbor. He continues to behave on the plane of knowledge as the
samaritan behaves in practice upon the plane of affection and
the concrete.

When the text reaches its conclusion, it remains for the lawyer to put into practice what he has just accomplished in understanding. It remains for him to deny his own overdetermination as a man of knowledge in order to realize in himself the determined definition of the neighbor in practical terms, just as the samaritan did: that is to say, in affectionate and concrete terms. In so far as he has not done this he can return to the overdetermination of the self-sufficient values of knowledge. He can continue to evaluate the degree of knowledge of other "teachers" or to have his own appreciated. This is to introduce differences between scholars and to qualify them with various overdeterminations; this is to act-- this time in practice--as did the priest and levite.

Overall Organization of the Debate

On two consecutive occasions Jesus attempts to lead the lawyer from a self-sufficient knowledge to the practice of love. The operation of negation takes place in the interpretation first of the Law and then of the story. In this latter instance, the operation consists in having him become, in terms of knowledge, like one of the characters in the story so that he might learn how to become like him in practice. We may say that a common matrix generates the story, its interpretation and the practical program to be realized.

In each of these realizations of the matrix the semes that it organizes are associated with various other semes. It is a matter of the lawyer doing like the samaritan and not doing exactly what he does. He first of all accomplishes this when passing from overdetermination to determination at the level of knowledge. And if he is invited to put this to practice, with his heart and in a concrete way, it would occur in circumstances quite different from that of encounter-

ing a half-dead man alongside the road from Jerusalem to
Jericho. The determined value to be posed might be associated
with the values of a living person in a form other than that
of restoring someone to health in spatial and corporal relations and at a monetary price.

It remains for us now to specify the divergence between
the two parts of the debate. This divergence is manifested
in the difference between the Law and the story, and between
eternal life which is to be inherited for oneself and pure
and simple human life which others are made to gain. The
discussion unfolds in the sphere of ethical and religious
values. However, a moral and religious authority is announced
in the commandment of the Law: "You will love." Similarly,
"eternal life" exposes its moral and religious quality. By
contrast, this quality has an effect upon a practice in which
the relations are established between men in both the story
and its interpretation: that is, we move from understanding
to human conduct and in this conduct from the heart to bodily
action.[41] Can we not recognize from the first phase of the
discussion to the second the passage from an overdetermined
definition of ethico-religious values to a determined definition by means of the value of a living man?

3. CONCLUSION: "THE PARABLE OF THE GOOD SAMARITAN"

Is the story that Jesus tells which engages the clever-
ness of the lawyer a "parable"? Is it not rather an example
which is to be imitated? This alternative runs the great
risk of being deceptive. It is necessary to describe texts
with a rigorous tool before attempting to arrange them into
categories. The problem which is raised for us is that of
the function of this story and its narration within the debate.
On the basis of what has preceded, we are now able to offer
some thoughts on the matter.

A Mirror Narrative

The story does not function as an illustration in relation to the commandment of the Law. It becomes an example to be imitated only if it is interpreted first of all on the knowledge plane and next in practice in concrete circumstances which differ from those of the story. The Law proposes a program which is to be carried out; the story forces us to construct the program through interpretation. This interpretation already begins the programming transformation. The know-how which we must set into operation in the daily circumstances of life is acquired through the course of an active reading, somewhat similar to the way in which we learn to simulate real situations.

To replace the story with the didactic lesson drawn from it would be in fact to take away from it its instructional character: learning how to learn, that is, learning from a fictitious act of learning what must be done in the changing situations of life. To substitute in place of the interpreted story a sentence such as, "Make yourself neighbor by showing mercy," would bring us back to the citation of the Law and to transform the role that this text gives to Jesus and the lawyer.

The action of the characters in the debate and that which is subsequently called for in the action demanded of the lawyer are reflected in the story as if in a mirror. There is a mirroring effect between the narrative and its interpretation and its imitation in a practice which remains to be discovered; but there is no identity of reflection. The mirroring effect permits us to recognize what is the same in other things. The characters in the debate act both in the same way as and in a different way from those of the narrative. This story, even understood as it is in the debate, calls for interpretations which should be unfolded in daily life.

A Text in Search of Characters

We have asked ourselves whether, for the purposes of representing the semantic values of the story, a pharisee or some other character would not work just as well as a priest or levite. This question is now clarified. We have seen how a lawyer may be likened to a priest or a levite and how Jesus teaches him to liken himself to a samaritan. The notion of character takes on its theatrical nuance here. An artist on stage becomes the character whose role he is given to play; in the same way a set of semantic values appears in a text in the linguistic guise of a character. If a "lawyer" is asked to act like a "samaritan" though he conducts himself as a "priest" or a "levite," it is clear that these names belong to the most superficial layer of their definition. We are led to imagine the constitution of a character by the crystallization and deposit of successive layers of elements. Depending upon the layer under consideration, different characters may be substituted so as to embody the same actor. Why not have another character take the lawyer's place in another language, in another semantic universe? A parable is a multitude of stories in seed-like form.[42]

A Position to be Filled

The story comes to a close before the complete restoration of the robbers' victim to health takes place. The story says just enough to support the interpretation which is

offered of it. The debate ends without the lawyer acting to
Jesus' final words. Does it say just enough for its context--
the Gospel of Luke--to assign it its function within the book?
We can certainly assume that. It would also be necessary to
find out if, elsewhere, Jesus acquires, and otherwise practices and perfects the competence that he puts into operation
here, and if other characters assume the lawyer's place in a
similar role. However, without waiting for the results of
this investigation and on the basis of our analysis, we are
permitted to think that the disappearance of the lawyer after
Jesus says "Go and do likewise" leaves vacant the receiver's
post in this speech for the sake of anyone who would care to
accept it.[43]

NOTES

1.   Literally, "Having done what shall I inherit ...?"
In working with the Greek text of the gospels we were led to
retranslate it in such a way as to make apparent the linguistic elements which function as indices for our analysis.

2.   In order to separate the story from the debate we
are making use of linguistic markers: the story is told in
the third person and in the aorist; the debate is characterized by the verbal tenses of the dialogue in the first and
second person.

3.   Let us be specific about our terminology. *Narrative
program:* an ordered series of states and transformations
based upon a relation of subject-object. *State:* a statement
with a verb of the category "having" or "being" marking a
relation of conjunction or disjunction between a subject and
an object. *Transformation:* a statement with a verb of the
category "doing" which brings about the passage from a state
of conjunction to a state of disjunction, or vice-versa. A
transformation requires an *operating subject* of the conjunction or disjunction between a *subject of state* and an object.
The two roles of operating subject and subject of state may
be held by one and the same actor (a *reflexive transformation)*
or by different actors (a *transitive transformation). Subject*

and *object* do not designate persons or things but correlated positions which may be manifested in the text by different linguistic elements; however, the one is never represented without the other.

4. We speak of *quest* or *desire* when a subject-object relation is indicated in a text and points to a *want* on the part of the subject.

5. Every transformation or *performance* requires a *competence*. We distinguish three elements of the competence which are necessary for the performance: the *want* (vouloir), the *power* (pouvoir), and the *knowledge* (savoir) relative to the *doing* which is to be realized. By means of these aspects of the competence, the subject-object relation, which was formerly only a *virtual* relation of conjunction, becomes an *actual* relation; the doing or performance, if successful, will result in a *realized* relation. The elements of the competence that must be had for the performance are to be viewed themselves as objects in relation to a subject. We shall call them *modal objects* in order to distinguish them from the *value object* that the performance sets out to obtain. We speak of modal objects because the want, power and knowledge relative to a doing are *modalities* of the relation between the subject and value object. For example, in the complex statement "Paul wants to buy a car," the statement "Paul wants" modalizes the statement "Paul is buying a car" in terms of wanting.

6. *Sender:* The communicative relationship links together three positions, *sender --> object --> receiver,* whether or not the object (modal or value) is transmitted or received. This tertiary relationship may be rewritten in the form of a binary relationship: an operating subject acts so that a subject of state is conjoined to an object.

7. *Helper:* A representation of the operating subject's power. It may be manifested by an actor other than the subject (the ally, the assistant, the auxiliary), by instruments or by an internal force belonging to the subject. We will call *opponent* any representation of power which is opposed to the subject's power; it may be the power of a subject who is an antagonist in an opposing program.

8. *Statement* and *enunciation,* or *story* and *narration,* are distinguished from one another in the same way that what is said is distinguished from the saying of it (the

speech act). Our analysis is concerned with the statement of the story. Its enunciation will be examined as it pertains to the function of the story told by Jesus in his dialogue with the lawyer.

9. *Anti-subject:* Stories often place two narrative programs in opposition to each other. The quest for an object is threatened or impeded by another subject's quest. In the former's program the latter is the opponent, while the former is the opponent in the latter's program.

10. *Discursive configuration:* An organized set of virtual *figurative trajectories.* Just as a lexeme is defined within a language by the total set of its possible uses (or "meaning") in statements, so also a discursive configuration organizes a set of possible figurative trajectories in the discourse of a society or an author: for example, the set of things that can be said about "highway robbery," "traveling," or "the inn" (even if these words are not employed). And as the lexicon classifies the uses of trajectories of possible meaning for the lexemes, we could well imagine a thematic dictionary of a society or an author which would be used to classify the potential figurative trajectories of the discursive configurations. As discourse or text retains from among the various virtualizations of a lexeme only those which are suitable for its sentences, so also a discourse realizes only one of the possible figurative trajectories of a discursive configuration.

11. An *actor* is defined by its *actantial role* in accordance with the narrative component of the discourse or text and by its *thematic role* in accordance with the discursive component. The actantial role is the status of a subject depending upon whether its relation to the object is potential, actualized (in terms of want and/or power and/or knowledge) or realized. Therefore, we will distinguish between the roles of a potential subject, of a subject according to one or more modalities and of a subject realized in the values of the object. The thematic role is the figurative trajectory as it is assumed by an actor: in our pericope, for example, robbers strip, beat and leave a man "half-dead"; robbers may be endowed with other figurative trajectories in order to assume other thematic roles.

12. The problem already arises in the sentence itself. How is the unity of meaning constituted assuming the multiplicity of words (and the multiplicity of their

possible "meanings")? The problem is more acute in a discourse since it is not a series of independent sentences.
We may speak of discourse only if we can postulate for the
totality of its sentences a common ground with respect to
meaning. The discourse engenders a homogeneous meaning
on the basis of elements which are capable of having multiple "meanings." It operates upon the similarities and
differences between these elements by either amplifying or
neutralizing their points of discord or harmony. This
phenomenon may be understood if we consider these linguistic elements (words, syntagms, sentences, etc.) as complex
groupings of more elementary features, or *semes*. The discourse selects those features which enable it to construct
its meaning. We recognize them by their repetitions and
their oppositions throughout the unfolding of the discourse
which causes the groups of semes, which it manipulates by
linking words together, to come together and to blend with
one another. Thus the meaning trajectories take shape, so
constituting the path of the discourse. It is the repetition of a common *semic feature* which enables us to distinguish an "economic" from a "moral" discourse, even if neither
of these words are employed. Within an "economic" discourse
other features may be repeated and/or opposed: for example,
that which is "worthwhile" and that which is not, as in a
"moral" discourse the one who is "honest" and the one who
is not. The homogeneity of a discourse depends upon the
semic categories which organize it, even without naming
them, through the selection of features pertinent to its
signification.

13. The priest and levite are marked with the feature
"religious"; the samaritan is marked by the feature "geo-
graphical." But we know that in the language of the time
the "samaritans" made up a "religious" community and that
the "priests" and "levites" were the cultic leaders of the
temple in Jerusalem. Moreover, the text introduces them
onto the scene on the road from Jerusalem.

14. The sign "/ /" brackets those terms that we
propose to designate as semes. The choice of these terms
carries with it a certain degree of arbitrariness since it
concerns, in principle, semic features which lay beneath
the words. These terms form an artificial language (or
metalanguage) which exists for the purpose of speaking
about the language of a text; they have a semantic value
only in their opposition to one another. /Overdetermined/
and /determined/ mean nothing in and of themselves; it is
the difference between these two terms which helps to
account for the difference that the text establishes

between "robbers," "a priest," etc., and "a certain man."
In the choice of these terms we shall attempt to stay close
to the language of the text in order to facilitate both contact with the text and the application of our analytic procedures. However, we thereby run the risk of reducing the
possibilities of formalization.

15. "By isotopy we mean a redundant set of semantic
categories which makes possible the uniform reading of the
story" (A. J. Greimas, *Du Sens*, p. 188). "The existence of
the discourse--as contrasted with a series of disconnected
sentences--can be asserted only if one postulates a common
isotopy for all of the sentences making it up, an isotopy
which is identifiable on the basis of the recurrence of a
category or a network of linguistic categories throughout
its unfolding" (*Maupassant*, p. 28). On the concept of isotopy and its use, cf. F. Rastier, "Systematique des isotopies" in A. J. Greimas, *Essais de sémiotique poétique*
(Larousse, 1972), pp. 80-106; C. Kerbrat-Orecchiono, "Prob-
lématique de l'isotopie" in *Linguistique et Sémiologie.
Travaux du Centre de Recherches Linguistiques et Sémiolo-
giques de l'Université Lyon II* (1976), n. 1, pp. 11-33.

16. Obviously these terms are debatable, but it is
their difference which counts. We have the opportunity
here to distinguish the exegesis or commentary from the
semiotic analysis. The commentaries are often concerned
with the motives presupposed by the priest's and levite's
conduct: concern for ritual purity which is threatened by
contact with a corpse? Fear of becoming mixed up in a
suspicious-looking affair? The text is content to oppose
movements in space in relation to the half-dead man and as
a consequence of a sighting: the threefold difference between priest, levite and samaritan is marked (in the repetition of the same linguistic phrases) by the compassion
which characterizes only the samaritan. We can account for
this fact by saying that the differences in the isotopies
of spatial and corporal relations are accounted for by a
difference in the isotopy of affectionate relations. And
it is this final difference that we render by the divergence between "passing by on the other side" (spatial),
"by avoiding him" (corporal), and "when coming close by
him .... he approached him" (spatial and corporal). The
text presents the behavior of the priest and levite as
contradictory to the samaritan in the isotopy of affection.

17. The reading which follows does not presuppose a
deep knowledge of this model. Suffice it to recall that
it is not a model of formal logic but rather a semiotic

model which is proposed to simulate the elementary structure
of signification in natural languages. It is therefore not
a matter of projecting a logic upon a text which would be
foreign to it but rather of entering into the investigation
of its logic by accepting the risk of discovering this model
to be non-operational. On the semiotic square see A. J.
Greimas, *Du Sens*, pp. 136-138, and the collective volume
Structures élémentaires de la signification, published under
the direction of F. Nef (Editions Complexe, distributed by
PUF), 1976.

18. Every language possesses pairs of contraries (for
example, masculine and feminine on the axis of sexuality).
By opposing two axes of contradictories the discourse can
establish terms as contraries even though they are not in
this relationship in the language. Two semes arising from
different isotopies are placed in relation of contrariety
and this relation will be recorded in the language for future
discourses. In our pericope the behavior of the priest and
levite on the one hand and the samaritan on the other represent contrary semes which belong in the first instance to
the isotopy of affection and in the second to the isotopy of
the concrete.

19. We speak of *figures* in the following sense: the
discourse or text manifests in the form of personages, processes, objects, places, times (etc.) ... complex semantic
structures and the analysis endeavors to distinguish the
elements (semes) which make up the semantic definition of
these figures. For example, to purchase a car may mean to
acquire a means for rapid transportation, a sign of social
prestige or a symbol of power. The same figurative object
covers diverse semantic definitions.

20. We consider that everything which depends upon
the competence to speak in a society and thus everything
which conforms to the relations of equivalence or opposition between elements of discourse in this society belongs
to the language (la langue) of this society. The discourse
may break apart this social order of discourse or repeat it.
Subversive discourse, for example, introduces a new system
of semantic organization.

21. The text itself lays down this rule for what is
to be considered normative by locating the route between
Jerusalem and Jericho. Positively speaking, what is normative is Judean. The samaritan is marked negatively, both
in terms of status as a foreigner in Judean space and in
terms of the system of values of Jewish religious discourse

such as can be determined, for example, in Luke 9:52-54 and 17:18.

22. For the system of values represented by the denominations of the personages (which refers us back to the language), the discourse substitutes another one in its place, a system represented by the roles that these personages play within this story. We may venture the following table:

	unaccepted		accepted	
	socio-professional	geographico-religious	geographico-religious	socio-professional
Language	"robbers"	"a samaritan"	"a priest" "a levite"	"an innkeeper"
Discourse	"robbers"	"a priest" "a levite"	"a samaritan"	"a samaritan" "an innkeeper"
	concrete	affectionate	affectionate	concrete
	excluding		including	

The divergence between the two systems is manifested in the inversion of the posts occupied in both, respectively, by the priest and the levite on the one hand, and the samaritan on the other. By way of their order of appearance onto the scene, the text brings the priest and levite close to the robbers from whom they are completely separated in the system of accepted values.

23. Strictly speaking, the term "to strip" in Greek has to do with the clothing rather than the belongings of the robbers' victim.

24. We speak of a semantic or semic *value* in order to designate a unity of the signified as it is defined by its differences with other signifieds within a system of relations. A value may be assumed by diverse signifiers (word order, complex expression, indeed one or more sentences) just as a coin, a bill or a check may have the same value, that value being defined by its differences from other values in the heart of a monetary system. In the semiotics of discourse the value is defined in function of the oriented relation *subject --> object* which constitutes the elementary statement. The syntactic position of *object* is the place of investment of the value or values sought after by the *subject* (See Note 19 and the example of the purchase of a car). These values semanticize the *object* and therefore the relation of *subject-object*. "The value which is invested in the sought-after object ... becomes the value of the subject who encounters it when seeking after the object; the subject is fixed in its semantic existence by its relation to the value. (A. J. Greimas, "Un problème de sémiotique narrative: les objets de valeur," in *Langages* 31, 1973, p. 16.) This explains why the states and transformations of the characters in a story must be analyzed with care. The notion of *value object* covers this distinction between the object as a syntactic (or actantial) position, and the *value* whose semiotic meaning we have just specified. We shall now compare and contrast this semiotic meaning with the *axiologic* meaning of the notion of *value:* "It will suffice to endow the subject with a *wanting-to-be* in order for the *value of the subject,* in the semiotic sense, to take charge of the *value for the subject,* in the axiological sense of this term" (Greimas, *Ibid.*). Up until now we have not made a distinction between these two meanings of the term in our use of the word *value:* in both of these meanings the value stands in relation to the subject. We have already come across the phenomenon of *axiologic valorization* in the division into either euphoric (positive) (p. 22) or dysphoric (negative) (p. 26) values. We call *deixis* the table of values which are either euphoric (or positive) or dysphoric (or negative).

25. Thus, we may characterize the process designated by "to put someone to the test" and "to justify oneself" with the aid of other biblical and Gospel texts, which are considered in reference to a common language. "To put to the test" is illuminated here by the context of the debate over doctrinal questions between knowledgeable men. As for "to justify oneself," the Greek translations and commentaries are hesitant: does the lawyer who has just appeared well-informed want to show that he was nevertheless right to question Jesus? Does he want to appear as a "righteous" man, concerned with the

proper understanding of his obligations so as to put them to
practice in a better way? At the narrative level these details are unimportant: it is a matter of bringing about the
acquisition of an object--the knowledge on the part of the
subject about the being of another. (Both of these roles may
be held by the same actor, as for example in "to justify oneself in one's own eyes.") The discursive analysis will be
concerned with the quality of self that the lawyer wants to
know about.

26. We might raise the question of the function of
this "doing" in relation to "inheriting eternal life" ("to
inherit" implies a role of sender not manifested here). In
order to determine this we would need to look at other texts
that presuppose this relation without clarifying it.

27. The common translation, "What *must* I do to inherit
eternal life?" runs the risk of introducing a having-to-do
that the Greek text does not make explicit in this instance.
Concerning the elements of competence, see n. 5.

28. This distinction is called for because of the
difference between the statements of state and the statements
of doing; see n. 3. All of these statements may be modalized
by want, power and/or knowledge.

29. See n. 5.

30. Even if he is not lying, the pretended ignorance
between "teachers" fools no one. This aspect of the question
depends upon the situation of discourse which the text may or
may not make explicit. In this case, it does not make it explicit; however, it does distinguish what is said (the question which is stated) from the saying of it (the act of stating it, called "to put to the test").

31. The *cognitive doing* may be either *emissive* (to dis-
pense knowledge) or *receptive* (to acquire knowledge). The
received knowledge is either *informative,* if it is enough
merely to receive it, or *interpretative,* if the receiver (the
one who acquires it) obtains it by an operation for which he
is the operating subject (he comes to be knowledgeable). The
interpretative knowledge is acquired by its receiver on the
basis of an initial informative knowledge. The *interpretative
doing* is to be distinguished from a *persuasive doing:* the
latter is the action of the sender who seeks to have his
knowledge accepted by the receiver; the interpretative doing
is the act of the receiver who appropriates this knowledge
according to his own system of values.

32. The future: "You will love" has this nuance in the cited text and the term "Law" specifies this nuance. The Law states an obligation to do.

33. Ultimately, "Do this and you will live" may be interpreted: "If you do this, you will live."

34. In order to have Jesus acquire this object, the lawyer performs a persuasive doing, with a view toward an interpretative doing by Jesus (see n. 28). The lawyer is situated in the sender's position.

35. We interpret "to love" as a succession of functions: an operating subject attempts to have a receiver (the one to be loved or the subject of state who is transformed) acquire a good. The two roles of operating subject and receiver may be held by one and the same actors (to love oneself or to love another).

36. This performance can have as its operating subject one or the other of two actors who become neighbors; it may even be a third who makes them neighbors. The story told by Jesus limits this set of possibilities.

37. He exercises a *performative doing* with respect to knowledge and then with respect to want. He causes the lawyer to be able to obtain knowledge and want.

38. It is the narrative and discursive coherence which brings us to understand "to justify oneself" not as "to be known as a righteous man" but in terms of the qualities of a good "lawyer."

39. Regarding this terminology, see n. 10 and 11.

40. Regarding this terminology, see n. 14, 15, and 17.

41. We are careful not to project upon the text the opposition which has become familiar to us all between the "religious" and "secular," the "sacred" and the "profane."

42. The difference between our analysis and any investigation which would begin with a definition of the parable should be clear: "If one selects as a field of exploration a body of texts traditionally and customarily classified under thus and such a label, we have no way of being assured that the common features, selected as definitive features of a genre, are truly that and do not happen to be also characteristic of a genre which is at first glance quite far

removed ..." (A. J. Greimas, *Maupassant*, p. 11). We cannot in principle pose the existence of a "parabolic genre" whose structural properties would remain constant. The analysis we have performed upon a "parable" may be practiced on other texts, be they parable or not, and the semiotic description of these texts forces us to revise the cultural classifications and to work toward a new typology of texts.

43. Bibliography: Our analysis should be compared with studies of our text in various commentaries upon the Gospels and in the well-known work of D. Buzy, *Les Parables* (Paris: Gabalda, 1932); J. Jeremias, *The Parables of Jesus,* trans. S. H. Hooke, rev. ed. (New York: Scribners, 1962); H. Kahlefeld, *Parables and Instructions in the Gospel,* trans. A. Swidler (New York: Herder and Herder, 1966); not to mention texts available in French. The Parable of the Good Samaritan has been and remains the field of numerous studies in which the tools of analysis inspired by linguistics and semiotics are tested. See G. Crespy, "La parable dite le bon Samaritain," in *Études théologiques et réligieuses* 48 (1973), 61-79; the works of J. O. Crossan, O. D. Via, D. Patte and R. W. Funk published in *Semeia: An Experimental Journal for Biblical Criticism* (1974), n. 1 and 2; and *Semiology and Parables: An Exploration of the Possibilities offered by Structuralism for Exegesis,* ed. D. Patte, Pittsburgh Theological Monograph Series, number 9 (Pittsburgh: Pickwick Press, 1976), papers presented at the conference on Semiology and Exegesis held at Vanderbilt University, May 15-17, 1975.

II.

"They Had Not Understood
Concerning the Bread ..."

Several Episodes
and a Single Narrative (Mark 6:30-53)

Mark 6:30-53

^{30}*The apostles returned to Jesus and reported to him*
all that they had done and taught. ^{31}*And he said to them:*
"Come away by yourselves to a lonely place and rest awhile."
For many people were coming and going and they had no time
even to eat. ^{32}*They went away by boat to a lonely place by*
themselves. ^{33}*Many saw them going and knew them and they*
ran there on foot from all the towns and arrived ahead of
them. ^{34}*And as they were landing, Jesus saw a great crowd*
and had compassion for them because they were like sheep
without a shepherd; and he began to teach them many things.
^{35}*Now, as the hour was growing late, his disciples came to*
him and said: "This is a lonely place and the hour is late.
^{36}*Send them away so that they may go into the country and*
villages round about and buy something to eat." ^{37}*But he*
answered them: "You yourselves give them something to eat."
And they said to him: "Shall we go and buy two hundred
denarii worth of bread and give it to them to eat?" ^{39}*But*
he said to them: "How many loaves do you have? Go and see."
And when they had found out, they said, "Five, and two fish."
^{39}*Then he ordered them to sit down in groups on the green*
grass. ^{40}*So they spread out in groups of 100 and of 50.*

*⁴¹He took the five loaves of bread and the two fish, and
lifting his eyes to heaven, he gave thanks, broke the bread
and gave it to the disciples to offer it to the people; and
he divided the two fish among them all. ⁴²And they all ate
and were satisfied. ⁴³And they gathered up twelve baskets
full of morsels of bread and what was left over of the fish.
⁴⁴And those who had eaten the loaves numbered 5,000 men.*

*⁴⁵Immediately he made his disciples get into the boat
and go before him to the other side to Bethsaida while he dis-
missed the crowd. ⁴⁶And after he had left them, he went up
to the mountain to pray. ⁴⁷And when evening came the boat
was on the water and he was alone on the land. ⁴⁸And seeing
that they were struggling to make headway because the wind
was against them, on toward the fourth watch of the night he
came to them walking on the sea. ⁴⁹But when they saw him
walking on the sea they thought he was a ghost and they cried
out. ⁵⁰For they all saw him and were terrified. But immediately he spoke to them and said, "Take heart, it is I. Have
no fear." ⁵¹And he climbed into the boat with them and the
wind ceased and they were completely astounded. ⁵²For they
did not understand about the loaves since their hearts were
hardened. ⁵³And after he had crossed the sea, he came to the
land at Gennesaret and they landed.*

When reading this pericope just quoted from the Gospel
of Mark, one usually distinguishes several episodes: the
return of the apostles from their mission, the instruction by
Jesus, the feeding of the five thousand, and the walk upon
water. A number of observations about this pericope invite
us, however, to consider it as a single story.

At the pericope's conclusion, the narrator indicates that
the disciples "had not understood concerning the loaves of
bread." The text itself causes us to read the episode of the

feeding of the crowd and the walk upon water as a unity of
meaning and thus forces us to seek out their relative function
within this pericope. The crossing of the sea, during which
time Jesus' walk upon the water takes place, leads us to con-
clude the pericope at v. 53 with the arrival upon the other
shore. We begin our text at v. 30 which describes the departure situation of an initial crossing of the sea and which
introduces onto the stage the story's three characters.

In the text thus delimited, we isolate three sequences:
- —sequence I: verses 30-34
- —sequence II: verses 34-55
- —sequence III: verses 45-55

The criterion which we have adopted for this segmentation
is the reference to the characters' movements and the spatial
coordinates of their attions. Two sequences are marked by actions which take place on water; they bracket a sequence which
deals with Jesus' instruction and feeding of the crowd, which
takes place on land.

Each of these sequences will become the object of a two-
fold investigation. First we shall seek to construct the narrative model, that is, to describe the narrative in terms of
narrative programs and actantial roles, being aware all the
time of the relative position of the characters (roles) in
their quests for objects (programs). Next, we will undertake
to describe the discursive component, that is, the construction of a code which in a systematic way represents the relations of semantic values (and of the figures which transmit
them) on the basis of which the discourse that we read produces its meaning-effect.

To do this we will pay strict attention to the way in
which the actantial roles and the narrative programs are manifested within the discourse by elements of the language (discursive configurations, figurative trajectories) which they

select in terms of particular semantic values.

In order to be as clear as possible, our description will follow closely the development of the text. We shall perform both steps of the analysis for each sequence, building partial models and reserving until the end of this study the construction of more comprehensive models.

1. INITIAL SEQUENCE: THE DIVERTED BOAT-CROSSING

1.1 *Narrative Component*

a. *From Report to Rest*

Sequence 1 opens with the gathering around Jesus of the apostles who have just returned from a mission. This reunion appears only in the figure of its completion: the end of a performance ("going and teaching") in which the apostles are the operating subject and Jesus is the sender who is capable of bestowing his approval upon the completed performance. Therefore, the narrative starts off at the level of the relation between sender-subject; we might call this the level of manipulation-approval.[1] This level crops up at several points in our text. The receiver of the apostles' performance does not appear here, though we find it represented by the people who come and go and who introduce a new lack into the story.

A narrative program then develops around the quest for the object "rest." Jesus, as sender, transmits the wanting-to-do (by command) and the knowing-how-to-do (by the statement of the process which is to be accomplished) to the apostles. In opposition to the crowd's disorderly movement,[2] the disjunction (acquisition of seclusion and distance) constitutes a qualifying performance: the acquisition of a power-to-do for the purpose of realizing the program of rest.

In the development of this program, Jesus and the apostles
make up a group subject: the Jesus-apostle group.

b. *The Deprived Rest*

Next we need to record a performance by the crowd. The
crowd is subject of a movement which is correlated to the
movement of Jesus and the apostles. With their head start
over them, the crowd is in a dominant position. It is not
merely a matter of catching up with the apostles and Jesus;
they arrive ahead of them. At the end of the crowd's performance the apostles and Jesus are deprived of the power-to-do
for their own program of rest. What is more, the failure of
this program permits the manifestation of a particular program
on the crowd's part. This narrative circle (Jesus' and the
apostles' performance *vs.* the crowd's performance) marks an
insistence upon the dysphoric[3] situation of the apostles and
not a simple return to the beginning point of the narrative.
On the narrative plane this circle establishes two programs:
the one with Jesus and the apostles that we just spoke about
and the one of the crowd. The crowd, which as a mass of
people coming and going was only a hindrance to rest, must
now be recorded as a crowd in movement within a particular
narrative program that we will oppose to the preceding one
(in the form NP2 *vs.* NP1). In NP2 the crowd's competence[4]
is made up of the knowledge acquired at the conclusion of an
interpretative doing ("the people saw them going away and many
understood"), and of the want for which the subject's movement
is often an indice. We are not yet able to specify the object
of the crowd's program, but we can note that the wanting-to-
be of the subject of state (the crowd) is dependent upon a
cognitive competence ("to recognize"), which is itself a consequence of the performance of an interpretative doing. The

interpretative doing appears in the correlation of the two
processes of "seeing" and "recognizing": this is a prospective interpretation[5]--a passage from appearing to being--
from the phenomenal plane to the noumenal plane which is
undertaken by a competent subject. This performance has, as
its object in this case, the doing of Jesus and the apostles
("the people saw them going away"). This mechanism is manifested several times throughout our text. In this instance
the crowd is the subject and the Jesus-apostles group is the
object; in Sequence II Jesus will be the subject with the
crowd as object; in Sequence III the disciples will be the
subject with Jesus as object. We will have the occasion to
return to these homologies at the conclusion of this study.

In order to obtain the object of its quest the crowd
must be in a state of conjunction with Jesus and the apostles.
The crowd's movement leads to the realization of this conjunction; it constitutes a secondary program with respect to the
crowd's principal program.[6] It is necessary for the apostles
and Jesus to be disjoined from the crowd in order to be able
to get some rest. Their movement leads to this disjunction
and constitutes a secondary program with respect to the program of rest which itself manifests the sanction of the apostles' teaching. Thus, we can be more specific about the narrative model of this initial sequence and the level of the
actantial opposition of the characters: oppositions between
the secondary programs and between the modal values.[7]

1.2 *Discursive Component*

a. *To Walk or to Sail*

It is the movement of the actors which is responsible
for expressing the opposition between the narrative programs

on the discursive plane. NP1 and NP2 are realized on different figurative trajectories (we could well imagine the crowd
overtaking the apostles in other boats), and the opposition
of both subjects may be read as the opposition of two types
of movement:

to sail by boat *vs*. to run on foot

This parallelism of figurative trajectories enables us to
specify in more detail the hypothesis that was offered concerning the relations between NP1 and NP2. The actors are
opposed to one another but are not situated upon the same
figurative trajectory. Their opposition cannot be simply
one of rivalry between subject and anti-subject in quest of
the same object whose acquisition for the one would be tanta-
mount to a loss for the other.[8] The crowd and the Jesus-
apostles group are opposed to one another in terms of the
means for effecting their movement, that is, at the level
of the secondary programs, as well as at the more fundamental
level of the values which govern the carrying out of these
programs.[9]

The two interrelated figurative trajectories form an
opposition, /land/ *vs*. /sea/, with the domination of /terres-
trial/ movement over /maritime/ movement. With the crowd's
success a certain feature characterizing the "sea" is negated:
namely, the determination which made the sea a limit--a
separation--a distancing vector. In Sequence III the same
relation of /land/ *vs*. /sea/ is represented by Jesus' walking.
If the sea, which has the character of "separating" is so negated, we can deduce that the crowd's performance in this initial Sequence brings about the transformation:

$$\text{/land} \lor \text{sea/} \longrightarrow \text{non/land} \lor \text{sea/}$$

on the basis of which a new organization of these places may
now be asserted.

72

b. *Going to a Solitary Place*

Within our semiotic perspective the departure of Jesus
and the apostles has its value within a system which accounts
for the movements of both this group and the crowd in a
taxonomic way.[10] In effect, the disjunction crowd *vs.* Jesus-
apostles, which is sought after at the beginning of the narrative as a condition for resting, may be realized either by
the crowd's movement (its dismissal) or by Jesus and the
apostles' movement (their departure):

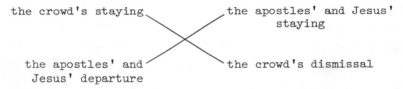

the crowd's staying   the apostles' and Jesus'
                                       staying

the apostles' and   the crowd's dismissal
Jesus' departure

The narrative in this case does not select the dismissal of
the crowd although this possibility is considered further
on in the text. The apostles and Jesus move, and the crowd
stays. Then the crowd as subject can effect an independent
movement which insures domination over the apostles and
Jesus within the framework of its narrative program. As
the subject of the doing, the crowd is the operating subject
of semantic transformations.

c. *Semantic Transformations of the Places*

The narrative's initial situation records an inauspicious
conjunction of the crowd and the Jesus-apostles group in three
ways: in terms of number ("many"), in terms of movement
("coming and going"), and in terms of time ("no time to eat").
With regard to this situation, the transformation which

intervenes owing to the crowd corresponds to a spatial orientation on the crowd's part. The Jesus-apostles group which was included in the crowd's movement of coming and going and incorporated within its space elsewhere becomes the place of the crowd's quest and one pole of its movement.

This movement establishes the opposition

city *vs.* this place

whereas the previous movement of Jesus and the apostles established the opposition

place where the crowd is *vs.* solitary place

By racing ahead of the apostles and Jesus, the crowd invests the place which the narrative reserved for them and which was only negatively defined as the place where the crowd is not, ("a solitary place, a deserted place") with itself. We note what is different about the place where the crowd is heading: "They ran to *this* place." In the operation realized by the crowd, we have the assertion of what was defined only in negative terms.[11] The narrative has constructed a place which is defined in positive terms as the apostles' and Jesus' place and as the place desired by the crowd. Even before the apostles and Jesus disembark, their place of arrival has been altered. It is in this way that the text diverts the group's crossing.

A systematic representation may now be given of the places constructed by this sequence of the text. A number of these places will be realized later on in the text.

74

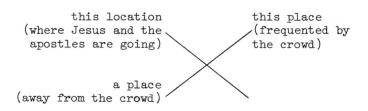

this location
(where Jesus and the
apostles are going)

this place
(frequented by
the crowd)

a place
(away from the crowd)

In the final analysis this double movement of the apostles and Jesus and of the crowd contributes to the construction of the *same* place. They are "conformed" actors whose programs are not contrary to one another; the places which characterize them are located on the same deixis.

Let us underscore the effects of this narrative and discursive interplay: it causes values to be determined for Jesus and the apostles by way of actors other than themselves, thereby producing the effect of ignorance or of discovery of the values which characterize them in this narrative.

d. *Conclusions*

In the double movement of the Jesus-apostles group and of the crowd there is a duplication of programs which weave together the narrativity of this fragment. The NP1 of the apostles in search of rest fails because of an opponent, the crowd, which neutralized the movement that would have kept the crowd at a distance. But by its own movement the crowd discloses itself to be the wanting subject in another narrative program, NP2. The text is more concerned with the representation of want (the crowd's) than with the lack experienced by Jesus and the apostles. The few observations made on the discursive plane come together at this point: in its movement the crowd realizes the positive determination whereas the apostles and Jesus represent the negative determination of the conformed values which belong to the same deixis.

The initial sequence establishes two comparable programs --NP1 and NP2--and marks the dominance of NP2 over NP1 by realizing the virtualization of NP1's power-to-do correlated with the establishment of the subject of the wanting-to-be in NP2. We can anticipate the narrative consequence of these programs. It calls for the realization of NP2 by the communication of its object to the subject of the wanting-to-be, and the modification of the subject in NP1 who must either be inscribed within NP2 on the basis of his virtualized position in NP1 or be restored to his position as competent subject in NP1. This will be the problem encountered by the disciples below. We may represent their actantial positions as follows:[12]

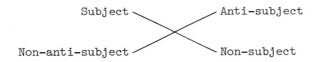

If the failure of the Jesus-apostles group to get away--a virtualization[13] of the subject-of-the-power-to-do in NP1--places them in the position of Non-anti-subject at the end of this sequence, then these characters must either gain the position of subject or be restored to the role of Anti-subject in opposition to NP2. What we have here is a problem of competence.

2. THE SECOND SEQUENCE: THE FEEDING OF THE CROWD

In order to set the boundaries for this second sequence we shall use again the spatial criterion. With the arrival on land (v. 34), the text records two figurative trajectories or processes: one of instruction and another of feeding in which Jesus represents the operating subject for a receiving crowd. The end of the sequence is more difficult to determine:

does Jesus' prayer on the mountain belong to the second or to
the third sequence? The movement of the group of actors in
vv. 45-46 leaves Jesus alone on stage for a performance which
might very easily mark the finale of the feeding sequence.
But the disciples are now involved in a new figurative trajectory beginning with v. 45. Therefore, we shall study the episode of the prayer on the mountain within the framework of
the third sequence.

2.1 *Narrative Component*

a. *The Shepherd's Compassion*

The arrival of the boat has a double function: as a
"getting out of the boat" it belongs to the preceding sequence; as a "landing" the arrival opens up Sequence III.

The initial statement of this sequence records the
transformation of Jesus' actantial role: he is inscribed
within the NP2 of the crowd in the role of the subject-who-
wants-to-do. This statement is manifested in two consecutive processes: "He saw a large crowd and was filled with
compassion for them." Jesus alone is the subject of both
of these processes; the disciples disappear from the scene.

Both of these processes constitute a performance of an
interpretative doing. Jesus acquires a knowledge of the
being of the crowd which he encounters again: "They were as
sheep without a shepherd." Sequences I and II are correlated
at the level of interpretative doing: the crowd interprets
Jesus' and the apostles' movement ("they saw them going away
and many recognized them") and Jesus interprets the crowd's
state ("he saw a large crowd and was filled with compassion
for them"). In Jesus' case the acquisition of knowledge
about the crowd's being implies the acquisition of a wanting-

to-do; that is, a reflexive establishment of the operating subject in program NP2. Therefore, the conjunction of Jesus with the crowd, which was sought after by the crowd, is accomplished (the realization of its secondary program). However, it is left unsaid whether the object proposed by Jesus is the same object as the crowd's wanting-to-be. That will remain undetermined until the end, for it is Jesus who defines an object of desire for the crowd by taking the crowd to be "sheep without a shepherd." The communication of this object to the crowd is realized without any glorifying performance on the part of the crowd: we do not know what the crowd understands to be the object communicated to it. To the extent that the crowd does not refuse the objects communicated by Jesus, we can postulate that the object proposed by Jesus and the object desired by the crowd are at least "conformed"--non-contrary and non-contradictory--if not identical to one another.

The conjunction of the subject of the wanting-to-be and the subject of the wanting-to-do on the shore of the lake constitutes the necessary condition for the realization of NP2, which then takes place in the form of abundant instruction ("He began to teach them many things"). This performance occurs without manifestation of an opponent to Jesus' ability. The text does not mention the content of Jesus' teaching of which we note only its inchoative aspect ("He began to teach them"). The opposition

inchoative *vs.* terminative

is manifested here, but the conclusion of the teaching is marked in a negative form: it is an endless teaching ("late hour"). This inversed correlation makes the teaching much more a type of behavior than a limited process. We shall return to this point after analyzing the feeding of the crowd.

b. 5 + 2 > 5,000

Jesus' teaching is characterized by its abundance ("many things") and by its temporal situation ("late hour"). It is interesting to note that the narrative duplicates this last remark: from the narrator's perspective it qualifies the object of NP2 with the feature /overabundance/; from the disciples' perspective it becomes the index of a disturbing situation, marking the object with the feature /excessive/.

In fact, the narrative causes "the disciples" to appear at the end of this teaching performance by Jesus. We now have a new figure for the character which has been designated up until now as "apostles." They intervene in the narrative in order to describe the situation created by Jesus' teaching in dysphoric terms: the overabundance is interpreted as disturbing with regard to a new program, "eating." In so doing the disciples are the subjects of a knowledge about the crowd's being (which needs to, but cannot, eat); however, as is the case with other characters, the narrative does not record those performances in which this knowledge is attributed. Moreover, the disciples are the subjects of a knowing-how-to-do and are able to foresee the subsequent processes in a program of food acquisition.

Let us keep in mind that in this program proposed by the disciples, the crowd would represent the operating subject of an appropriation of food after a movement in the direction of inhabited places and a purchasing performance: the acquisition of an object of exchange which requires that the crowd disjoin itself from the Jesus-apostles group. In other words, the effect which brought about the crowd's transformation from being conjoined as disturbers to wanting-to-be-conjoined as receivers to the Jesus and disciples group.

With his injunction ("Give it to them yourselves"), Jesus leads the disciples from this program of possible buying to a program of impossible giving--an impossibility that is underscored by the disproportion between what they have and what they must have, as much with respect to money (200 denarii are needed) as with respect to food (there are only five loaves of bread and two fish). The program proposed by the disciples is virtualized at the level of the wanting-to-do: they propose the buying and Jesus orders the giving. In this new program the disciples, deprived of the power-to-do, are subjects of the having-to-do. As in the initial sequence, we find two secondary programs in operation that we can represent as follows:

By their statement the disciples manifest a knowing-how-to-do, that is a certain programming: if one lacks food or if one wants to supply food, it must be bought. Out of the necessity of going and buying the order of values governing the disciples is revealed. When on Jesus' command the purchase is reversed and so becomes a gift of what is possessed, a new knowing-how-to-do must be acquired, a new order of values within which the apostles must act. The discussing between Jesus and the disciples is sufficiently developed in order that the parallelism in the two programmings might be manifested in the questioner's replies. The disciples declare themselves unable to realize the program (buying and giving) that they themselves propose. Here again it is necessary for a secondary program to be virtualized so that another program may be asserted and realized.

With the disciples' response as to the number of
loaves of bread and fish, the principle performance of
attribution begins in accordance with the program proposed by Jesus. Jesus is the operating subject, but the
disciples' position is more complex. They are passive
subjects of wanting (having-to-do and not-wanting-to-do).
The text does not specify the disciples' position with
respect to the power-to-do and on the plane of knowing-
how-to-do they seem to be governed by the system of exchange.

The performance is asserted in the process of "taking
the loaves of bread," "lifting his eyes to heaven," "giving
thanks," "breaking the bread"; we shall be more specific
about the semantic value of this process below. But for
the moment we are interested in the form of communication.
The attribution of food to the crowd, as with that of knowledge through teaching, takes place in a participatory communication. In the same way, the teaching transmission does
not take knowledge away from Jesus, just as the acquisition
of food by the crowd (dinner guests) takes nothing away
from the disciples who distribute what they have. There
will even be some leftovers, just as the teaching will be
prolonged until a late hour.

We may thus represent the form of the communication[14]
in the program proposed by the disciples and in that which
Jesus realizes as:

1. exchange: $S_1 => [(0_1 \wedge S_1 \vee 0_2) -> (0_1 \vee S_1 \wedge 0_2)]$

2. participatory
   communication: $S_3 => [(S_2 \wedge 0_2 \vee S_1) -> (S_2 \wedge 0_2 \wedge S_1)]$

wherein S_1 = crowd   => = transforming doing

       S_2 = disciples   -> = passage from one state to another

       S_3 = Jesus $\wedge$ = conjunction

       O_1 = money $\vee$ = disjunction

       O_2 = food

In the communication of food as well as with that of teaching, the narrative gives no indication of an opposition to Jesus at the level of the power-to-do. The opposite program appeared (in the debate with the disciples) only at the level of the knowing-how-to-do, and of knowing about the order of values governing the subjects' performances. Jesus' performance in NP2 takes the figurative trajectories of teaching and feeding in which the dinner guests are fed beyond their needs. At a later time we shall investigate more carefully the relationship between these two figurative trajectories.

This second sequence introduces the attribution of an object from the moment of the manifestation of lack up to its communication, and does so twice. Jesus is the operating subject for each attributive performance, and we might expect to find at the conclusion of each performance a glorification of the subject by the receivers. We note the reference to the large number of guests and the leftovers that were gathered up (this reference is attributable to the narrator). These features--the description of an overabundance of the object--may be the substitutes within the discourse for a recognition performance that the narrative does not manifest. Let us note as well the particular position of Jesus' prayer on the mountain. It may well be a secret form of the subject's recognition.

2.2 *Discursive Component*

a. *To Teach and to Feed*

The analysis of the performances in this second sequence reveals the recurrence of participatory communication in the two figurative trajectories of teaching and feeding: Jesus distributes (causes the distribution of) food as well as knowledge. Similarly, in the debate between the disciples and Jesus we noted an opposition with respect to the places: the disciples represent a system of distribution of places where the feeding occurs in a location suited for it ("hamlets and villages") which is not the place of Jesus' teaching ("desert"). This diversifying of places is negated by Jesus, and the crowd is fed in the place where it is taught. The actions of teaching and feeding establish the same sort of participatory communication. But we have noted that the object of teaching (the teaching content) is absent. We also made note of the inchoative aspect of this process. By contrast, the feeding of the crowd clearly sets the communicated object before us in precise detail ("five loaves, two fishes") and describes the performance from beginning to end even to the point of mentioning what is left over and the dismissal of the dinner guests). All of this takes place as if the process of teaching were there for the purpose of providing, by juxtaposition within the narrative, an equivalent for the mode of communication and the object communicated in the feeding. Through this process the narrative constructs a metaphoric relationship between teaching and feeding: that is, between the knowledge transmitted and the food distributed. The teaching is a type of nourishment, but in order for Jesus to teach the crowd, it first must be fed. The application of the somatic plane to the noological plane constitutes a particular symbolic or noo-somatic plane within which the somatic objects that are communicated realize the attribution of knowledge.

A new program is proposed and realized as a result of the failure of NP1. It corresponds to a new definition of the sought-after object: the likening of teaching and feeding to one another, a specific and particularly effective mode of communication. It is the realization through speech of a performance without confrontation. It is a transformation of a dysphoric situation (one teaches at the wrong time and in the wrong place; one eats at unusual times and places). It is a matter, then, of realizing an /overly proper/ solution on the basis of the failure of the /proper/ solutions (to rest apart from the crowd; to send those who are buying away into the villages).

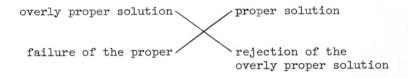

We are then in a position to investigate two things: on the one hand, the relation between this teaching-feeding accomplished by Jesus and the teaching of the apostles in the first sequence; on the other hand, the function of these performances by Jesus within the pericope as a whole. In the role of "apostles" the disciples enter the story as competent subjects of a performance (going and teaching) which is completed and should be followed by a time of rest. The analysis of sequence I permits us to record the failure of this resting program as due to the loss of the subjects' power-to-do. On the basis of this virtualization, sequence II may be interpreted as the proposal of a contract to the disciples on the grounds of a redefinition of the object which Jesus' teaching and feeding performances manifest. The acceptance of this contract remains problematic, for the passage from one program to the other calls for the virtualization of the subjects in the initial program and a performance of interpretative doing. The crowd and Jesus realized this performance in a comparable way:

"they saw ... recognized" <−> "he saw ... was filled
                                        with compassion"

However, the disciples have yet to accomplish it. This is what is at stake in sequence III.

b. Bread and Fish

The representation of the object in this second sequence presents a problem. It is particularly developed along the feeding trajectory. We note the duplication of the represented objects: bread and fish. Our semiotic analysis must investigate this duplication and the relative value of each of the objects.

Bread and fish appear first of all in the narrative as representations of the impossibility of feeding the crowd. They represent a disproportionate deficiency (5 + 2) as opposed to the 200 denarii called for by the number of dinner guests (5,000) in the buying program. Likewise they appear as a representation of the object of which the disciples will be the receivers ("How many loaves of bread do *you* have?"). The transformation from the impossibility of feeding under difficult conditions to an overabundant feeding will be operated by a manipulation of the figures of the object. Therefore, we shall pay very close attention to the values which these figures transmit. The problem is presented especially with the "fish," for the "loaves of bread" could in this instance be simply a hyponymic figure[15] for any kind of nourishment. Thus they appear in the discourse:

$$\text{"to buy 200 denarii} \qquad \simeq \qquad \text{"to buy something}$$
$$\text{worth of bread"} \qquad\qquad\qquad \text{to eat"}$$

The reference to the fish draws attention to the opposition on the food axis "bread" *vs.* "fish." This is a fleeting reference in the text since in the estimation of the number of guests (v. 44) there is mention only of "those who had eaten the bread." The fish play a prominent role in the narrative only at the very moment of the feeding performance.

In this instance we will interpret the bread and the fish in relation to the system of places in which their communication occurs and in connection with the other figurative elements that this communication introduces.[16] "He took the five loaves of bread and the two fish, and lifting his eyes toward heaven he blessed and broke the bread and gave it to the disciples ..." The communication of the object by Jesus is bracketed between the two consecutive processes of "taking" and "giving" which frame the "look toward heaven." The transfer of the object which stands between the disjunction (object taken away from a subject and a place) and the conjunction (object attributed to a subject and a place) takes place in the passage by way of an "elsewhere" ("to lift the eyes toward heaven and say the blessing"). Jesus is the operator of this transformation which conjoins "heaven" and "the word" with the transformed objects. This transformation corresponds to a reorganization of the spatial locations of the story: the "land," "sea" and "heaven." The bread which is a hyponym for food is introduced into the

narrative (v. 37) in conjunction with the inhabited places
where it can be bought; it is the figure of a /socio-economic/
land, but it will be consumed in the desert, a /non-socio-
economic/ land (a place where buying is impossible) that will
be transformed by this same communication into /pastoral/ land
("on the green grass"). Within the framework of our pericope
we will take the fish as representing another place--the "sea"
--about which we have already been able to observe certain
semantic and figurative characteristics. In this sequence,
both in contrast to heaven and in conjunction with it, the
text lays out /land/ and /sea/ as values which are conjoined
in the figure of the bread and fish distributed to the crowd.
We were able to observe in sequence I the failure of the apostles' crossing ahead of the crowd (which "ran on foot"): this
was the negation of the sea as /separation/. In sequence III
we will find this negation of the sea and this assertion of
the land in Jesus' walk upon water, a figure in which /land/
and /sea/ are connected to one another. By negating the determinations of /separation/ from /land/ or from /sea/, each
sequence in our text negates the disjunction /land ∨ sea/ in
order to assert the conjunction /land ∧ sea/ by presenting
the third term /heaven/ in the second and third sequences.

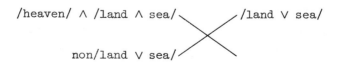

/heaven/ ∧ /land ∧ sea/   /land ∨ sea/

non/land ∨ sea/

We shall leave the fourth term of this system unstated; it
will be manifested later on.

Thus, a spatial isotopy could be proposed in this story
in which the operations upon the values contribute to the production in the story of a "new creation": this is the establishment of a new land and a new sea which closely approximates

what goes on in apocalyptic stories.

c. *The Crowd of Dinner Guests*

The crowd enters into the figurative trajectory of the
first two sequences and we can now provide a full accounting
of the actantial and semantic transformations which affect
it. In the first sequence, the cleavage between the movements of the apostles and the crowd permits us to determine
the latter's role as subject of the wanting-to-be in NP2.
This position is confirmed in sequence II where Jesus is the
operating subject who transforms the crowd from virtual subject (in a disjoined state) to a realized subject (in a conjoined state). Thus, we may represent the crowd's actantial
roles in the following way:

sequence I: anti-subject of   --->   Subject of the
               the power (NP1)   wanting-to-be (NP2)

sequence II: virtual subject   --->   Realized subject
               of state (NP2)   of state (NP2)

In the figurative trajectories of the previously analyzed
discourse, these actantial roles select the thematic roles.
The differences between these roles enable us to describe the
crowd's semantic transformations.

The crowd appears first of all in the text in the figure
of "everyone coming and going": that is, in a *sociological*
isotopy having the values of /number/ and /unstable movement/.
The initial transformation of the crowd which is realized by
means of its movement, preserves the value of /number/ ("the
people," "many," "all of the villages") but adds /orientation/
to the movement. In Jesus' interpretative operation ("compassion") the crowd's thematic role is recategorized in terms

of a pastoral isotopy ("they were as sheep without a shepherd") in which the object of the crowd's secondary program is made to appear as the figure of the missing shepherd. As a subject of state in the processes of sequence II, the crowd takes on the roles of the one who is both /taught/ and /fed/. This second role is the only one described in detail. "He ordered them all to lie down to eat on the green grass. They spread out in groups of 100 and 50." The /number/ of the crowd is continued but /instability/ gives way to /organization/ wherein the crowd becomes the table guests of a meal arranged according to Jesus' orders. It is possible to see in the "green grass" a figure corresponding in this instance to the continuation of the pastoral isotopy (manifested above by the sheep without a shepherd) as support for the deixis of gratuitousness which is established at the start of sequence II, and contrasted with the deixis of economics suggested by the disciples' proposal which Jesus rejects. This group of textual semantic references is organized on the basis of a code which permits us to note the way in which the different qualifications of the crowd become significant in their differences:

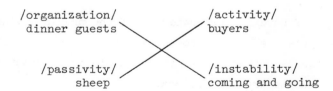

d. *The Construction of the Places*

We have already noted the semantic structure of the places in sequence I. By going ahead of Jesus and the apostles, the crowd realized the double operation of leaving the place where it had been staying in order to rejoin (and, by its presence, to determine) the apostles' place. In sequence

II the system of places receives additional characterization. An opposition of /urban/ *vs.* /pastoral/ comes to light when Jesus' interpretation recategorizes the crowd as being in a disjoined state (without a "shepherd"). The location of the teaching of the crowd (sheep without a shepherd), which is designated by the disciples as the "desert," is a /pastoral/ place distinguished semantically from the "villages and towns" where the disciples propose to send the crowd. For those actors marked by the deixis /urban/, the non-inhabited place is the "desert."

Throughout sequence II the figure "green grass" transmits the positive characteristic of the deixis; the system of places may thus be represented as follows:

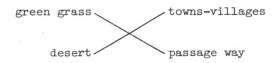

We establish "passage way" as the fourth term by homologation of the system of places and the system of the crowd's thematic roles. The "passage way" corresponds to the crowd of people coming and going.

e. *The Figures of the Actants*

We have noted in the initial sequence that the duplication of secondary programs produces a complex actantial structure which accounts for a system of actants.

This arrangement reappears in sequence I with the debate between Jesus and the disciples. The discursive organization of these programs produces the actors who are responsible for the actantial roles. We are interested in this instance in the figure of the sender. We will see in "heaven" the figure of the receiver of the values which are put into circulation by Jesus in the acts of teaching and feeding. "Lifting his eyes to heaven, he gave thanks." This figure is associated here with "speech" and "prayer." The figurative trajectory responsible for the program of feeding proposed by the disciples permits us to take "village" as a figure of the anti-sender. This is the place from which the crowd left for its first transformation; it is there that the disciples wish to send the crowd in order to buy the food. This place manifests socio-economic values. Beginning with the second sequence, the non-anti-sender may be represented by the "group of disciples," a non-socio-economic group which becomes the source of the food ("You yourselves give them something to eat"). And it is the food which comes from the disciples that will be used by the sender "heaven" for the purpose of feeding the crowd. The figure of the non-sender will be sought for in an isotopy related to the socio-economic isotopy and within which "heaven" represents a figure of the positive aspect: sequence III will present the non-sender in the figure of a "hardened heart."

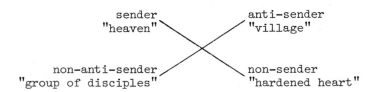

3. THIRD SEQUENCE: THE AMAZEMENT

We divide up this third sequence on the basis of a spatial criterion. In v. 45 Jesus has his disciples climb back into the boat and in v. 53 we record their arrival upon another shore at Gennesaret. The space in which the disciples' narrative program will unfold is therefore

clearly marked. In this case we have a maritime episode to
be correlated with the first maritime episode in the text
and to the non-maritime episode in the desert and on the
mountain.

The striking feature of this sequence is the episode
that we ordinarily associate with the title "the walk upon
water." It is one thing to account for this episode as an
autonomous story and quite another to do so within the
framework of a much larger whole within which it is integrated. Therefore, it is in function of its position within
the text that we have to analyze this sequence in terms of
its narrative programs and its figurative trajectories.

3.1 *Narrative Component*

a. *Jesus' Solitude*

We have observed that the feeding of the crowd in the
narrative does not lead to a glorifying performance by Jesus.
The third sequence opens with the dislocation of the group
of actors who were previously gathered together. Disciples
and crowd are sent away from the place that Jesus alone
occupies in the narrative. But this sending away does not
signal an actantial or categorical opposition between Jesus
and these actors. As for the crowd, the program introduced
in sequence I and interpreted by Jesus in sequence II is
realized; as for the disciples, their being sent off ahead
of Jesus ("Go before him to the other shore") may be seen
as homologous to the values manifested in the overabundant
communication of the object.

The dismissal of the other actors has the effect of
leaving Jesus alone on stage and of underscoring this solitude. Jesus is by himself at the beginning of this sequence

as he was alone at the beginning of sequence II ("as he was getting out of the boat he saw"). In both instances, Jesus' solitude is associated with mediating places in the narrative: the "shore" (land *vs.* sea), the "mountain" (land-sea *vs.* heaven), whose position functions as a point of connection between the sequences and between specific performances ("to have compassion" and "to pray"). On the narrative plane we will describe both of these processes as two correlated functions on the plane of manipulation-sanction: the one corresponds to the acquisition of a wanting-to-do by the subject; the other corresponds to the sanction in which the sender evaluates the subject's performance in terms of the values that it represents. Jesus' prayer, which we have already interpreted as a "blessing" in the feeding of the crowd, on this occasion occupies the position which is anticipated for the sanction. Having taken place in solitude, the sanction remains in the position of non-appearing (the secret) in relation to the other actors; the subject has yet to be manifested. The appearance which is conformed to its being needs to be communicated and received. These remarks lead us to situate Jesus' prayer on the mountain in the third sequence.

b. *To Walk or to Row*

In this sequence the narrative inaugurates a new narrative program in which the disciples are the subject operators ("he made his disciples get back into the boat and go ahead to the other shore towards Bethsaida"). Jesus' injunction communicates the having-to-do and the knowledge-how-to-do to the disciples since the different processes to be accomplished have already been stated. But the realization of this program is barely manifested: the narrative is focused upon Jesus. No process of movement is mentioned on the part of the

disciples. We simply record the static situation of the
boat in the middle of the sea and the loss of the disciples'
power-to-do because of an anti-subject ("the opposing wind").
This deprivation transforms the disciples into virtual subjects of the power-to-do for the sailing program.

The disciples' situation is integrated as an object of
Jesus' knowledge ("seeing"). We cannot establish the relation
of implication between this knowledge about the disciples'
being and Jesus' walking upon water with any certainty, nor
can we assert that the latter leads to the restoration of the
disciples' power-to-do. Jesus walks upon water and joins up
with the disciples. This movement performance succeeds ("he
went past them") whereas the disciples' performance fails.
On the basis of an identical principal narrative program of
crossing the sea, the narrative establishes two sub-programs,
one of walking and the other of sailing. Jesus is not the
anti-subject with regard to the disciples, for his walking
upon water does not deprive the disciples of their power-to-
sail; however, it does produce other effects. At most, it
casts light on the failure of the disciples' secondary program
and the virtualization of their competence by means of discursive juxtaposition. We encountered an analogous scheme in
the other sequences. While crossing the sea by boat, the
apostles and Jesus are seen from a distance by the crowd which
runs along on foot; the purchase of food in the villages proposed by the disciples is made unnecessary by the overabundant
gift of food by Jesus. This parallelism between both secondary programs enables us to pose a relationship between two
types of power-to-do, that is, two types of modal values, by
manifesting different figurative trajectories within the same
discursive configuration.

In the comparison which is then established between the
secondary programs, the text asserts the values represented

by Jesus and negates the values represented by the sailing
of the disciples, whereas no particular figurative actor
establishes a connection between both operations by means
of a hierarchically superior narrative program that the
narrative could manifest. The narrative constitutes Jesus
and the wind as similar actors: the wind virtualizes the
operating subjects of NP1 and Jesus asserts the values of
NP2.

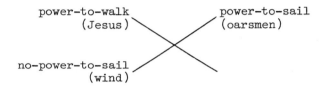

c. *From Fear to Amazement*

With an opposing "but when they," v. 49 begins with a
performance of interpretative doing in which the disciples
are subject. It is a prospective interpretative doing since
the knowledge about Jesus' appearance, which is in this case
a knowledge about the doing ("while seeing him walking on
water"), precedes the affirmation of knowledge about the
being ("a ghost"). Thus, two planes are distinguished from
one another: a phenomenal plane--that of appearance--and
a noumenal plane--that of being. A fiduciary type of relation is established between these two planes. Not being able
to deduce the being from the appearance, the subject of the
interpretative action decides that a certain relationship
exists between the appearance and the being.[17] This situation is clearly manifested in the text: the fiduciary relation is indicated by the reference to believing ("they thought
that he was a ghost"). Thus, the text causes the veridictory
value of the disciples' interpretation to appear with the

result being a false knowledge about Jesus: they are not satisfied in not recognizing Jesus walking on water (non-power-to-know); they falsely assert a qualification by taking him for a ghost (power-not-to-know).[18] These distinctions appear in a clearer form in the following model:

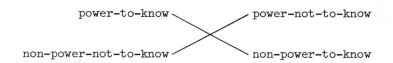

This model shows that the ghost is a figure for the *power-not-to-know* since the interpretative performance takes place and because the affirmation that he is a ghost is a consequence of it. However, in manifesting both the deceptive fiduciary operation (to believe that) and the disciples' incompetence, the narrative forces us to take this ensemble (the disciples' interpretative doing and affirmation of the ghost) as a figure of *non-power-to-know* which characterizes the disciples at this moment in the narrative. We can then make a distinction between two levels in the definition of the disciples' state: a level of *recognition* (realization of interpretative operations) and a level of *knowledge* (realization of fiduciary operations logically presupposed by the interpretative operations). The relation between these two planes is a relation of performance to competence.

In communicating their knowledge about Jesus, the disciples' interpretative performance consists in attributing a role to Jesus within a narrative program which is reconstructed by the subject of knowledge. In this case, Jesus is endowed by the disciples with the role of opponent which is manifested by the figure of "trouble" and "fear," corresponding to the role of virtual subject that the disciples claim for themselves. At the conclusion of the disciples' interpretative performance, the narrative result may be summarized as follows. The narrative has opened up several planes upon which the disciples occupy a deceptive position, a disjoined situation which will be resolved later on in the text:

-- subject disjoined from the power-to-sail
-- subject disjoined from the power-to-know
-- subject conjoined to a false knowledge about Jesus' being
-- subject disjoined from the power-to-want ("fear")

In v. 50 we start a new phase of this third sequence ("but he") which would be the phase of the disciple's restoration for which Jesus is the operating subject.

On the plane of knowledge (so far a false knowledge about Jesus' being), the declaration, "It is I," communicates true knowledge. However, this restoration of knowledge calls for some comment. Jesus' declaration is made in a direct style and the process of enunciation is given in detail ("he spoke with them"; "he said to them"). We will oppose this to the manifestation of the disciples' knowledge: the declaration about the ghost is fully contained within the statement without a shifter of the enunciation.[19] The disciples are not the subject of the speaking but of the cries. In other words, we will ask ourselves what lack of knowledge Jesus' declaration fills. "It is I" says something only about the actorial identity of the one who "walks" and who "speaks," and does not otherwise determine the thematic role of the one who walks on the sea. Jesus' affirmation is an affirmation about the subject's being. It implies a process of recognition which is of an inferential nature in which the knowledge about being precedes the knowledge about being and appearing.[20] Finally, let us note that the knowledge is communicated to the disciples according to the transfer formula:

$$sender \longrightarrow object \longrightarrow receiver$$

We see the difference between the communication of knowledge and the acquisition of false knowledge by the disciples at the conclusion of their interpretative doing in which they are the subject of a reflexive appropriation which sets a particular fiduciary type of competence into operation (in their case, a deceptive one). Therefore, what is the disciples' situation with respect to knowledge after Jesus' declaration? There is a communication of true knowledge, but there is no positive manifestation of the reception which would complete the narrative statement in the correlation

$$communication + reception$$

Jesus' declaration allays their fear ("take heart"), but the narrative does not manifest the disciples' state subsequent to this injunction. Jesus' climbing into the boat realizes the conjunction of Jesus with the disciples on the somatic plane. At the same time, it is the neutralization of the opponent to the sailing program, although it does not positively manifest the restoration of a power-to-sail. The disembarking is clearly indicated, but the anticipated place is not reached. Once again these performances on the pragmatic level are integrated within the cognitive plane: the end of the narrative records the disciples' state and presents their amazement as the sequence of the non-knowing ("they did not understand about the loaves") and the non-power-to-know ("hardened heart").

This presses us to make a distinction between fear

and amazement on the narrative plane. The former corresponds
to the virtualization of the disciples, which is brought about
by the acquisition of false knowledge. It affects the disciples' power-to-want. The amazement points to a logically
prior state: the disciples were conjoined to a true knowledge
about Jesus' being, but remained disjoined from the power-to-
know. The virtualization remains at the level of interpretative competence and within the narrative space that we are
analyzing, the establishment of the disciples as a competent
subject remains incomplete.

c. Conclusion

This third sequence manifests the articulation of the
pragmatic and cognitive planes: the pragmatic plane is
integrated as an object of interpretative doing. On the
pragmatic plane, the disciples are the virtual subject of
the ability-to-do in contrast to Jesus who is a competent
subject (sailing *vs.* walking). The disciples become subject of the interpretative doing, having as their object
this performance by Jesus. The result of the interpretative
doing ends in the disciples becoming the virtual subjects
of the power-to-want ("fear"). Therefore, there is a progression in the disciples' virtualization. The liquidation
of these disjoined states does not restore the disciples
to their previous competence. Rather, the discourse makes
apparent a level of competence on which the disciples remain the virtual subject of the power-to-know and wanting-
to-know. The reference to the "loaves of bread" which is
then made by the narrator forces us to articulate this deep
level of interpretative competence together with the previous sequences of the story. We will do this further on.

3.2 *Discursive Component*

The movement on the sea with respect both to Jesus and the disciples is accounted for in two different figurative trajectories: the one has to do with sailing, and the other with walking. We have already encountered oppositions of this sort in the initial sequence.

We take these manners of movement as metonyms for the places where they occur and which the discourse holds in opposition: "the boat was in the middle of the sea and he was alone on the land." In the story of the walk upon water, in contrast to the immobility of the disciples at sea, we note the figurative manifestation of the dominance of /land/ in the paradigmatic relationship between the value of /land/ *vs.* /sea/. In the first sequence, both the crowd's running on foot ahead of the apostles and Jesus manifested the same system of values.

Sequence II showed us that the transformations affecting the elements /land/ and /sea/ were in the service of a transformation of their junctive relations (conjunction *vs.* disjunction):

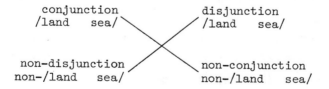

If the /sea/ was negated by the crowd's movement as is the case in the action of the "wind" and in "Jesus' walk upon water," it takes the form of a distinct figure which is both separat*ed* and separat*ing* from the land. The crowd, by its overtaking-movement, negates the /separation/ which constitutes the secondary value for the apostles and Jesus. Jesus walks on water; however, the walk is for the purpose of joining up with the disciples and ultimately of Jesus' taking his place with them in the boat. In sequence II, the manipulation of "bread" and "fish" corresponds to the same code. The transformation of the values /land/ and /sea/ which are represented in the food items is accomplished in their conjunction with /heaven/ which can, as a connecting element on the figurative plane, represent the sender. This organization of values is encountered once again in sequence III. In this instance, Jesus is not defined solely by the walk upon water. The "mountain of prayer" represents the passage in Jesus' trajectory between the performances in the desert and that of the walk upon water, which is the mediating place of the elements recategorized by the semantic transformations in sequence II. And it is as operating subject that Jesus realizes his walk upon water. This pragmatic manifestation is registered upon a figurative trajectory which is comparable to the one in which the disciples move. It is the conjunction of elements that the disciples were called upon to interpret and to understand. Thus, to recognize Jesus walking upon water or to understand about the loaves of bread is to interpret the same organization of values under different figurative forms.

Therefore, we can propose this taxonomic representation of the places and figures based upon the existence of cosmological places (heaven, land, sea), figures which mediate between these places (mountain, wind, shore), transfer objects (bread, fish, word) and corresponding interpretative operations (prayer, amazement, compassion):

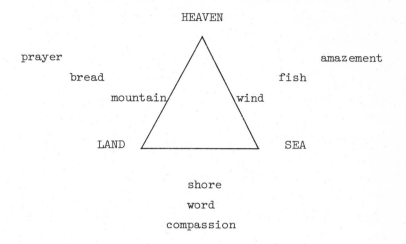

This system of places is established in sequence III
and Jesus is the operating subject for their conjunction.
It is in this role that he presents himself to the disciples
in his walk upon water. We therefore think that the figure
of the "ghost" which the narrative produces as a false representation of Jesus must be analyzed semantically as the opposite figure, the contradictory to the conjunction /land ∧
sea ∧ heaven/ which defines Jesus.

We have recorded the prayer on the mountain as a secret
form of the sanction. On the level of appearance, there is
no positive figure for the operating subject (except for his
identification, "It is I"); there is only the contradictory
figure, the ghost, and the reference to the disciples' incompetence in recognizing Jesus. This all takes place as if
this third sequence occupied the position of a glorifying
performance corresponding to Jesus' principal performance
in sequence II. Indeed, the cognitive level is clearly
manifested here, but on the one hand this glorifying performance is deceptive, and on the other the text manifests
values which are contradictory to the ones that the principal

performance has established. Even though the actions of teaching and feeding involve a power-to-do without any opposition, the recognizing performance is deceptive; there is a failure in the process of making-known.

4. GENERAL REMARKS

4.1 *Narrative Component*

a. *The Recurrence of a Narrative Form*

In all three sequences we were able to recognize the recurrence of a common narrative form: the semiotic existence of a subject A is manifested in its relation to an object O. A narrative program is begun for the purpose of realizing the conjunction (S ∧ O) by establishing a competence on the part of the operating subject. In all three sequences this competence is virtualized either by an opponent or by the proposal of another program, and this virtualization creates a dysphoric state for the subject who is disjoined from the value object and deprived of the modal values making up the competence necessary for realizing the program. The restoration, i. e., the realization of the initial program, is accomplished by means of another competence, by another operating subject and in another figurative trajectory in such a way that the mode of the object's transferral and its values are found to be transformed at the conclusion of this process.

This narrative with its three sequences balances the secondary programs of a principal program and manifests the success of an operating program in opposition to the failure of another secondary program. We have labeled these secondary programs NP1 and NP2. We can represent their correlation

with the two schemas of a semiotic square: the failure of
NP1 (which we write as non-NP1) implies the success of NP2
in our narrative, and it is clearly an assertion since on
each occasion NP2 succeeds without the confrontation of an
anti-subject, except for the third sequence where only the
values of non-NP2 are presented for the recognition of Jesus.

Our text offers several realizations of this narrative
form: in the separation of the apostles and Jesus who are
headed off by the crowd; in the feeding of the crowd brought
about by the gift of bread and fish; in the crossing of the
sea by Jesus who goes past the immobilized disciples; and
finally, in the recognition of Jesus with the characteristics
that we have already mentioned.

Being situated at the level of the secondary programs,
that is to say at the level of the competence of the operating subject, both sub-programs NP1 and NP2 characterize,
by their opposition to one another, two orders of values in
which the operating subjects are related; they also call
attention to the receivers upon which they depend. This is
the reason why we were able to construct a system of receivers
(see p. 90).

The final realization of NP2 is established beginning
with the failure of NP1 even though it cannot be said that
the operating subject of NP2 includes the virtualization of
NP1 within its own program. We cannot claim that in this
story Jesus tries to place his disciples in impossible situations but the narrative does just that. From this particular
syntagmatic position of the success of NP2 no doubt comes the

"miracle effect" which appears in the reading of the text:
Jesus' performances are realized in the depths of failure
and impossibility. The realization of NP1 would be the
prime solution, one that is "proper" for the situation where
one finds oneself (in order to avoid the crowd, to feed it,
to cross the sea, or to recognize Jesus). The failure of
this solution leaves an "overly proper" solution in its place.

The "non-overly proper" position corresponds to the
negative side of the "overly proper" object and to its dysphoric evaluation. The overly proper resolution is marked
by an over-abundance (euphoric); it is recategorized as
excess (dysphoric) which creates a new situation that has
to be resolved. This situation is realized in our text in
connection with Jesus' teaching and the late hour during
which it unfolds.

b. *The Progression of the Story*

The narrative form that we have just constructed is
that of a change in programs--from NP1 to NP2--and with each
occurrence an interpretative performance is established between two series of pragmatic performances. When this performance precedes the realization of NP2 it corresponds to
the acquisition of knowledge about the nature of the values
and/or the knowledge-how-to-do which is necessary for the
realization of NP2. When it follows the realization of NP2
this performance occupies the position of the glorifying
performance in which it is necessary to acquire knowledge

about the nature of the operating subject of NP2 and the
nature of the values of this program. In each sequence of
the story there is something to be learned; we are able to
follow a progression in the narrative in the manifestations
of the interpretative doing.

In the first sequence, the knowledge acquired by the
crowd ("to see" and "to recognize") implies their running
ahead of those who are sailing, and is correlated in sequence
II with the knowledge acquired by Jesus ("to see" and "to be
filled with compassion") which implies the teaching. This
initial narrative block in its cognitive aspect constitutes
the manifestation of *volition* (wanting-to-be, wanting-to-do).
In sequence II the interpretative doing precedes the realization of NP2: it introduces in the debate between the disciples and Jesus the paradigmatic relation of NP1 and NP2 with
respect to the power-to-do which will be put into operation
with the feeding of the crowd. Sequence III is more complex.
It manifests the disciples' interpretative doing following
Jesus' pragmatic performance upon the sea in the position of
a glorifying performance and for the purposes of acquiring
knowledge about the being and the power-to-be of the subject.
But in the quest for knowledge itself we have again encountered the basic narrative form presented above: the failure
of NP1 in the recognition of Jesus (he is taken to be a
ghost) and the assertion by Jesus himself concerning his
identity.

This narrative progression in knowledge enables us to
account for the following statements within the framework
of the narrative grammar: "They were filled with amazement.
Indeed they understood nothing about the loaves of bread,
for their hearts were hardened." These statements manifest
three planes of non-knowledge: the "amazement," the "lack
of comprehension concerning the bread" and the "hardened

heart." We offer the hypothesis that what we have is a rereading of the whole narrative on a cognitive isotopy and from the point of view of the disciples. We discover here traces of the narrative progression that we have just described among the three sequences. The amazement appears to us to be the mark of the disciples' incapacity to realize the passage from non-NP1 to NP2 at the moment of the recognition of Jesus' power-to-be. The lack of comprehension about the bread marks the disciples' incapacity to make the passage from non-NP1 to NP2 at the moment of the acquisition of the knowing-how-to-do (to buy *vs.* to give). The "hardened heart" represents at the end of the story the mark of the disciples' incapacity to realize the passage from non-NP1 to NP2 at the moment of the acquisition of the wanting-to-do: what we have in the disciples is the figure opposite to Jesus' "compassion."

Throughout the entire three sequences, the passage from non-NP1 to NP2, in the various figures that it assumes, is proposed to the three actors in the narrative. The crowd realizes the transformation which makes it the subject of the wanting-to-be in the first instance. In the second, Jesus is defined as subject of the wanting-to-do by his compassion and the power-to-do in the performance of teaching and feeding the crowd. In this realization of NP2 the disciples, whose power-to-do and knowledge-how-to-do in NP1 were virtualized, share in Jesus' performance although the text does not express their acquisition of the values at work in this performance. It is for this reason that we have recognized them as being in the position of non-anti-sender. The positive assertion of NP2's values is put in question in sequence III in the figure of the recognition of Jesus. We have seen that it does not lead to recognition.

The first and third sequences in our story manifest the

correlated contents in which the principal transformation,
operated in the narrative at the level of the topical contents, is to be measured.[21] This transformation is performed
by the realization of the program NP2 on the crowd's behalf
in the teaching and feeding. We had noted how at the beginning of the text, the plane of manipulation-approval was
brought forward in the approval of the sender Jesus as contrasted to the teaching of the apostles. On the same plane,
the third sequence manifests the manipulation of the disciples by the sender Jesus.

CORRELATED	Approval apostles (sequence I)		Manipulation the disciples (sequence II)
TOPICAL		Realization subject of state crowd (sequence II)	

The entire text may be read on the narrative plane as a
complex installation of a contract in which a subject (the
apostles), virtualized in a given program in which it appeared
to be competent, is presented with the quest for and realization of new values. The establishment of these new values
in the story occurs in the pragmatic performance of Jesus on
behalf of the crowd. They are next proposed to the disciples
on the basis of the interpretation and recognition of the
pragmatic performances. Sequence III, which takes up once
again the figurative elements of sequence I, registers in a
negative mode the acceptance and recognition of the values
put into operation by Jesus in the realization of NP2. The
narrative is not complete.

4.2 *Discursive Component*

In the progressive analysis of the text we have constructed a certain number of partial systems, accounting for
the meaning effect in the specific parts of the text which
organize the figures into limited isotopies. At the end of
this study we can attempt in a hypothetical way to construct
a single model which describes in a systematic way the organization of the most general semantic categories which are
selected in the interrelation of the narrative's lexematic
figures. In order to do this we account for the fact that
a fixed narrative form articulates the contents in the correlation of NP1 and NP2. Likewise we take into account that
for each realization of this narrative model the articulation
of the secondary programs is manifested by making parallel
two figurative trajectories belonging to the same discursive
configuration. The semantic values which the code that we
seek to construct articulates, must select those figures
manifesting the characteristic states of the subjects in
each of the discursive realizations of NP1 and NP2. The
semantic code takes the form of a semiotic square which is
formed from the correlation of two isotopic schemas: one
Distinctiveness, the other *Affinity.* These designations are
arbitrary; they correspond to features selected by the organization of the partial systems that we have constructed
throughout our analysis and by the possibilities that these
systems possess for homologation.

This fundamental organization of values corresponds to
the organization of discursive elements (discursive configurations, figurative trajectories) which make up the text.
These discursive elements are established on four registers
or semantic planes which are the figurative isotopies on the

basis of which the variations in figures may be recognized.
We have selected the plane of *cosmological* figures, where we
have identified the elements of space and their relations;
the *sociological* plane where we observed the transformation
of the crowd's roles; the *communicative* plane which records
the transfer objects and their modalities; and the *cognitive*
plane where we observed the transformation of the disciples
by their acquisition of knowledge. The semantic code accounts
for the significative differentiation of the figurative trajectories on the basis of these four planes.

The value /affinity/ is transmitted by the figures of
/over-abundance/, /communion/ and /recognition/. It is set
in contradiction to the /non-affinity/ which is supported
by the figures of /excess/, /crowd/ and /non-recognition/,
characteristics belonging to the crowd at the beginning of
the text and then of the disciples in their interpretative
doing. On the schema of *Distinctiveness* the value /distinc-
tiveness/ corresponds to everything that is measureable--
separation, exchange, succession and division of times and
places. We found the figures of this value on all four
semiological planes. The contradictory value /non-distinc-
tiveness/ is manifested by the deceptive states of the subjects who are engaged in the program of /distinctiveness/,
whether it be in the maritime movements which are either
headed off or fail, or in the proposals for exchange which
are negated, or in the reconsideration of the division of
times and places.

The following model sums up these facts. The most
general semantic values are further specified here by some
of their semantic characteristics.

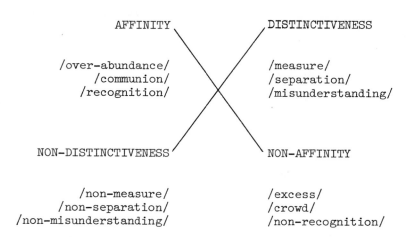

AFFINITY

/over-abundance/
/communion/
/recognition/

DISTINCTIVENESS

/measure/
/separation/
/misunderstanding/

NON-DISTINCTIVENESS

/non-measure/
/non-separation/
/non-misunderstanding/

NON-AFFINITY

/excess/
/crowd/
/non-recognition/

We have seen in the narrative analysis how each schema
of the model may correspond to either of two narrative programs. The narrative is organized in terms of the comparison
of these two programs. The two secondary programs in each
sequence are directed toward the acquisition of the means
for realizing a principal program. Situated so they are at
the level of competence, they are significative of the relations of the subject with the sender and the values which
ought to govern the actions of the subject. As values which
are characteristic of the secondary programs, /affinity/ and
/distinctiveness/ represent two modes of competence on the
part of the operating subject in the processes which are supported by the semiological planes of the discourse. The
passage from NP1 to NP2 corresponds on the semantic plane to
the relation of implication of /non-distinctiveness/ to
/affinity/, which is contrasted with the opposite implication
of /non-affinity/ to /distinctiveness/. These implications
represent the change of isotopy--the passage from one schema
to the other--and characterize on the narrative plane either
the manipulation (attribution of the knowledge about the

values of a program to a subject by a sender) or the sanction
(assertion of the values in whose name the subject realizes
the program, and the disclosure of the value of the objects
in this program). The particular effect of the model in this
narrative would be to make evident in a privileged way the
operations of assertion and the actors who are opposed to one
another (especially in the case of Jesus and his disciples)
according to the type of assertion that they manifest, that
is according to the deixis that they realize.

The functioning of the semiological planes equally contributes to the characterization of this narrative. We have
noted this with regard to the teaching and feeding: the possible homologation of the operations realized upon different
figurative trajectories produces a particular representation
of the values of the objects and we were able to compare the
somatic and noological, the cosmological and the sociological
planes in order to define the new object of value proposed
to the disciples.

The trajectory of our analysis and the semiotic description that we have given of the Markan text is at this point
no doubt incomplete. We wanted to show with a specific text
how it is that what we customarily read as a series of episodes constitutes a unity of meaning which can be accounted
for on the narrative and the discursive planes.

NOTES

1. In the unfolding of the canonical narrative program
we can distinguish two different planes:
--the plane of performance which emphasizes the transformations of the subject-object relation
--the plane of manipulation-sanction which emphasizes
the sender-subject relation

The story opens with manipulation: there is a communication of knowledge concerning the being of the values. This corresponds to the establishment of the subject by the sender and belongs to the "contract" phase of the story. The story closes with the sanction; this corresponds to the evaluation of the performances accomplished by the subject and belongs to the "glorifying" phase of the story. Thus, we can distinguish between a plane of values which governs the subject's performances and a plane of the setting-into-motion of these values in the performances.

2. In our description the term "crowd" designates a character which can be presented in the narrative in the form of different figures.

3. In the realization of a narrative program, the objects and actors may be distinguished according to whether they are or are not favorable to the narrative's realization. In the axiological evaluation of the semantic content we will make a distinction between the contents of the two deixes (see Chapter 1, n. 24). On both of these two planes these distinctions are designated by the opposition:

euphoric *vs.* dysphoric

4. See Chapter 1, n. 5.

5. "If we designate the plane of appearance as the *phenomenal* plane and the one of being as the *noumenal* plane-- these two planes being understood as having a semiotic existence--we will say that the interpretative doing consists in passing from one plane to the other in establishing a *fiduciary relation* between the two planes by successively asserting first the one and then the other of the two modes of existence. In fact, it is this relationship which, when articulated in different ways, is constitutive of a field of *fiduciary values*, taking the lexical form in English of "certitude," "conviction," "doubt," "hypothesis," etc., a field of modal overdeterminations the organization of which is still difficult to imagine." (A. J. Greimas, *Maupassant*, pp. 107-108)

6. A narrative program is considered to be *complex* when the acquisition of the *principal value object* necessitates obtaining *values* which we might call *secondary* values which constitute the object of *sub-programs* or *secondary programs*.

7. On *modal values* or *modal objects* see Chapter 1, n. 5.

8. This type of program realizes the formula of exchange:

$$(S_1 \wedge O_1 \vee S_2) <==> (S_1 \vee O_1 \wedge S_2)$$

in which the symbol " $\wedge$ " indicates a state of conjunction and " $\wedge$ " a state of disjunction.

9. In fact, the secondary programs have to do with the acquisition of modal objects (establishing competence). Therefore, they are characteristics of the relations between the operating subject and his sender. The latter is always present within the story as the representative of the values in circulation in the principal narrative program.

10, The form of this model is that of the semiotic square (cf. Chapter 1, n. 17). It articulates two axes of contradictory relations (also termed *schemas*) which define four terms: S1 *vs.* non-S1; S2 *vs.* non-S2. These terms are defined by other relations. Contrarity articulates S1 and S2, on the one hand and non-S1 and non-S2 on the other, and characterizes both *axes* of the model. Implication articulates S1 and non-S2 on the one hand and S2 and non-S1 on the other. These two latter relations define both *deixes* of the model. The terms which make up the deixis are called *conformed* terms: S1 and non-S2 are conformed terms.

On this point read A. J. Greimas, "Les jeux des contraintes sémiotiques," *Du Sens* (Seuil, 1970), pp. 138-140; English translation, "The Interaction of Semiotic Constraints," *Yale French Studies* 41 (1969), 86-105.

11. The performances that can be registered at the narrative anthropomorphic level (the level of actantial roles in the narrative programs) correspond at the deep level to the logical operations effected upon the semantic contents: for example, negation or assertion. See A. J. Greimas, "Éléments d'une grammaire narrative," *Du Sens* (Seuil, 1970), pp. 157-183.

12. "Analytical experience--both our own and that of other semioticians--has clearly shown that in order to account for relatively complex texts it is necessary to envision the possibility of breaking down any actant into at least four actantial positions which we might present by making use of the terminology proposed by Claude Picard:

114

Actant — Antactant

Negantactant — Negactant

(A. J. Greimas, *Maupassant*, p. 63.)

13. The existence of a subject is defined by its relation with an object, and both terms are always correlated. Thus we can state in precise terms the relation S   O: the relation is *virtual* if the subject is disjoined from its object, and the operation of this disjunction is called *virtualization*; it is *realized* when the subject is conjoined to its object, and the operation of this conjunction corresponds to the *realization* which is the conclusion to the narrative program. See also Chapter 1, n. 5.

14. On this point see A. J. Greimas, "Un problème de sémiotique narrative: les objets de valeur," *Langages* 31 (1973), 29-34.

15. "The term 'hyponomy' designates a relation of inclusion which is applied not to the referent but to the signified of the lexical items concerned. It is related to the logic of classes. Thus, *dog* maintains a certain meaning relation with *animal*; there is an inclusion of the meaning of *dog* within the meaning of *animal*. We can say that *dog* is a hyponym for *animal*." J. Dubois, *Dictionnaire de Linguistique* (Larousse, 1973).

16. In the space that we have delimited for our study we will refrain from making any comparison between this communication of food and the narrative of the "Last Supper." It could be done, though requiring that we account for the substitution of "wine" for "fish" as a figure conjoined with bread in another textual setting when passing from one story to another.

17. See above, n. 5.

18. We have analyzed the "ghost" in this situation only from the narrative point of view. But it is not unimportant to the signification of the story that Jesus be taken for a *ghost* (in other passages of the gospel he is taken for John the Baptist or Elijah). The semantic analysis of this figure belongs to the discursive analysis that we will carry out below.

19. There is a shifter of the enunciation when the

subject of the enunciation delegates the speech process to
a subject within the discourse.

20. See above, n. 5.

21. The distinction between *correlated* and *topical*
contents is necessary because of the fact that ordinarily
within stories the transformation of the contents manifested
in the initial and final sequences happens as a result of
the transformation of another type of content realized by
the principal performance.

III.

"We Must Make Merry ..."

Controversy and Parables (Luke 15)

[1]The publicans and sinners were all drawing near to hear him. [2]And the pharisees and scribes murmured saying, "This man receives sinners and eats with them." [3]Then he told them this parable:

[4]"What man among you having a hundred sheep and losing one of them does not leave the ninety-nine in the wilderness and go after the sheep which is lost until he finds it? [5]And when he has found it lays it on his shoulder rejoicing, [6]and when he comes home he calls together his friends and neighbors saying, 'Rejoice with me, for I have found my sheep which was lost.' [7]Even so I say to you there will be more joy in heaven over one sinner who repents than over the ninety-nine who have no need of repentance.

[8]"Or what woman having ten coins if she loses one does not light a lamp and sweep the house and search carefully until she has found it? [9]And when she has found it calls together friends and neighbors saying, 'Rejoice with me, for I have found the coin which I had lost.' [10]Even so I say to you that there is joy before the angels of God over one sinner who repents."

[11]And again he said:

"There was a man who had two sons. [12]And the younger one said to his father, 'Father, give me the share of

inheritance which is coming to me.' And he divided up his possessions between them. [13]Not many days later the younger son, after gathering together all that he had, left for a distant country and there squandered his inheritance in loose living. [14]When he had spent everything, a great famine arose in this country and he began to be in want. [15]So he went and joined himself to one of the citizens of this country who sent him out into the fields to feed the swine. [16]And he would have liked to have fed on the pods that the swine ate, but no one gave him anything. [17]But coming to his senses, he said, 'How many of my father's servants have bread enough while as for me, I perish with hunger! [18]I will rise up and go to my father and I will say to him, 'Father, I have sinned against heaven and before you. [19]I am no longer worthy to be called your son; treat me as one of your hired servants.' [20]And he arose and went to his father. But when he was yet at a distance, his father saw him and had compassion and ran and embraced him and covered him with kisses. [21]And the son said to him, 'Father, I have sinned against heaven and before you. I am no longer worthy to be called your son.' [22]But the father called his servants: 'Bring quickly the best robe and put it on him; and put a ring on his finger and sandals on his feet; [23]and bring the fatted calf, kill it and let us eat and make merry, [24]for this my son was dead and is alive again, he was lost and is found.' And they began to make merry.

[25]Now his elder son was out in the field. And as he was drawing near to the house he heard music and dancing. [26]He called one of the servants and asked him what was going on. [27]And he said to him, 'Your

brother is home and your father has killed the fatted
calf because he has returned safe and sound.' [28]*He*
became angry and refused to go in, and his father came
out and entreated him. [29]*But he answered his father,*
'Lo, all of these years I have served you and never
disobeyed your command and you never gave me a kid
so that I might make merry with my friends. [30]*But*
when your son comes home, who has wasted your posses-
sions with prostitutes, you kill the fatted calf for
him.' [31]*But he said to him, 'My son, you are always*
with me and all that is mine is yours. [32]*We must*
make merry and be glad for your brother was dead and
is alive, he was lost and is found.'"

The fifteenth chapter of Luke is built around two poles:
on the one hand a controversy situation and on the other a
fictitious discourse by Jesus. The controversy opposes the
scribes and pharisees to Jesus over the matter of eating with
sinners. It does not develop into a polemical conversation:
Jesus' adversaries are content to "murmur" in commenting upon
his behavior. Jesus speaks at length and offers two comparisons and a parabolic story. His opponents do not respond.
It would be possible and quite simple to lift out one of the
three "parables" in order to analyze it independently of its
context. However, the relation which exists between narrative and discourse, a pragmatic doing and a cognitive doing,
leads us to proceed initially with an overall analysis.

The presentation of the controversy provides the framework of events for the discourse. The latter prolongs the
story since it constitutes Jesus' reply to his opponents'
murmuring and, in turn, is transformed into a story. Thus,
several narrative scenes are distinguished within the text:
the one in which Jesus, the sinners, the scribes and

pharisees act; we shall call this the "primary story"; a
second scene in which the characters in the parabolic story
act (the father, the two sons, etc.); we shall call this
the "secondary story." Between these two we find a type of
"intermediary story" which introduces onto the stage all of
the characters from the primary story in new roles and complementary characters. The first part of this analysis will
be devoted to the clarification of the relations existing
between these three narratives. We will be concerned in
particular with the problem of the thematic and actantial
roles. The second part of the analysis will take up in detail the analysis of the parabolic story of the two sons.

A. "THERE IS JOY OVER ONE ..."

The division of the characters into three groups corresponding to the three stories provides us with a principle
for segmenting the text. The three narrative levels are, in
fact, manifested in successive sequences: the disagreement
between Jesus and his opponent (15:1-2); the invitation to
understand (15:3-10); the adventure of the two sons (15:11-
32). Two kinds of relations--paradigmatic and syntagmatic,
relations of equivalence and of transformation--exist between
them.

1. SEQUENCE I: DISAGREEMENTS BETWEEN JESUS AND HIS OPPONENTS (15:1-2)

This initial sequence is characterized by the introduction of two incompatible, narrative programs, by the
duplication of the doing of two operating subjects and by
the establishment of a system of thematic roles.

1.1 *The Narrative Programs*

The relations among the three groups of characters
(Jesus, the publicans and sinners, the scribes and pharisees) are established as follows: an object (word) could
eventually be transmitted by Jesus to the sinners. The
latter move "in order to hear him." They are the subjects
of a wanting-to-be capable of becoming the state subjects
conjoined with their object after the performance. Jesus
is the operating subject to the extent that he accomplishes
the transmission of the object. He manifests a wanting-to-
do, a power-to-do and a knowing-how-to-do. The text does
not state this directly, but the remark made by the scribes
and pharisees presupposes it: "He welcomes sinners and he
eats with them." The mandate which establishes Jesus in
this actantial role and precedes its acceptance is only
represented indirectly in the receivers' movement. These
various operations and their own sequences are compatible
with and complementary to one another. They are inscribed
within a single narrative program, NP2,[1] which is aimed
toward the transmission of the word to the sinners.

The scribes' and pharisees' reaction, by contrast,
is not expressed here. It corresponds to an opposite program, NP3. It is not manifested as a program of the attribution of an anti-object, but rather as an attempt to put
in question NP2 by attempting to discredit its operating
subject. If there is a possibility to virtualize NP2, it
exists only indirectly, not because the anti-subject would
be able directly to impede or to halt the performance of
NP2, but because a deprecating interpretative doing is
applied to this performance.

1.2 *The Duplication of the Doing*

While the two narrative programs are completely opposed
to one another, they are not perfectly symmetrical. In NP2
the performance is defined under the category of a pragmatic
doing: to eat and to teach. In NP3 it is defined under the
category of interpretative doing. The operating subject of
NP2 acts. The operating subject of NP3 interprets. This
dissymmetry in operations, which is quite visible in the
initial sequence, will be attenuated in what follows when
Jesus, in turn, will offer his own interpretation of the
facts.

The use of a system of actants which is more complex
than the simple opposition of subject *vs.* anti-subject can
enable us better to describe this actantial distribution.[2]

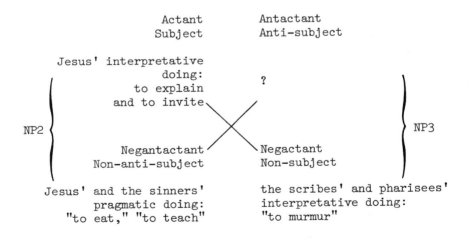

Each schema of the semiotic square corresponds to a
different isotopy. The distinction between roles is therefore in function of a double opposition: syntactic, NP2 *vs.*
NP3; and semantic, /to act/ *vs.* /to interpret/. Jesus assumes

both roles in succession first by acting and then by explaining. His direct opponents assume only one role. An empty spot in the deixis corresponding to NP3 signals the incomplete character of the representation of values by the characters. In this way this sequence opens up to the rest of the chapter and the Gospel story.

1.3 *The System of Thematic Roles*

We must not expect from so short a pericope very many explicit manifestations of the figurative trajectories and their interactions. What is to follow therefore will have to be subject to verification later on. Three groups of characters are named: "publicans and sinners," "pharisees and scribes," "him" (an anaphoric pronoun referring to Jesus). Next, they are qualified by their action: the first group "comes near in order to hear Jesus"; the second "murmurs"; and Jesus "welcomes the sinners and eats with them." The semantic features of the appellations are combined with these features of the qualificational definition in order to indicate the role of each character.

a. *Roles Manifested by Appellations*

From the point of view of the semic values contained within their appellations and recorded in the cultural dictionary of the figures, the "publicans and sinners" belong to the same configuration (religious and social) as do the "pharisees and scribes." They are its negative representatives; they have transgressed the values exemplified by the others. We may say:

$$\frac{\text{pharisees and scribes}}{\text{publicans and sinners}} \simeq \frac{\text{the ones who keep the law}}{\text{the ones who transgress the law}}$$

This double role is acquired prior to the characters' entrance into this text. It is therefore open to transformation due to the fact that a third character enters onto the stage along with them and so they will have to be defined in relation to him.

From the point of view of his appellation, Jesus does not belong to the religious configuration. His proper name singles him out as a particular individual who is not endowed with a social role. The anaphoric pronoun which designates him here refers obviously to everything that the development of the text has previously manifested with regard to him, but what it retains does not appear at once in the form of a title designating a role. It is the third person, in between the ones who keep and the ones who transgress the law, which constitutes his initial narrative title. Being distinct from first the one and then the other, Jesus does not represent a particular configuration:

$$\frac{\text{Jesus}}{\substack{\text{scribes, pharisees +}\\\text{publicans, sinners}}} \simeq \frac{\text{non-marked configuration}}{\text{marked configuration}}$$

b. *Roles Manifested by Actions*

The pertinent roles in the text under analysis must be deduced from the series of operations performed by these three characters. Publicans and sinners come near in order to hear Jesus. The action is defined as an oriented movement. This displacement may be interpreted as a figure of desire: S   O.

The intensity of this desire is represented by the durative
and unanimous nature of the movement: "... *all were* drawing
near him." The object of this wanting is indicated: they
are looking for a word. The text does not specify the content of this word. But there is no doubt as to the discursive configuration introduced here: it is that of communication. It defines Jesus as speaker, the publicans and sinners
as hearers, and the object as word or signs. However, it is
difficult to decide what is the actual figurative trajectory
and therefore the thematic role: is it a relationship of
professor to students, of master to servants, of preacher to
congregation?

The denunciation of Jesus' behavior by his opponents
reduces the ambiguity and selects the roles. By saying
nothing about the teaching and by emphasizing the welcoming
attitude and the common meal, the denunciation sets forward
the affective and festive aspect of the communication as
well as its effect in establishing significant relationships.
As speaker, Jesus represents a friendly word which welcomes
and an efficient use of sign which transforms his hearers
into dinner guests.

$$\frac{\text{Jesus}}{\substack{\text{publicans and} \\ \text{sinners}}} \simeq \frac{\text{holder of the word}}{\text{beneficiary of the word}} \simeq \frac{\text{subject}}{\text{receivers}}$$

Within the same figurative trajectory the thematic roles of
Jesus and his interlocutors are similar. They are distin-
guishable from one another only by the difference in actantial
positions.

It is clearly the opposite case with the scribes' and
pharisees' role. They murmur. As before, this is a use of
the word and a position in the chain of communication, but

in order to disapprove, to suspend the feast and to cancel
its communal effects. We may say:

$$\frac{\text{Jesus}}{\text{pharisees and scribes}} \simeq \frac{\text{friendly word}}{\text{denouncing word}} \simeq \frac{\text{welcome and meal}}{\text{murmur and denial}} \simeq$$

$$\frac{\text{proposed communion}}{\text{demanded separation}} \simeq \frac{\text{powerfulness of signs}}{\text{control over signs}}$$

The difference is no longer simply actantial, but axiological. If we take into account the connotation associated
with the murmuring as indirect condemnation, as unstated in-
dignation, we could fill out the picture in this fashion:

$$\frac{\text{Jesus}}{\text{scribes and pharisees}} \simeq \frac{\text{straightforward word}}{\text{non-articulated word}} \simeq \frac{\text{explicit}}{\text{unacknowledged}}$$

c. *The System of Roles*

When entering into a common text the characters retain
the determinations which are attached to their appellations
and acquire others. This process is subject to strict constraints which impose upon each of the roles so constituted
a definition correlative to all of the others. In order to
construct this system we must know the universe within which
the roles (the invariant of the system) are defined as well
as the criteria or variables of distinction.

The invariant in this case is the universe of signifying
action, of the word and of its effects. The diversity of
roles is produced by the variety of actantial roles and the

duplication of narrative programs.

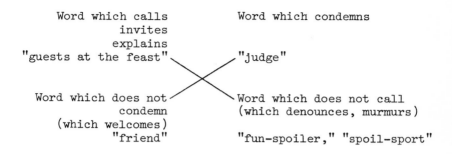

This model still lacks detail and precision, for the primary narrative is not complete. Moreover, it will not be complete since the chapter ends with the parabolic story and does not return to the reaction of the characters presented here. The whole of the underlying semantic universe will be manifested by other means.

2. SEQUENCE II: THE INVITATION TO UNDERSTAND (15:3-10)

This second sequence is introduced by an enunciative formula: "Then he told *them* this parable: ..." It shows on the one hand that this discourse prolongs the primary story and corresponds to a performance by Jesus which is prepared for in the first two verses, and on the other hand that the receivers of this verbal performance are not clearly identified. "Them" can refer back to the scribes and pharisees by themselves, but it does not necessarily exclude the publicans and sinners. This is essentially an explanatory and hortatory performance. Jesus becomes the operating subject of a self-interpretative and persuasive doing. From a thematic point of view an additional detail is provided: Jesus' word takes the form of a "parable."

Indeed, the reported discourse does not have the appearance of being an explanation or a didactic justification. It is transformed into a story. A two-fold change takes place: from the primary narrative to the discourse and from the discourse to a narrative activity which establishes characters, programs and new roles on a second stage. This duplication of the primary narrative by a secondary narrative is carried out in sequence III. At this point it is only clearly leaning in this direction. This is one reason for speaking of an "intermediary story." In fact, the characters remain in part the characters of the primary story: "What man among *you* having a hundred sheep ..." They are questioned right away by Jesus: "I say to *you*, even so ..." However, the time, place and roles are different and other characters which are absent in the primary story enter on the stage. Within the sequence itself a difference is established between the comparison of the shepherd ("What man among *you* ...") and the woman who manifests a greater distance in regard to the characters in the primary story.

The narrative character of the discourse combined with the partial identity in characters gives the effect of similarity which invites us to follow in the analysis of sequence II the same procedure as that taken in sequence I: a study of the narrative programs, of the different types of doing and of the thematic roles.

2.1 *The Narrative Programs*

In contrast to the primary story which presents an apparent polemical structure, both comparisons seem to be stories with a single narrative program. There is nothing standing in the way of the liquidation of lack nor in the way of the attribution of the object. There is nothing which stands in the way of the recognition of the realized subject. This narrative program includes the establishment of a subject (in the name of a common and incontestable instinct which rules out any refusal of the mandate), the qualification, the performance, the attribution and the recognition. It culminates in the unquestioned joy and the feast which characterize the positive final contents.

However, we cannot fail to record an opposed program; at the very least it brings about the disappearance of the sheep and the coin and the obstacles to their recovery. But on the one hand it is implicit (neither the anti-subject nor the opponent are represented) and on the other hand, it is not prolonged after the performance. There is no dispute over the rejoicing. If we were to compare this organization to the one found in the primary story we could offer two observations:

(1) In the intermediate narrative there is no representation of the anti-subject. The lack does not follow upon a misdeed. The shepherd has lost his sheep, the woman has lost her coin. No one has taken them from them. The liquidation of the lack does not presuppose any confrontation. In the primary story, by contrast, the anti-subject is represented--the pharisees and scribes (non-subject)--but only in the order of the interpretative doing; there is a confrontation, but it follows the performance of restoration. At the very least we have a difference in focalization.[3] In both comparisons everything centers upon the shepherd and the woman who are the only active characters in the story. They lose, they seek and they find. In the primary story nothing is said about the loss and recovery even though several characters may, as is the case elsewhere in sequence III, assume these functions.

(2) However, we could have more than a difference in focalization. By suppressing all opposition at the moment of the object's attribution and recognition, the intermediary story produces an effect of unanimity which breaks with the murmuring and contestation. The effect appears to be crucial. It is due precisely to the suppression of NP3, and this absence is the result of the transformation brought about by Jesus' discourse. It is correlated with a change in role: the characters who assume the actantial role of operating subject in NP3 (pharisees and scribes) are transformed in the comparison with the shepherd into operating subjects of the positive program (NP2). Their relation to the sheep is one of wanting-to-do and of wanting-to-be. They themselves call for the celebration. This is a complete reversal of actantial positions. Combined with the modification of thematic roles, it produces a true recategorization.

As for the initial negative program corresponding to the misdeed and to the lack in sequence II, it is missing in the primary story which starts off with an attempted restoration.[4] Sequence III, by contrast, will manifest both of these negative programs of which one is opposed to the possession of the object and the other to its recovery. The table found on the following page represents these three possibilities.

2.2 *The Diversity of Doings*

In each of the comparisons three types of performances follow upon one another: (1) the somatic performance of searching for and recovering the lost object; (2) the persuasive performance of extending an invitation for a communal rejoicing; (3) the assertive performance (communication of knowledge) about the joy in heaven. The first two performances are brought about by the shepherd (or the woman), the

	NP1	NP2	NP3
Seq. I		$S_1 => [(S_2 \lor O_1) \\ -> (S_2 \land O_1)]$	$S_3 => [(S_1 \land O) \\ -> (S_1 \lor O)]$ Interpretative doing (Contestation) bearing upon NP2
Seq. II	$S_x => [(S_4 \land O_3) \\ -> (S_4 \lor O_3)]$ Misdeed and lack (realized condition)	$S_4 => [(S_4 \lor O_3) \\ -> (S_4 \land O_3)]$	
Seq. III	$S_6 => [(S_5 \land O_4) \\ -> (S_5 \lor O_4)]$ Misdeed and lack (event recounted)	$S_5 => [(S_5 \lor O_4) \\ -> (S_5 \land O_4)]$	$S_7 => [(S_5 \land O) \\ -> (S_5 \lor O)]$ Interpretative doing bearing upon NP2

S_1 = Jesus

S_2 = publicans and sinners

S_3 = scribes and pharisees

S_4 = shepherd and woman

S_5 = father (and son)

S_6 = younger son

S_7 = older son

O_1 = word

O_3 = sheep and coin

O_4 = familial values

O = recognition of subject's being

$=>$ = transformation doing

$->$ = passage from one state to another

actor in the statement. The enunciator of the intermediary story is responsible for the third and it is intended for his questioners. It therefore prolongs the primary story in a direct way.

The effect of this organization is reached when Jesus states the heavenly reaction to the conversion of a sinner. He thereby produces an interpretation of his own behavior and negates the pertinence of his opponents' murmuring. The relation between what he does (welcoming the sinners, eating with them) and what he says is a relation of appearance to being, of the phenomenal to the noumenal. The knowledge thus communicated is knowledge about the object's being. It is therefore capable of modifying the wanting of his interlocutors. The affirmation of heavenly joy is very much a manifestation of the interpretative doing which is opposed to what the murmuring manifested. It makes clear the incompatibility of the scribes' and pharisees' negative attitude with the heavenly reaction.

This declaration acquires its persuasive value from the similarity established between heavenly joy and the shepherd's behavior: "Even *so* ..." The persuasive doing is already at work in the micro-story whose logic imposes an attitude upon the principal character, the shepherd (who is found to be at the same time one of the ones who murmurs), which is contrary to the attitude he adopts as interlocutor. In this way the murmuring is put in contradiction with a type of universal commonplace. As such, the murmuring is overdetermined and is rendered more unacceptable.

The second comparison no longer allows for the same identification of the operating subject of the search--a woman--with Jesus' interlocutors. But coming as it does after the first comparison, it duplicates it in a superlative way and gives accent to the generality of the behavior described:

the woman corresponds to the man, the piece of money to the sheep, the house to the wilderness, etc. The logic of participation in joy does not admit of any exception.

We see that the intermediary story as a whole refers as much to the tactic of persuasive doing as it does to narrative know-how. In the parabolic mode it is the controversy which is prolonged. Jesus' opponents are called upon to react and, once disqualified with respect to their own system of values, are invited to accept the one belonging to Jesus, a system of values which has currency in heaven itself.

The relation among the different types of doing within the chapter as a whole may be represented in the following table:

			Murmuring (reference to a legal norm)	Dissuasive doing
First part of the initial sequence	Phenomenal (appearing)	Hypothetical narrative sequence Lack Attribution Collective joy	Description (reference to an experimental norm)	Persuasive doing
	Noumenal (being)	Secret narrative sequence Heavenly joy	Assertion (reference to a heavenly norm)	
	Summing up:	Familial story	Narration (reference to a symbolic norm)	
Pragmatic doing	Interpretative doing			

2.3 *The Thematic Roles*

Two configurations appear: the first is pastoral, the
second monetary. They give rise to the characters: shepherd,
housekeeper; the objects: sheep, coin; the places: wilderness, house. Both are equally foreign to the configurations
identified in the primary story. But a third configuration
appears in the final declaration. It is a religious configuration including the angels of God, the sinner, heaven. It
is homologous with one of the configurations in the initial
story and possesses at least one element in common with it:
the sinner.

a. *The Figurative Trajectories*

There is a common activity, a very specific activity,
which both shepherd and housekeeper hold in common: to lose,
to seek, to find, to rejoice, with the accent placed upon
the searching. It is the persistence of this searching which
is underscored. This selection, which determines the object
as being lost, sought for and recovered, enables us to confirm the sheep and the coin as being two representatives of
a common class of objects: objects which may be lost, sought
for and found. Consequently, both configurations are reducible to a third, more general configuration: the economic
order. The coin is the monetary unit employed in the exchange
of goods. The sheep as a farm product may be as well. This
equivalence outweighs the difference between them that the
opposition /animate/ *vs.* /inanimate/ would represent. Sheep
and coin are primarily thematic elements of economic value.
In the parabolic story of the two sons, that which will be
lost and found will no longer belong to this order of values,

an order that only inheritance (and perhaps the kid, as well) will bring to mind. From the outset of the text the difference is expressed in these terms:

$$\frac{\text{sheep and coin (and kid)}}{\text{younger son}} \simeq \frac{\text{economic values}}{\text{human values}} \simeq$$

$$\frac{\text{inheritance}}{\text{familial status}} \simeq \frac{\text{relation of possession}}{\text{relation of communication}}$$

The operating subjects--the shepherd and the house-keeper--are therefore considered first of all in their common role as owner. This is clearly what the texts say: "What man among you having a hundred sheep ...."; "What woman having ten coins ..." But this role itself is trans-formed and as a result of this transformation it will be set in harmony with the father's role in the secondary story and with Jesus' role in the primary story. We begin to see that the chapter's unity is built by the successive homolo-gations of figurative elements and by their integration within the unified organization of thematic values.

b. *The Transformation of Roles*

The transformation is manifested by the decrease in value of the large quantity and the great increase in value of the small quantity. This shift, which is perceivable first of all at the level of the object in the form of an opposition between the unity and what remains out of the total (99 or 9), also signals a modification of roles. It belongs to the owner's role in its purely economic aspect not to neglect the smallest part of his goods, to care for

and to recover it. However, it is not part of the owner's
role to prefer a unity as over against a larger quantity.
Nevertheless, the text clearly seems to suggest this first
in a negative and then in a positive way in the first comparison ("What man ... does not leave ...") and in an exclusively positive way in the second comparison ("What woman ...
does not light a lamp and sweep the house and search carefully until she has found it."). The new relationship which
is established between the male and female owners and the
object possessed is more on the order of attachment to a
value which is precious and sought for in and of itself
than of a simple possession. This order selects the features
which give their behavior their affective tones and generates
the figures in terms of a sentiment code: "lays it on his
shoulder rejoicing ..." This joy is motivated not by the
reconstitution of the initial possession but by the discovery
of the lost object. The role of possessor of economic goods
is bent in the direction of a role which is difficult to name:
one who loves, perhaps, in the strong sense of the term--a
friend and protector. The owner possesses more or less, and
the amount is a matter of importance to him. The one who
loves is linked to each object that he values and which becomes, in its own right, significant in his eyes, ceasing by
the same token to be a numbered possession.

The evaluation of the thematic roles on the basis of the
discursive configurations observed in the text corresponds to
the construction of sememes on the basis of lexemes.[5] It
therefore represents the passage to the pertinent semantic
values and enables us to build up semiotic models. This is
the way in which they could be presented if we were to compare
the one with the other:

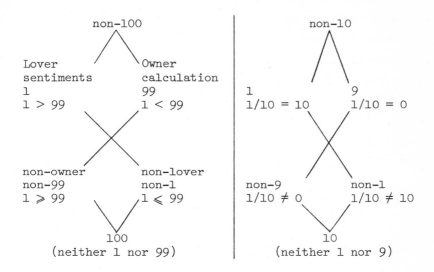

c. *Additional Remarks on the Thematic Roles*

By virtue of the relation of similarity established between what takes place in the wilderness and in the house and
what takes place in heaven, we may consider that the thematic
roles are harmonized on both sides and that the economic configuration is integrated along with the religious configuration into a common thematic organization. The additional
characterizations contained in the declaration relating to
the joy in heaven will permit us to describe the common system in more detail. These details have all the more interest
for us, for they are subsumed under an interpretative doing
and therefore represent the plane of being in agreement with
the plane of appearance.

Within the religious configuration a selection is made
which is limited solely to the parallel between the sinner who
repents and the 99 righteous who have no need of repentence.

The parallel is explicit in the initial declaration and implicit in the second: "... there will be more joy ..." *vs.* "... there is joy over one ..." The distinction between the unity and the larger quantity and the over-evaluation of the unity presupposes the same choice of semic features both here and in the two micro-stories: it is not the quantitative aspect of the object which is pertinent and which defines the thematic role of the subject.

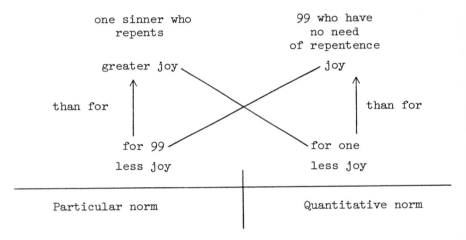

From the point of view of the context in which this semic feature is found, an important difference must be noted: it is no longer the object, whether lost or found, which needs to be counted and evaluated but the performance of a subject in transforming his own state--"a single sinner *who repents*." The relation to the subject of the joy is modified. It loses all connotation of possession or property. This actantial shift entails a modification in the organization of recognition. The joy no longer sanctions the recovery of an object but the success of a performance by a subject. The one who rejoices is no longer the one who searched for and then found, but those who are both witnesses and the actors. The joy

defines a place (heaven) and a group (the angels of God). As
for the 99, they are defined in a symmetrical way by the absence of performance and not by what they would represent as
goods possessed and preserved by a subject. The joy on their
behalf is not excluded; it is simply smaller.

This more obvious incompatibility of roles with the
economic characterizations confirms that their definition,
within the micro-stories of the sheep and the coin, must be
sought for in a direction which is more affective than economic. Conversely, the experimental and uncontestable character which is attached to the relations of the economic order in return marks the religious universe about which Jesus
speaks. His declaration harmonizes the order of appearance
(experience) and of being (in heaven and from the point of
view of heaven). It manifests what is true in the harmony
between two practices and establishes it in correlation with
a particular thematic role which is capable of subsuming all
of the figures employed.

d. The System of Thematic Roles

The harmonization of roles centers in this instance
around the type of relationship which exists between subject
and object, with the object capable of being either an economic value or a performance accomplished by another subject.
The equilibrium of the system presupposes that the consideration for the object's value in and of itself--of the subject's
interest in the case of the sinner who repents--predominates
over the consideration for the possessor's joy. We may say:

$$\frac{\text{shepherd and housewife}}{\text{owner of sheep or money}} \simeq \frac{\text{lover}}{\text{possessor}} \simeq \frac{\text{heaven (angels of God)}}{\text{malcontents who murmur}}$$

Obviously, both domains (animals and money) from which the
representatives of these roles are taken are not totally adequate. The shepherd and the woman retain something of their
role as owners and the gap which exists between what happens
in heaven and on the earth is bridged only through the assertion of similarity: "Even so, I say to you ..." Many aspects
of the roles are yet to be manifested. The parabolic story,
which occupies only two thirds of the text, presents additional possibilities which the discourse is not going to develop.

3. SEQUENCE III: THE ADVENTURE OF THE TWO SONS (15:11-31)

   This sequence will become the object of a detailed analysis which we shall introduce by indicating the mode of articulation of this parabolic story with the two preceding sequences.
   It is introduced by an enunciative formula which is
different from that which introduced the second sequence:
"And again he said ..." The receiver is not mentioned. The
text then places itself at a distance with regard to the primary story. This distance will eventually be accentuated by
the fact that the characters are in this instance entirely
different from those of the primary narrative and by the absence of any questions to the interlocutors. The structure
of the third sequence, therefore, is simpler than the structure of the two preceding sequences. It is because of this
narrative autonomy, this "shifting"[6] which permits the adventure which is told to unfold in its own time and place and
according to its internal logic, that we speak with regard to
this part of the text of the "parabolic story" and the "secondary story."
   Curiously, in spite of this strict distinction among

narrative scenes, the parabolic story echoes all of the important elements of the primary story and the intermediary story: the disappearance and lack, the return and the recoveries, the feast and the meal, the murmuring and the dispute, the invitation to understand and to enter into joy. It is therefore a sort of condensation of the chapter as a whole, a mirroring point which reflects the chapter's main lines. However, the dominant concern of this organization perhaps resides in the new configuration which it lends to these figures: the familial configuration. This is a family story, as it had previously been an animal story and a money story. The relation of this familial configuration to the religious configuration, which constitutes the point in common of the two initial sequences, is closer. The sin and the sinner now appear in the narrative scene and heaven is conjoined with the actor-father ("I have sinned against heaven and before you.") in such a way that the absence of the concluding declaration about the heavenly joy is compensated for in advance by this conjunction. It is the whole of this overall shift which we must now study.

B. "THERE WAS A MAN WHO HAD TWO SONS ..."

In approaching this third sequence as a pertinent element of the entire chapter, we shall have to take into account at one and the same time its narrative autonomy and its dependence with regard to the global signifying system. We must therefore concern ourselves simultaneously with the description of the narrative programs, the levels of doing and the thematic roles and their correlation with those in the preceding sequences.

In order to facilitate our observations about the text we will subdivide it into three sub-sequences: the degradation

(15:11-16), the reintegration (15:17-24) and the debate
(15:25-32). Three kinds of criteria which are represented
in the following table justify this segmentation: the
situation in space, the orientation of the action and the
position of the father in relation to his sons.

	Sub-sequence I	II	III
Place	Foreign country	House	Outside of the house
Action	Leaving Lack	Return Attribution	Refusal to enter Denunciation
Actors	Father and two sons	Father and younger son	Father and older son

1. THE DEGRADATION (15:11-16)

The first sub-sequence is more complex than its name
implies. The degradation is, in fact, manifested only at
the end of a process within which successful and deceptive
performances blend together. Moreover, the point of view,
namely that of the younger son, on the basis of which success and failure are judged, represents only one aspect of
the situation. Therefore, the analysis must restore the
complexity of the narrative network and the discursive
system.

1.1 *The Narrative Programs*

a. *An Explicit Program*

It seems that we can organize a group of operations in
a program centering about the younger son. It has to be with

the request for a share of the inheritance, the departure
for a distant country, the use of possessions and the attempt to procure new goods for oneself through association
with a foreign employer. The initial performance which is
manifested in the form of a demand accepted by the father
and followed by the attribution of an object is converted
into a secondary sub-program. The inheritance becomes a
modal object, a figure for the power-to-do and the power-
to-be. The acquisition of this competence permits the start
of a principal performance which ordinarily is preceded by
a movement of the invested and qualified subject. This
principal performance consists in the exchange of the inheritance as over against another object which is not represented
in the text, but which is considered as attributed as the
value object. The linguistic statement: "He squandered his
fortune in loose living" provides us with only an interpreted
representation of the performance and its object. With the
manifestation of the underlying narrative statement there is
an interference here of the axiological elements of the enunciator who modifies the thematic roles and their mode of articulation with the actantial roles. We shall come back to
this. We can produce the narrative formula underlying this
type of transformation:

Simple acquisition: $S \Rightarrow [(S \vee O) \rightarrow (S \wedge O)]$

Exchange: $S \Rightarrow [(O_1 \wedge S \vee O_2) \rightarrow (O_1 \vee S \wedge O_2)]$

When O_1 = object-power (Op) as is the case here ("His
fortune"), then the acquisition of O_2 coincides with the
loss of power:

$$S \Rightarrow [(Op \wedge S \vee O) \rightarrow (Op \vee S \wedge O)]$$

Accordingly, the performance is limited within time.
On the one hand, this limit is correlated in this instance
with the inexhaustible nature of the qualification, and on
the other hand with the intervention of a cosmic agent (the
famine) whose position, consequently, must be defined. Thus,
there is a return to the secondary sub-program with a view
toward reestablishing the competence. The foreign employer
now occupies the father's place in the communication of the
modal object. However, the end of this qualifying performance
is opposed to the preceding one: there is no attribution of
power. The employer is a deceptive actor: "He would have
liked to have fed on the pods ... but no one gave him any."
There is no longer any sender. A transformation has thus
taken place, and it is that which we must now describe.

b. *An Opposite Program*

If the principal agents of the degradation are easily
identifiable--the famine and the foreign employer--it is, by
contrast, difficult to say at what moment the course of events
is reversed and, therefore, where for the first time the opponent to the younger son's program is indicated. We have
noted that the acquisition of the value object coincided with
the exhausting of the power. We must call attention as well
to the fact that the value object itself is not represented
as a lasting object which can continue to exist after its
attribution. It is a consumable object which obeys the same
law as the power that makes its acquisition possible. Therefore it disappears when the power runs out. This is what the
statement already referred to says: "He squandered his fortune in loose living"; and what is confirmed in the opposition
between "After having gathered together all that he had ..."
and "When he had spent everything ..." The exchange which

constitutes the performance is a sort of unequal exchange
leading itself to a disjunction of subject and object. The
anti-power, represented by the famine, presupposes this initial phase of the degradation. This natural calamity is not
in and of itself the anti-subject; it reveals--more than it
causes--the son's uncertain status. It shifts the lack from
the area of food and moves it toward elementary, psychological needs. In so doing, it reveals the priority of the lack.
Therefore, it is within the operation of the principal program that we must look for marks of the opposite program
which ends up in a dominant position.

How are we to account for this particular type of opposition? We cannot think in terms of two contrary, narrative
programs wherein the one negates the other in confrontation
since both programs are accomplished simultaneously: the object is acquired at the same time as the power is used up;
the subject is realized at the same time as he is alienated.
Rather, what we have here is a single narrative program which
is duplicated through a play upon being and appearance. The
same series of actions is able to establish the apparent
realization of the subject and his actual alienation. The
textual manifestation states very clearly what is the case
from the point of view of being: famine and foreign employer
eliminate all ambiguity: "and he began to be in want." It
is now clear that the son's trajectory leads to the desire
for food and that he was motivated only by this want which
appears in other forms and which in the final analysis is
deceptive.

Just as the subject has invested himself, we can say
that this lack is also the result of his own misdeed. By
wanting and believing himself able to acquire the value object, he alienates himself from it. We can represent his
modal position in the following model:

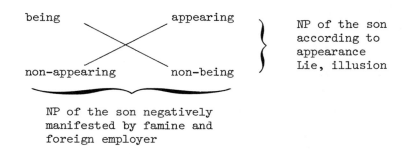

being   appearing

non-appearing   non-being

NP of the son
according to
appearance
Lie, illusion

NP of the son negatively
manifested by famine and
foreign employer

c. *The Single Program of Degradation*

Once the unity of the narrative program is established,
whose repetition is explained as the truth effect,[7] it remains for us now to describe it. It is a negative program
since a lack and misdeed are recorded in it. It is negative
in relation to an implicit, positive program which has no
other representation than that of its sender, the father of
the two sons. We do not yet know what it corresponds to,
but we can see that by breaking away from the sender, the
younger son is separated from the value object and enters
the space of the anti-sender which is clearly represented
by the distant country, or anti-house. The intermediary
stage of the exchange of objects corresponds to the transition point between what is true and false, that is the passage by way of lie and error.

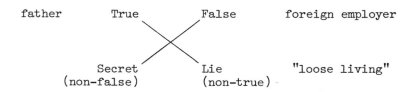

father   True   False   foreign employer

Secret   Lie   "loose living"
(non-false)   (non-true)

1.2 *The Diversity of Doings*

All of the explicit narrative operations in this initial
sub-sequence take place on the somatic order: the exchanges
are exchanges of goods. The practical nature of the performances and the objects is particularly clear beginning with
v. 14 where the problem of food comes to the foreground. However, we can note that the duplication of the narrative program in terms of being and appearing entails an interpretative
operation by the operating subject. The subject must understand the object in one mode or another; the object is, in
effect, proposed in a two-fold way: as apparent and true.
He does this through an interpretative operation thereby establishing his knowledge about the object and conditioning
his wanting. The son's demand, "Give me the share of the
inheritance which is coming to me," contains, although implicitly, this interpretative doing. It is presupposed by
the valorization of the inheritance and the object that it
enables him to acquire. It is this interpretative doing
which renders the performance problematic and leaves it open
to being deceptive. It is opposed to the enunciative interpretation of the text itself which while situating the son's
adventure in its own axiological perspective, states then
and there its negative quality: "He squandered his inheritance in loose living." In this text, both of these points
of view correspond, the one to the phenomenal plane and the
other to the noumenal plane.

1.3 *The Thematic Roles*

Because the preceding observations have already taken
into consideration certain aspects of the semantic investments

of the actors, they anticipated the thematic roles in the
analysis. It suffices now to give an initial systematiza-
tion that the analysis below will have to verify.

Three configurations provide the essence of the figures
in this sub-sequence: family, merry making and subsistence.
They are related to one another through consideration of
economic means.

a. The Family Roles

1. The familial configuration furnishes a group of
pre-organized roles: father, sons and brothers. The mother
is lacking but her absence does not pose a problem for the
reader because of the legal turn taken by the story. In
fact, the paternal role is limited to the activity of dividing up the family possessions. This limitation is a result of the younger son's request. Therefore, it presupposes
an initial restrictive determination of his own role. This
son becomes the one who demands economic goods; he is first
a potential owner soon to become an active owner. At this
point he does not leave the familial configuration but transforms the father into a distributor of wealth and the parti-
cipative object circulating within the familial space into an
object which can be divided up, appropriated by each person
and spent. The position of the elder son who has not yet
demanded a share is itself modified: "He divided up his
possessions between *them*."

The transformation of familial roles then accomplished
in the direction of the economic configuration prepares for
and makes possible the passage of the younger son into the
configuration of leisure and the life of amusement. He remains a son, but he is now "prodigal," that is, defined exclusively by his capacity to spend his inheritance. The

spatial figures are correspondingly transformed:

$$\frac{\text{son}}{\text{owner}} \simeq \frac{\text{father}}{\text{distributor of possessions}} \simeq \frac{\text{participatory value}}{\text{appropriated value}} \simeq$$

$$\frac{\text{to have}}{\text{to spend}} \simeq \frac{\text{familial}}{\text{economic}} \simeq \frac{\text{house and homeland}}{\text{distant country}}$$

2. "When he had spent everything ...": with the reversal of the situation there is correspondingly a reversal of roles. The prodigal son becomes poor and his desire is diverted towards food. His role is articulated now in terms of the famine and the foreign employer. The former pertains to a cosmic configuration; the second to a socio-professional configuration. It is indicated negatively, however, by means of the roles actually introduced here.

b. The Role of the Foreign Employer

The step taken by the younger son to attach himself to the foreign employer and to exchange his labor for food calls attention to the initial contract between father and son. This would enable him to subsist despite the poverty and famine: it is the equivalent--even though he is in a foreign land and it is for the purpose of acquiring the food object-- to a demand for the division of the possessions. In the related figures of employer and his servant the roles which are assumed remain definable in correlation with the familial system, but according to an order of opposite values: the employer's behavior is the opposite of that of the father. He refuses to give the requested object. The son's fate is the opposite of what it was: he does not receive his share

of the goods. Beneath these differences is the permanence
of a system of familial roles which insures the deep semantic homogeneity, or isotopy, of the story. Thus we will be
able to compare the roles. The correspondences are established as follows:[8]

	Paternal role	Maternal role	Place	Son's request	Basis	Result
First contract	father	guaranteed food	house	share of goods	inheritance rights of the son	positive
Second contract	employer	famine	distant country	food (for swine)	labor (watching over swine)	negative

We must distinguish carefully in the series corresponding to the second contract the dysphoric aspect of the elements and their axiological negativity. The dysphoric aspect
is clear. It is a result of the opposition to the unfolding
of the son's program. This is the case with the famine, the
labor and the refusal to provide food. By contrast, the axiological value is more difficult to establish. From this point
of view we must distinguish those things which have the tendency to be confused: the role of employer and the refusal
to give food. The employer transforms the son into a watch-
man over the swine. He is the antithesis of the father. This
role is right away a negative one. However, we observe that
he refuses to provide the usual food owed in exchange for labor. The text neither specifies nor underscores the point for

it is not essential. It is enough for the characterization
of its negativity that the action proceeds in the direction
of the son's alienation. There is little doubt about this.
Also the space in which he places him--"in the fields to feed
the swine"--is the most negative part of the foreign space.
It is unnecessary to attribute to him additionally the refusal
to provide pods whose meaning is, moreover, of a different nature.

The refusal to give the swine's food can only be said to
be negative if the request is a positive one. However, though
we do not usually comment on this, the desire for the swines'
food is a behavior which is marked axiologically in a negative
way, that is as anti-cultural, a return to the natural, animal
order. This point of view is registered without any ambiguity
in the discursive dictionary which applies to this text. It
is an overestimation of economic-biological values; it is an
excessive request. To oppose it in this case with a refusal
is a positive act. However, it is not said whether the employer is the agent of this refusal. There again a concern to
polarize attention upon his injustice often results in going
beyond the given in the text. It is possible that this employer is unjust; however, that is not pertinent here. The text
is content to record the non-attribution: *"no one* gave him
anything"; thus, the non-realization of the desire by the absence of the sender.[9] In this foreign space there is nobody
to give pods to the starving son. The distribution of economic-biological values is not carried out. It stands as a
limit, unassuming perhaps and difficult to interpret, but
nonetheless significant. It obstructs the realization of the
desire to eat the swine's food and makes the prolongation of
his stay in the foreign country impossible. It thus puts an
end to the process of degradation which has followed its
course to the detriment of the younger son.

152

This son-servant is himself redefined within this
semantic universe. His role as keeper of the swine confirms his disjunction from the familial space and involves
his incorporation into animal space which is impure, unclean and anti-cultural, and presupposes the most extreme
separation from the role of a son. Being desirous of the
swine's food, he is threatened with becoming the very opposite of son. The non-attribution of this food prevents
this negative transformation: being less well fed than the
swine and against his own will, the son is distinguished
from the animals. But this distinction is a lack. We see
here once again that we must not interpret the situation
in ideological terms. His misfortune would have continued
had he found someone to give him the pods "that the swine
ate."[10] Now let us sum up this analysis in a semiotic square:

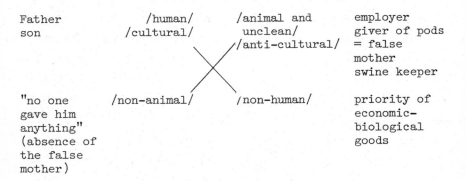

| Father
son | /human/
/cultural/ | /animal and
unclean/
/anti-cultural/ | employer
giver of pods
= false
mother
swine keeper |
| "no one
gave him
anything"
(absence of
the false
mother) | /non-animal/ | /non-human/ | priority of
economic-
biological
goods |

It can be seen that the intermediary phase which is
given the name "prodigal life" already involves the introduction of values from the negative deixis, even though the
play of the veridiction still maintains the illusion. Likewise we have confirmation of the axiological distinction between the role of the employer who alienates the son and
prolongs his stay in the foreign country (he confers upon

him the new role of "swine keeper") and the reintegrating
role by the absence of the attribution of animal food to
the son.

c. The Role of the Famine

The famine is an ambiguous actor from the actantial
point of view: it is negative with respect to the younger
son's narrative program since it accentuates and radicalizes
the lack, and positive with respect to an initial program
which is opposed to the son's since it manifests the negative character of the break with the sender and leads,
therefore, to the interruption of the experience. From a
thematic point of view, the famine is characterized as a
lack of food for men and more specifically as a break in
the contract to provide food which exists between man and
the earth. For this reason, we speak of "calamity" or
"natural disaster." Consequently, the famine is a negative
figure of the food-producing earth. As the feminine and
maternal position, it completes the organization of roles
within which we have placed that of the compassionless
employer and his exploited servant. By this fact it re-
calls the system of familial roles which predominates
from the story's beginning and leaves it to be understood
that a certain image of the mother as the one who dispenses
goods and food is pertinent here. However, it is significant that this maternal, food-providing position only appears in a deceptive representation (and outside the country: "in a distant country"). By breaking with the father
and joining himself to his share of the family possessions,
the younger son has also broken with the true female sender.
Furthermore, there is no one who can transmit food to him.
The foreign land ceases to feed men; this signals absence

of the true mother.

We cannot call enough attention, on the other hand,
to the fact that by causing the non-food-producing earth
to enter onto the scene, the narrative presents two characterizations. The first is in relation to the reorienta-
tion of the desire and to the manifestation of the lack.
The food becomes "longing." The lack is registered in the
body (which will become "belly to feed"). And it is understood that it already was a matter of desire for this object
and of this lack in the son's fate. The second characterization is related to the orientation of the performance which
henceforth will be entirely deceptive (this was not the case
up until now): there is no attribution of a food-object.
The famine represents the non-attribution of ordinary (human
and cultural) food. The refusal to give the son pods represents the non-attribution of an excessive (unclean and anti-
cultural) food. In the meantime, the contract with the employer, which is a negative performance, will have aggravated
the situation and confirmed the break with the father. The
model can now be given in somewhat more detail:

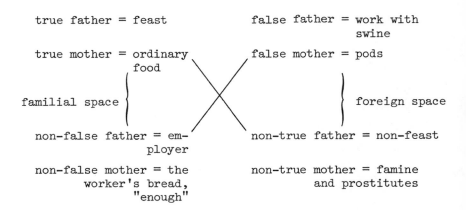

true father = feast   false father = work with
                                                 swine

true mother = ordinary   false mother = pods
              food

familial space {   } foreign space

non-false father = em-   non-true father = non-feast
                 ployer

non-false mother = the   non-true mother = famine
          worker's bread,   and prostitutes
          "enough"

Conclusion: This initial sub-sequence thus establishes a double narrative program: one which unfolds at home under the sign of the father and an actual gift of economic goods; and one which unfolds in a foreign country under the sign of a deceptive contract and the refusal to give the necessary food. The appearance of what is positive, which for the moment reverses the second program, does not withstand the veridictory operation which ultimately manifests its deceptive character. The subject of state in this second program remains disjoined not only from the value object temporarily acquired through exchange, but also from an implicit and elementary value object whose possession he had undervalued and whose conservation he had neglected.

Correspondingly, a semantic system selects and distributes the semic features in such a way as to define as many of the figurative trajectories as is called for by the narrative structure and to establish the thematic roles suited for the actantial roles in the constitution of the actors. These thematic roles are definable beyond each of the discursive roles cited, but it is the familial configuration which provides the best explanation. We will confine ourselves therefore to two forms of the paternal role: the one which dispenses the inheritance or the employer of swine herdsmen; two forms of the son's role: the successor to the father through the possession of the family goods or the one who works with the swine and is a consumer of animal food; and finally two forms of a role that we can for convenience sake call the maternal role since it is related to the food: a normal feeding function which the text manifests only in a collective, negative form (famine) and in an excessive and abnormal feeding function, but which is in this case entirely virtual—that of giving animal food to a man.

It will be observed that we have been careful not to decide prematurely and in function of a preconceived idea lying outside of the text on the positive or negative nature of the roles and the behavior. Both the one and the other are correlated in an exclusive way. A thematic ambiguity corresponds to an actantial ambiguity: the limit is difficult to fix between that which announces or initiates his reintegration. Interference from the point of view of the actors themselves and from the enunciator complicates the analysis. Suspending the food-providing role of the land or depriving the son of the swine's food aggravates his physical misery. However, putting an end to the "prodigal life" manifests the genuine significance of the departure and makes the return possible. Therefore, it seems necessary to react against the usual reading of this text in which these operators and operations openly represent the negative values of the main axiological system. What follows in the rest of the story will determine this point.

2. THE REINTEGRATION (15:17-24)

It would take too long to pursue the analysis in as detailed a way. Therefore, we shall center our attention in this second sub-sequence upon the points which prolong the suggested perspective without of course neglecting to register resistance by the text or invitations to improve upon the models employed so far.

2.1 *The Narrative Programs*

This sub-sequence is notable for the simplicity of its narrative structure. A single program unfolds in accordance with a classical succession of states and actantial roles:

virtual subject, invested subject, qualified subject, actualized subject, realized subject. The marked steps of this process are quite obvious. The contrast is in the form of a self-mandation and reflexive attribution of programmatic wanting and knowledge, the "I will rise up ..." movement, and principal performance which assures the communication of the object and the recognition. There is nothing opposed to the realization of this program; there is neither an anti-subject nor an opponent. The principal performance does not give the appearance of a confrontation. Three points deserve further consideration.

a. The Orientation of the Narrative Program

The orientation can be deduced from the direction of the movements. The principal movement--"He rose and went to his father"--is carried out in the direction opposite that of his departure to a distant country. It is a return. Therefore, it must correspond to a program which is opposite the one that we called the younger son's program or a NP of degradation. If we call NP1 this program of degradation and NP2 the one which concerns us at the moment, we may write: NP2 = non-NP1. As NP1 itself was opposed to a NP0 (implicit in the first sub-sequence), such that NP0 = non-NP1, we can see that NP2 = NP0. To the extent that NP1 has been described as a program of degradation with respect to a complex value object represented by the younger son's integrity, NP2 will be a program of restoration.

In addition to the major physical, bodily movement of the son, the text mentions two others: a noological movement ("coming to his senses ...") and the father's movement ("He ran and embraced him"). The son's return in and of itself marks the reversal of the performancial process at the level

of wanting and the establishment of the subject, and initially makes the knowledge about the new object—the bread—
stand out. The movement's reflexive aspect indicates the
actorial identity of the sender and the subject. Also, it
suggests that NP1 depended upon a sender external to the
son or, at the very least, a sender distinct from the most
internal point of the son.

b. *The Actorial Representation*

The younger son himself undertakes NP2 in its initial
phase. However, in either part of the operations that he
personally brings about, an actorial repetition is observed.
Before the decisive about-face occurs, we observed that the
absence of someone to distribute animal food to the son represented a limit to the degradation, a lack present within
the anti-program. Therefore, we must now record the non-
attribution of the pods as an initial figure for the positive
subject and the initial effect of the domination of NP2 over
NP1. Perhaps we should have even pointed it out above in the
unfolding of NP1 and recorded as virtualities of NP2 everything which tended to restrict the amplitude of performances
and to limit the attribution of the object in NP1: the ex-
haustible nature of the inheritance, the famine and the impossibility of alleviating the need for sustenance by working.
The more the son's desire is restricted to the point of being
concerned only with his bodily survival, the more impossible
the attribution becomes.

At the moment of his return, a new change in actors substitutes the father for the son. This substitution is represented by the movement of the father which transforms the return into an encounter and marries it with the discovery of
the sheep and coin by a shepherd who goes into the wilderness

and a woman who searches all through her house. If the reversal in movement accounts for the son (who corresponds better to the "sinner who confesses"), the conclusion of the
movement places the father at center stage. Therefore, this
organization brings together traits from each of the performances mentioned in the preceding comparisons.

The substitution of the father for the son at the conclusion of the performance is manifested more clearly yet in the
differentiation between the statements of a contract for obtaining the servants' bread and the actual attribution of the
object. The father takes the initiative and that provokes a
sort of acceleration in the story. If the communicated object
does not exclude the sought-after object, it does go beyond
it in the direction of recognition. The son's particular
problem is itself overridden by the establishment of a collective actor of merry-making. Thus, this sub-sequence presents at one and the same time a very great actantial simplicity and a great actorial complexity.

c. *The Attribution of the Object*

The son asks for bread. The father gives him a robe,
a ring and sandals and organizes a festal meal. The difference especially affects the discursive analysis but enters
into the description of the narrative program to the extent
that the redefinition of the object at the moment of the principal performance and of the attribution is echoed in the previous sentences and ultimately can specify the correlation between the different programs. It appears here that the re-
focusing of the narrative upon the manifestation of filial
dignity and upon the participatory nature of the object confirms both the negative nature of NP1, which gave value to an
appropriated and an economic-biological type of object, and

its deceptive character, since the initial stages unfolded
however in a quasi-festive mood (what is sometimes called
the "pleasure" of the prodigal life).

2.2 *The Diversity of Doings*

The movement of son and of father is a somatic operation. The program which is considered by the son: "treat
me as one of your servants ..." may be considered as belonging to the somatic order since it leads to the attribution
of bread. But the operation by which the son tries to get
his father to accept his project points to a persuasive doing.
It does not have a direct effect since the father does not
pursue it. It can no longer be said that he fails since the
realization goes far beyond his proposition. The ultimate
unfolding of the performance will exceed the somatic plane.
In clothing the son with signs of his socio-familial status,
the father brings about an operation which concerns the being
and appearance of the subject more than it does what it is he
has. This is at the same time a realization and proclamation
of his status as son. The body is of interest here, but from
the perspective of the signification. It becomes signifying.
The starved and perhaps poorly dressed son is presented with
fine clothes and a festal meal. The concern is both for the
knowledge and the body. We shall call the level at which
operations such as these are defined as "noosomatic."[11]

The second sub-sequence differs therefore from the first
by its stress upon the noological level. It occupies an intermediary position between the first level where the somatic
doing dominates and the third where the interpretative doing
dominates.

2.3 *The Thematic Roles*

Two roles are asserted more clearly here: that of the father and of the son. They are not new; however, their fundamental components appear more clearly.

a. *The Paternal Role*

The borrowing that the text does from the familial configuration is asserted and expanded on the one hand in the direction of the professional dimension of the family which appears as a business made up of laborers, servants, activities, payment, and lifestyle; and on the other hand in the direction of feelings, manifestations of affection and signs expressing position with respect to one another. The pole around which all of these figures are organized is the father, one figure among all the others, but also the key to the system of roles. By describing him we can identify the axes upon which the significant oppositions which are pertinent to this story are defined.

(1) The father is the representative of the law. For this reason he is connected to heaven and defines the transgression. The son's words, "Father, I have sinned against heaven and before you," are very clear on this matter. The reinterpretation or recategorization of the past adventure in the ethical code presupposes the prohibition represented by the father. From this point of view the minimum difference between "against heaven" and "before you" is very significant. The ultimate indicator and place of the law is heaven. The violation is defined as being "against heaven." However, it is the father who is the more immediate indicator: his presence signifies the law and identifies the error.

(2) The father has the power to establish the social and filial roles of each one of the laborers, servants and son. He exercises this power by his word (he either calls his son or no longer calls him) and this by means of signs. We recognize here the problem of the semantic characterization of the objects transmitted at the moment he encounters his son: robe, ring, sandals and meal. These objects do not have a utilitarian value even if they are able to resolve the son's hunger and lodging problems. They are signs. The socio-cultural code which associates a precise value with each of these elements could be ignored; but we cannot fail to record their overall signifying importance.[12] As signs they declare the call to be and to appear to be son. They represent the father's word.

Thus, the opposition is made specific between the effects of an intervention by a foreign citizen who negates the values of humanity, that is of the culture at the son's home, conjoins him to the swine and reduces him to the point of wanting to feed on the pods, and the authoritative word of the father who disjoins him from the purely utilitarian and biological order in order to conjoin him to the meaningful order. This transformation is accomplished all at once (there is no initial meal to ease the son's hunger before the celebration[13]) by a complete reversal of values and along a trajectory which made the representation of the anti-values possible. Thus, what the father's intervention excludes appears more clearly. The incompatible values therefore appear as well in three homologous squares:

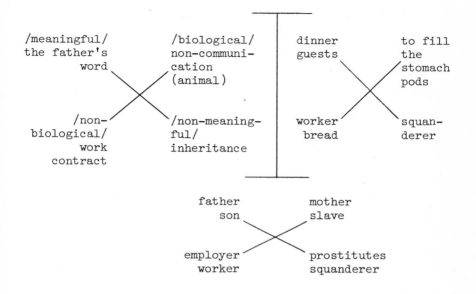

(3) The father maintains the lack at a level at which
it manifested itself and in the form in which it appeared:
the father neither attributes the swine's food nor the worker's bread. He does not seem to understand the son's request.
The response that he gives exceeds the request and alters its
aim. This difference, which is essential to the organization
of meaning in this narrative, is difficult to give expression
to. It opposes "longing" which is directed towards food to a
possibility of being and appearing to be son not through the
direct negation of the lack but by entering into the meaningful universe which is characteristic of the father. It presupposes the categories of /biological/ *vs.* /meaningful/ which
appear already in the preceding models.

This component of the paternal role affects the condition
of its operation, that is to say, the restoration performance.
We see that from beginning to end the father does not stand in
the way of the manifestation of anti-values. He accepts the
division of the goods; he does not hinder the son's departure

and he lets the adventure take its own course. When he receives this son who is marked by his deceptive experience,
he has him enter without prior condition into the meaningful
order and into the feast. This is a son who is starved and
reduced by his previous activities to being no more than a
figure of the bodily need whom the father clothes with tokens
of his filial status. This is a son who is marked by death
and therefore is non-existing, lost and who comes back to
life. However, death which sums up the adventure designated
by the son above as "sin" is defined by an overabundance of
longing by the overevaluation of the biological. Life, by
contrast, is defined by the possibility of gaining access to
the feast, of allowing oneself to be clothed at the father's
word. We must add here a fourth square which is homologous
to the preceding three others:

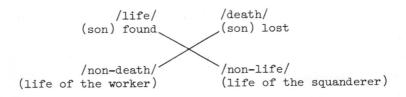

It is verified that the greatest danger to which the
son was exposed throughout the course of his stay in a foreign country was to waver without returning from his quest
for the goods representing exclusively biological anti-values.
The absence of a sender of the pods afforded him some protec-
tion. The trajectory in the order of anti-values has shown
in which figures (inheritance, for example) they were able
to appear, thereby affecting the knowledge and soliciting the
wanting of the subject. Behind these anti-values we have suggested that there exists a negative, maternal role (the false
mother); the famine (non-food-producing land) announces its

entrance onto the cosmic plane, and the statement "no one gave him anything" its absence on the social and relational plane. We shall return to this point.

(4) The father organizes the feast. Not only does he establish his son in the appearance of his true being, but he also establishes a collective actor who is capable of introducing the object transmitted as sign. The effect of the injunctive word is extended to the entire group: "... Let us make merry." The word suspends the course of utilitarian activities and clothes the entire group with a signifying character. It causes the group to enter into the paternal and filial universe. It abolishes the master-slave relationship in order to generalize the father-son relationship. The business becomes family at celebration. The order of signs centered around the new son begins to impose itself. It excludes all other figures.[14] There is no individual response on the son's part to the father's word, but simply a collective word. The house becomes the place where the values associated with the father figure are manifested. It is filled with music and dance. Moreover, the space is divided into two parts: outside is the locus of work in the fields and its utilitarian preoccupation.

/meaningful collectivity/   /utilitarian collectivity/
communion   work hierarchy
festive group   master-slave relation
house   fields

/non-utilitarian collectivity/   /non-meaningful collectivity/
(to be with the father always)   (meal with friends)
(communal possession)   (calf)
(family work)

It is all the more important to integrate the feast
within the paternal figurative trajectory since from the
point of view of his thematic role the father is conjoined
as a visible link to heaven ("against heaven and before
you"). Thus, on the one hand, the family feast is homologous to the "joy in heaven," and on the other hand homologous as well to the interplay of correspondences between
the primary story and the secondary story with Jesus' eating
in the company of sinners.

b. *The Maternal Role*

(1) The father's compassion. There seems to be some
difficulty in integrating two details within the semantic
complex proposed as a definition of the paternal role, a
definition which we have centered upon the law and the injunctive word. It concerns the compassion and the manifestations of the affective relation: "He ran and embraced him
and covered him with kisses." The precise reason why this
integration would be open to question does not rest in the
sentimental character of the behavior which we would judge
to be incompatible with the father's character. To make
matters worse, this would be psychologizing. It is the
thematic function, that is the articulation of these attitudes about the values. Indeed, the compassion is definable
as the knowledge about misery, participation in the suffer-
ing and the wanting to act, in order ultimately to do away
with it. The compassion is directed toward the lack in the
same way that it is manifested at the end of the son's adventure and represents the contract which is able to remedy
it. Therefore, this would be the only paternal behavior
directed toward the attribution of bodily goods presently
lacking, thereby presupposing a wanting-to-respond to the

son's implicit request: "Treat me as one of your servants" (who have enough bread).

Compassion is therefore the figure representing the absence of the law, at least in its heartless character, and as foreign to any consideration of the person. Thus, compassion is more complementary to the paternal role than it is intrinsic to it.

(2) To embrace the son and to cover him with kisses implies a bodily conjunction and a communication by means of somatic contact which are foreign to the order of injunctive and decisive word which will dismiss the project imagined by the son without even replying to it. This valuation of the bodily here and there in the order of signs goes together poorly with the third aspect of the paternal role which only takes affect with the description of the bodily lack. Moreover, we could add to both of these problematic actions the initial non-refusal to divide up the possession because it has the same value.

There remain no fewer than three features now belonging to the paternal figure and they are evoked as positive features. We may consider them either as complementary traits and marginal to the thematic role, after having well noted the difference between them and the principal traits, or instead as elements of another thematic role not represented in the text (or, at least, not named through the intermediary of a personage). Since this role is often invested in another character, we may consider the comparison, the kisses and the division of possessions (participation in the food-providing family land) as figurative elements of the maternal role. This completes the organization of family roles and fills a void at the level of the system which is often felt in the reading.

(3) However, it is not without interest that we return
to the fact that the representation is exclusively masculine
and paternal.[15] This signifies that in addition to the roles
being clearly distinguished, the representation of the figures
is indifferent to the /masculine/ *vs.* /feminine/ distinction.
We have already observed this with regard to the two comparisons in which a shepherd and a woman successively play the
same role, which is also primarily paternal and, in a complementary way, maternal. It is possible, however, that the affinity between the monetary object (coin) with the feminine
figure and the animated object with the masculine figure already suggests the tendency for the goods which are appropriated as "inheritance" to represent the abnormal dominance of
the maternal role. Be that as it may, the story shows that
the true mother (and the land in its food-producing role) is
found only in comparison with the true father, and that the
break with the true father can only be an opening for the
domination of the false mother who feeds her children as one
would fatten swine. If this extreme humiliation is avoidable,
it is not possible at any rate to escape the experience of
famine, that is from the absence of the true mother. In this
parable the land provides food only if it remains conjoined
with the father in the form of family business or as revered
inheritance. Consequently, it is only in finding the true
father after having broken with the owner of the swine, that
the son has any chance of finding a food-providing mother
(and land).

c. *The Role of the Son*

We will take up only two aspects of this role:
(1) The choice between the status of servant in the family business or of acknowledged son corresponds to two forms

of the role. "Servant" is equivalent not to being non-son, which presupposes a presence in a foreign land, but to not-appearing-to-be-son, in accordance with the declaration, "I am no longer worthy to be called your son; treat me as one of your servants." This title is strictly opposed to "swine herdsmen" in the employment of a foreign employer, who would be the anti-son. The proof for this is that the servant receives (more than enough) bread, that he is disjoined from the false mother who feeds her children as she would a herd of swine; he is also sheltered from the famine.

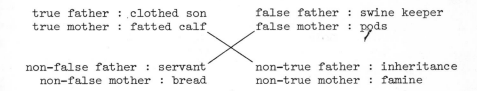

```
true father : clothed son        false father : swine keeper
true mother : fatted calf        false mother : pods

non-false father : servant       non-true father : inheritance
non-false mother : bread         non-true mother : famine
```

"Son" admits of an additional characteristic under the category of appearing which corresponds to the function of clothing-ornament and of feast-message. The servant is fed; the son is clothed and feasted: this is the role under the modality of what is true.

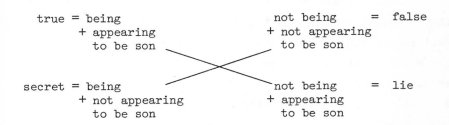

```
true = being                  not being      = false
    + appearing                  + not appearing
      to be son                    to be son

secret = being                not being      = lie
    + not appearing              + appearing
      to be son                    to be son
```

Correspondingly, the truth of the father's role is linked to his power to manifest as meaningful, that is to clothe, the son's body. With respect to these modalities, we also see that the inheritance is the appearing-to-be-son disjoined from

170

being son. In terms of its semic definition, this implies
a dominance of the mother as sender of consumable goods and
withdrawal of the father as sender of meaningful values.

(2) The manifestation of the role of son also sheds
light on the two symmetrical roles of father and mother as
well as on their hierarchical relationship. The more the
role of son is estranged from its definition as being true,
the more the dominance of the maternal pole is affirmed,
that is the importance of food and of the biological body;
also the more the deceptive character of the attribution
and the gravity of the lack is asserted.

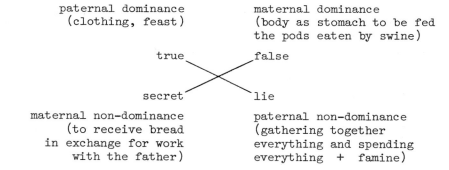

paternal dominance
(clothing, feast)

maternal dominance
(body as stomach to be fed
the pods eaten by swine)

true   false

secret   lie

maternal non-dominance
(to receive bread
in exchange for work
with the father)

paternal non-dominance
(gathering together
everything and spending
everything + famine)

The disappearance of the inheritance, which represents
the deceptive content, is therefore not an obstacle to the
position of the true contents. The former simply presupposes
the negation of the maternal dominance or the willingness to
eat at any price and to preserve the body. By returning to
a relationship with the family land in paternal mode,[16] the
work relationship which is substituted for a relationship
of inheritance is supplied to him in the absence of goods.
This is what the elder son does not understand.

3. THE CONFRONTATION (15:25-32)

The third sub-sequence prolongs the story in the form
of a confrontation with a character who has up until now not
entered the scene--the elder son. This sequence gives the
impression of being marginal in relation to what precedes,
first of all because it unfolds outside of the house in contrast to the feast, and secondly because the opposition which
is manifested here does not stand in the way of the realization in process.

3.1 *The Narrative Programs*

There is a confrontation, hence two opposed programs:
the one which the son represents, the subject of anger and
denunciation; the other of the father, the persuasive subject. Their relations to the programs already described
are established in the following way: the father's program
is in continuity with NP2 and NP0; that of the elder son is
opposed both to NP2 and NP1, in opposition both to the father and the younger son. If we term this NP3, we can write:
NP3 = non-NP1 and non-NP2, which means that for NP3, NP1 =
NP2, which is contrary to the point of view of the narrator.

We might add that in his discourse the elder son al-
ludes to a previous program whose characteristic feature is
its having been deceptive: he has worked and not received
his reward (in food). Therefore, he too is the subject of
a lack. This program calls to mind that of the younger son,
NP1, in its final stage at least (work for an employer).
The major difference is that the elder son has respected
the moral norm and he seems to have found in that a reason
for not accepting the lack.

3.2 *The Diversity of Doings*

The modification of the relation between the programs
is the result of a cognitive doing: a reinterpretation of
the previous somatic and noosomatic operations.   Moreover,
the sub-sequence begins with a series of transmissions of
knowledge: the son hears the music, a servant informs him
of the news.   The anger is a somatic manifestation of an
interpretative doing which engenders an anti-wanting: "he
did not want to go in" is equivalent to "he wanted not to
go in" (he refused to go in).

The father sets into motion a persuasive doing--("he
entreated him ...")--and an explanatory and justifying doing;
he opposes the necessity for holding the feast to the elder
son's pejorative interpretation.

This debate remains as inconclusive on the cognitive
level (the sanction of the explanatory doing and the persuasive doing is lacking) as it does on the somatic level
(no movement toward the feast is mentioned).

This sub-sequence, in which the cognitive doing dominates, brings to mind the situation of the parable's enunciation.   The secondary story is joined together to the
primary story, and perhaps it is this coupling of one with
the other which is indicated in this absence of a conclusion.   In fact, the parabolic narrative reaches the interpretative and explanatory stage here and, therefore, from
this point of view joins together with Jesus' position in
the whole of his discourse.   With regard to the initial
sequence, Jesus' discourse belongs to an interpretative
order (cf. the table on p. 133):   it is the anti-murmuring.
It situates Jesus in the position of the father in opposition to the elder son.   The result is that the final sentence--

"we must make merry and be glad ..."--points back to the enunciative situation in a particularly appropriate way.

3.3 *The Thematic Roles*

It is the character of the brother and the relations between brothers which dominates at this point, although the father is far from being absent; the controversy opposing the two brothers concerns him as well and is brought into the open before him.

a. *The Role of Brother*

The brother role is introduced in two figurative forms: the elder brother and the younger brother. This initial distinction is echoed in the following oppositions:

$$\frac{\text{worker}}{\text{squanderer}} \simeq \frac{\text{frustrated}}{\text{depraved}} \simeq$$

$$\frac{\text{faithful companion to the father}}{\text{lost traveler}} \simeq \frac{\text{brother all of the time}}{\text{brother at the feast}}$$

In order to arrive at a correct representation of the system of roles, we must divide each figure into two parts. Indeed, it is clear that the younger son appears in two forms: as the elder son sees him and as the father sees him: "your son comes home" *vs.* "your brother." Similarly, the elder son appears in two forms: he is one person in his own view and someone else in his father's view.

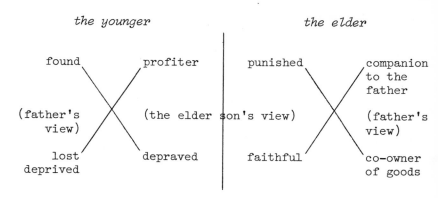

This model brings three aspects of the brother role into view.

1. This is a dialectical role which is intrinsically marked with the possibility of division. Each brother can be the image in reverse of the other. The division is brought about in the competition between the two positions on the negative deixis (the elder son's view) and is resolved on the positive deixis (the father's view).

However, both roles here hold a point in common: the registering of a bodily lack as represented by the frustration of being in want of food. This lack generates a performance which takes two forms: the request for and the squandering of the inheritance with prostitutes or the yearning to have a calf at a feast with friends. The exclusion of these two forms of conjunction is a principal component of the brother's role (we find the categories of /masculine/ [friend] *vs.* /feminine/ [prostitutes] and the figurative indifference with respect to them). This thematic role always requires an actorial duplication, which itself makes possible the actantial duplication (there are always at least two brothers and they may be opposed). Therefore, it is perfectly fitting for the expression of the total resolution of the lack, the symbolic resolution coexisting with the somatic lack.

2. It contains the taking of a position with regard to the paternal pole as a representative of the law. The ethical isotopy appears in both of the brother's discourses: "I have sinned," says the younger; "I have never disobeyed your commandments," declares the elder brother. This consideration does not appear in the father's discourse, but he does not deny it. Moreover, in the presence of both sons he introduces the obligation in the form of an injunction: "Bring quickly ... Let us make merry," and in the form of a declaration: "We must make merry ..." This obligation is reinforced in both cases by the necessity for breaking with a type of food; the longing or yearning[17] for this food leads the subject to the conjunction with negative values: on the one hand the pods and on the other the calf. It is this break which integrates the non-liquidated lack into the process of reintegration. A search for an undesirable resolution haunts this story. It can even affect the irreproachable servant and represent another form of transgression. The father figure, who is omnipresent in his prohibiting value, sometimes suspends the course of this search either at the last moment or at the least expected moment.

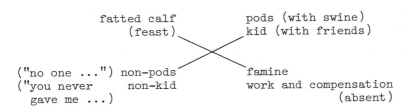

```
          fatted calf          pods (with swine)
            (feast)            kid (with friends)
                         ╲   ╱
                          ╲ ╱
                           ╳
                          ╱ ╲
                         ╱   ╲
("no one ...") non-pods        famine
("you never    non-kid         work and compensation
   gave me ...)                            (absent)
```

The non-attribution of both kinds of food is presupposed by the entrance into the father's order and of true brotherhood. Each of the brothers must submit to the lack and bear the weight of it. Does the elder son, in his anger, come to regret it? He excludes himself from filial and fraternal space; he refuses to come into the feast. The father must take responsibility himself for the non-attribution of the kid and for explaining the meaning of this. In the most noble appearances he represents the object that, in some way, must be lost and accepted as having been lost, without ever being assured of being protected from the yearning that it may give rise to.

3. The father gives meaning to the lack of a kid by affirming two things: the father and elder son's living together and the co-ownership of the possessions. "You are always with me ..." is equivalent to giving value to the paternal role and to the identification of the father and the son by their presence within the same space. Correspondingly, it is confirmed that the departure of the younger son was a break with the father. "Everything that is mine is yours," states the priority of the father's possessions and the inseparable character of the paternal and maternal poles. By not searching for a foreign (female) sender for the longed-for goods, the elder son receives them as his own, that is as the father's possession with which he can be identified. It is this identification that the father's persuasive discourse attempts to make in the welcoming of the brother. There is only one solution to propose to the recalcitrant brother in order to satisfy his desire: to come into the feast where he will find inseparably bound together his place as brother, his place as son and his place as a child fed from the family land: "My *child,* you are always with *me* ... but your *brother* ..."

b. *The Role of Father*

The manifestation of its components is confirmed and
clarified now. It is clear that the episode is not superfluous. The most characteristic element is the power of
the word, which is introduced directly, to make the recalcitrant son enter into the feast, that is to say to make
him leave behind his aggressive refusal and to suspend his
regression to the past where the figure of the missing kid
deforms the image that he has of his father and brother.
He brought about a comparable operation when he caused the
younger son, who was led back to the house on account of
the lack of goods, to enter into an order of signs.[18]

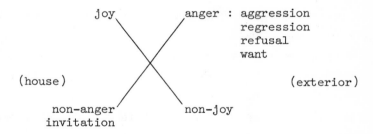

In the double exercise of the paternal role that the
parable successively introduces, the thematic invariant is
therefore unquestionable: the law, the word. Its introduction through the reconversion of figures into thematic roles
or realized sememes opens up an endless route for the analyst,
but along the way it is possible to mark stopping points when
it is judged that the journey may be pursued henceforth along
another way.

CONCLUSION

It might seem useful to take up once again the entire chapter in order to show how the diverse models are articulated and how the structures of the primary, intermediary and secondary stories are superimposed upon one another. That would truly occasion a repetition, for the possibilities of homologation have already been mentioned. On the other hand, this is a task that the reader of this chapter should perform for himself as a verification of the proposed analysis. Finally, the Gospel text does not return to the primary story. The succession of three sequences and their growing extension constitutes the only help provided to the reader for the evaluation of the chapter's unity. The narrative is transformed into discourse, which itself undergoes a metamorphosis back into the story by recategorizing the characters in diverse configurations up to the one that is the most productive and integrative: the familial configuration. The familial configuration is not the final word upon the message of this chapter (or of all the Gospel narrative), but it is a key enabling us, more easily with this key than others, to gain access to its code.

NOTES

1. It is for the purpose of having the correspondence between these three narrative levels of the text appear more clearly that we label this narrative program NP2, even though it is brought to light before the others. We will thus keep the same numerical order for the homologable program. We will find later on a NP1 which is logically prior to NP2.

2. See Chapter II, n. 12. Greimas proposes and makes use of this schema in his work, *Maupassant* (Paris: Seuil, 1976), p. 63.

3. We call "focalization" the centering of the story upon one point or another of a narrative program, upon one narrative program rather than another, upon an actor, an episode, etc.

4. Moreover, this initial narrative program has, in the intermediary story, only a limited function: it is the simple condition of beginning the transformations with both comparisons being more narrative formulations of a general truth than a genuine story; they do not contain a series of operations which are presented as complete but anticipate the connection of consecutive performances in the realization of a hypothetical situation. What is important to bring out here is the logic of this chart-like series of events.

5. The *lexeme* is the *signifier* corresponding to a *sememe* or structured ensemble of *semes*. The lexeme is stable but it may correspond to a very large range of sememes. Between the multiple possibilities of meaning that a lexeme has when considered outside of its context and the meaning actually produced in a fixed syntagm there is always a gap. The reader must overcome this gap in order to insure the correct comprehension of the sentence. Likewise, the analysis assures the exact description of the semantic system. On the scale of discourse, the relation between *discursive configuration* and *thematic roles* is precisely the same as that between lexeme and sememe. We must overcome the same gap in order to insure the description of the elements of

meaning. We see that the construction of sememes or thematic roles is not without restriction. It is conditioned by the presence of other lexemes or other thematic configurations and thus brings us back to a problem of intersecting figures.

6. Following Prof. Greimas, we shall say that "shifting" (débrayage) is that phenomenon which, in a text or part of a text, removes the marks of enunciation and delegates to the actors in the statement all of the expressive function that the enunciator henceforth assumes only in an invisible way.

7. Although the figures which most frequently manifest the veridictory dimension of the text (lie, secret) are not very visible here, we speak of *veridiction* in order to account for the illusory effect that reverses the values of a narrative program in the eyes of a character. The illusion (or error) is in a symmetric relativity with the lie. So we can reestablish the total system of veridictory figures as modalizations of the assertion and knowledge such as will be employed further on:

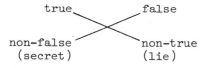

These figures can be defined on the basis of a more elementary opposition:

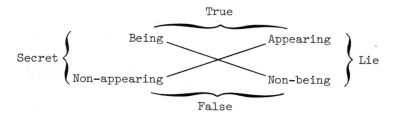

8. We must carefully distinguish in what will follow the *figurative* level which is observable in the text and the *thematic* level, which is constructed. The thematic level is articulated in a more systematic way: by choosing to describe it from the familial point of view, we have the possibility of having two complementary roles appear in the single character of the father. This is a useful distinction for exposing the entire system of roles. Out of convenience and in

reference to the complete state of the system of family roles, we name that which has a relationship to food, "maternal." It is not in any way a matter of inventing a new personage but a means of ordering the invested contents actually represented in the characters.

9. The text here does not use the term "want" but rather "longing": "And he longed to fill his stomach with pods ..." Later on we will make use of this lexematic difference in order to sum up the opposition between NP1 and NP2, for example. The term "wanting" in semiotic metalanguage corresponds equally as well to "wanting" or "longing" in the natural language. By contrast, in psychoanalytic metalanguage the difference between the two words is very pertinent. Our use of the term "longing" will be situated instead at the level of the natural language within which this difference, while pertinent, is less precise.

10. To be persuaded of this, we will proceed as do linguists, by commutation, by asking ourselves: if someone gave the swine's food to the son, or if he secured it on his own, what would have to be changed in the narrative and how would it proceed?

11. The term "noosomatic" doing comes from Greimas. He also uses it in the same sense as the term "signifying somatic doing"; cf. *Maupassant*, p. 212.

12. The *Traduction OEcuménique de la Bible* states on p. 249 in Note o that: "*The ring* is a sign of authority ... *sandals* are the garb of a free man, in contrast to that of a slave."

13. We see that the concern for plausibility is totally missing from the parable: the son has not eaten a thing since the beginning of the famine!

14. We should also note the reversal which affects the animal actor. Instead of the swine which are fed (in order to fatten them up), it is the fatted calf that is killed in order to provide food for the feast. However paradoxical this assertion may seem it must be said that according to the axiology of this text it is more positive to be killed and eaten at the meal offered by the father than to be only a flock of animals out to pasture, ultimately to become objects of exchange, that is a source of profit and utilitarian nourishment.

The fatted calf thus becomes a new figure for the lack

(*vs.* the swine) and it is to be perceived that parallel with the longed for but undesirable object which takes the diverse forms of pods and kid (as well as received inheritance), the lack itself goes through several figurative variations (misery, yearning, loss of life ...). We should add that in this parable, only the festal food is obtained by means of a being put to death: "... take the fatted calf, kill it ..."

15. Only the discourse of the elder son will mention a relation to the feminine figures in the younger son's adventure ("Who wasted his possessions upon prostitutes"), thus causing the predominance of the maternal pole to appear in the programs of degradation: the son leaves the father and joins himself to prostitutes.

16. We could extend this analysis by analyzing both in this and other parables the figure of agricultural work, the relation of man (father) to the land (mother), with the dominance resting with the paternal pole in culture. We could see the opposition between a presupposed relation to the land through the raising of swine and the consummation of uncooked vegetables and another presupposed relation to the land through the consummation of bread and the fatted calf (cooked). Clearly such a study is possible within a literary corpus reflecting a society in which man is the cultivator, as is the case in a portion at least of the biblical literature. Other problems would be raised if this role were entrusted to the woman. However, several combinations are possible between the roles and the figures.

17. We do not hesitate to declare the "imaginary" character of the object-kid longed for by the elder son: it never has and never will exist as a pure object of regressive discourse. This is a good illustration of the distinction recorded in the lacanian metalanguage between "imaginary" and "symbolic." The object which is sought after by the younger son is no less "imaginary" even though it falsely appears to be more "real."

18. The character of the elder son is indispensible to the manifestation of the role of "brother." On the one hand, it completes the figurative manifestation of "longing" by the "yearning" for compensation; on the other hand, it completes the figurative manifestation of the reintegration without liquidation of the lack: a living brother should cause the kid to be forgotten!
    It is especially by this means that the parable questions the scribes and pharisees of the primary narrative

at the level of their wanting and longing. On this problem of "wanting" see the very interesting study by Louis Beirnaert, "La parabole de l'enfant prodigue lue par un analyste," in *Exegesis* (Delachaux and Niestlé, 1975), pp. 136–144. Several other studies are devoted to this parable in the same volume.

IV.

To Fish/To Preach

Narrative and Metaphor (Luke 5:1-11)

by JACQUES GENINASCA

¹*One day while the people pressed upon him in order to hear the word of God, he was standing by the Lake of Gennesareth* ²*and he saw two boats by the lake; the fishermen had climbed down from them and were washing their nets.*

³*Now, climbing into one of the boats which belonged to Simon, he asked him to put out a ways from the land. Then he sat down and taught the people from the boat.* ⁴*When he had ceased speaking, he said to Simon, "Put out into the deep water and lower your nets for a catch."* ⁵*And Simon replied: "Master, we have toiled all night long and have caught nothing; but at your word I will lower the nets."* ⁶*And when they had done this, they caught a great number of fish to the point of bursting their nets.* ⁷*They called to their partners in the other boat to come and help them, and they came and filled both boats so full that they began to sink.*

⁸*But when Simon Peter saw it, he fell down at Jesus' knees saying, "Depart from me, Lord, for I am a sinful man,"* ⁹*for all who were with him were amazed at the catch of fish which they had taken,* ¹⁰*and so also were James and John, the sons of Zebedee, who were partners with Simon. And Jesus*

said to Simon, "Don't be afraid. Henceforth you will be catching men." [11]*And when they had returned the boats to the land, they left everything and followed him.*

The study presented here would never have appeared had it not been for circumstances which led me to participate in the colloquy organized by CADIR (Centre pour L'Analyse du Discours Religieux) in July of 1974. The limits of this study are those imposed upon it by the author's lack of specific training in the matters of biblical exegesis and by the nature of its object: a pericope taken from the Gospel according to Luke.

As far as the indispensable knowledge of biblical studies is concerned, I have relied upon the competence of the team of specialists with whom I have had the pleasure and fortune of collaborating. I have taken the text which is proposed for analysis as an isolable segment of the Gospel of Luke and I will consider the pericope of the "Abundant Catch" as an autonomous story having a beginning and an end upon which it is legitimate to test the operational character of a series of hypotheses which were formulated in order to give an account of so-called "literary" texts.

A priori, such an operation does not exclude reflection upon the miracle as genre nor upon the place occupied by the pericope under study within the larger text in which it is incorporated. But it must be admitted that a study devoted to the miracle genre or to a Gospel as a whole must begin with a tentative analysis directed toward one or more representative samples selected and delimited intuitively. The choice of a pericope from the Lukan text is therefore in compliance with heuristic constraints and is partially dependent upon chance.

NATURE OF THE OBJECT UNDER STUDY

The nature of the text is not the nature of the narrative.

The type of narrative analysis guiding our research
emerged out of and was developed within the domain of oral
literature. It has retained from its origin the tendency to
neglect the text which conveys the story to us in reaction
against purely philological studies.

For theoretical reasons which are at times poorly understood, scholars orient their work in the same direction and
are led to separate the narrative analysis (conducted at the
immanent or semiotic level of the narration) from the discursive analysis (carried on at the *apparent* or linguistic level).
In fact, there are no existing rules today which make possible the passage between these "two levels of representation
and analysis"[1] either in one direction or the other. Because
the narrative is articulated in narrative elements the boundaries of which do not necessarily coincide with those of the
textual sequences[2] (we can expect to encounter instances of a
syncretic or discontinuous manifestation of statements, sequences or narrative syntagms), it is not all clear how we are
to establish in an explicit way the relation which connects
the manifestation with the plane of the content.

Lévi-Strauss situates myth "simultaneously in and beyond
language" (le langage).[3] According to A. J. Greimas, the narrativity is "organized prior to its manifestation."[4] It all
occurs as if the nature of the story were independent of the
verbal manifestation which carries it to us; the story is
therefore able to outlast its translations. However, the absence of criteria enabling us to decide whether or not two
texts are in a paraphrasing relationship and upon a theory of

translation makes any analytic enterprise problematic which would not relate directly to the original text. We cannot arrive at the narrative structure in a decoding procedure without treating the discursive structures, even in the case where the latter are logically subordinated to the former. We run the risk of error or, at any rate, of depriving ourselves of any kind of control by leaving unformulated those operations which assure the passage from the manifestation to the plane of the content.

The Moment of Discourse

By refusing to identify the discourse with the manifestation of the narrative structures, we shall in the context of our study call discourse that constructed *(sui generis)* unit which is distinct from the text-occurrence. Its function consists in the rearticulation of elements on the plane of the expression and the plane of the content of the message's natural language. The unity of the discourse whose structure is independent of sentential structure is not linked to a given natural language. Being made up as it is of the relation of two sub-elements which we shall call discursive elements, at the moment of its realization the discourse corresponds to an indefinite number of phrastic statements. The segmentation of the text is supposed to identify a series of successive segments whose limits coincide with those of the discursive elements.

The discursive elements are defined entirely by the relations that exist between them:

(a) a relation of equivalence, by virtue of which all of the content of the first element is represented in either an identical or transformed way in the second element. The nature of the transformation is linked to the operations that may be shown on the plane of the content.

(b) a relation of succession, determining the orientation of paradigmatic equivalences and their perception in
terms of transformations. This second relation presupposes
the relation of equivalence. We shall call this the relation
of transformation.

The relations which are constitutive of discursive elements bring to mind the two axes of language (the paradigmatic and the syntagmatic) though with one important difference.
The paradigmatic relations are given *in praesentia* in the discourse and the successions have as their function the ordering of the elements of each paradigm into a signifying series.

Formally defined, the discursive elements are devoid of
content in and of themselves even if their function is essentially a semantic one. It is their relations which condition
the signification of the text as an articulation of meaning.

Introducing the moment of discourse forces us to redefine
what it is we mean by "narrativity." The narrative dimension
of a text will no longer be identified with the series of narrative statements or with a process, but will correspond by
definition to the set of discursive transformations which provide the place where the text's narrativity is to be seen.

The analysis of a story presupposes the possibility for
constructing the discursive relations on the basis of the
text-occurrence. Such a proposition does not assume that the
nature of the story is to be confused with the nature of the
text.

The coincidence of discursive and textual spaces justifies the operation of segmentation which must occur at the
beginning of the analytical procedure. Although a single discursive element may serve as the space for several processes
distributed over several isotopies--to coincide, for example,
with the complete manifestation of a process a and with the

partial manifestation of a process *b*--we do not foresee the
possibility of *the simultaneous existence* of several segmen-
tations of the text.

The possibility of segmentation is linked both to the
presence of demarcating signals and to the prior knowledge
of the relations which must exist between the contents of
the segments obtained. The establishment of semantic cor-
relations for its own part is a function of the presence of
an index which assures the selection of elements of content
placed in a relation of equivalence by the discourse.

The Parallelisms and Their Function

We know that repetition can function as a signal for
the existence of a signal. Under the form which we will
label "parallelism," repetition will help make concrete the
demarcating signals and the indices which the reader needs
in order to construct the discourse. Readily observable in
the text as discrete entities, parallelisms tend to be organized into a system only in those texts characterized by
an increase in the *poetic function* (attention which is directed toward the message as such). They are linked by nature to the fabricated aspect (l'aspect bricolé) of the message and, contrary to the relations of equivalence which are
logically prior to them, they do not possess a proper structural status.

To the extent to which their actualization is a function
of the constraints and limits of the natural language employed, parallelisms do not survive the test of translation.
The disappearance of certain parallelisms, no doubt, corresponds to a loss of information (which can be compensated for
by the appearance of other signals with the new text). It
does not exclude the possibility of preserving the nature of

the story based upon the possibility of the reader constructing the original system of equivalences which is hypothetically independent of a given natural language.

Any series of terms which is capable of repetition may
give rise to a parallelism. There is a class of parallelisms
that is not linked univocally to a given natural language.
We have in mind the concatenations of different kinds of sentences (assertions, questions, imperatives) or the succession
of statements which are connected together at different enunciative moments.

Parallelisms are to be found as well on the plane of the
content though this does not necessarily imply the repetition
of linguistic elements. They consist in the repetition of
sequences which may be interpreted chronologically as *departure + trajectory + arrival*. Figurative trajectories such
as these exist prior to the text which develops them even
though they belong to a certain level of the content (one
cannot perceive them if one is unable to propose a semantic
interpretation of the sentential statements). They function
as signifiers with regard to the discourse and contribute to
the construction of discursive elements whose relations determine the signification of the message in its totality.

The construction of the signification of a story implies
that the analysis be able to construct it as discourse. In
fact, it is with regard to the moment of discourse that one
can describe the "specific properties which are manifested by
the language utilized in myths"[5] or in narratives in general.

Appeal to the translation makes imperative the part of
the analytic procedure which must furnish the necessary conditions for the correct decoding of the message on the basis
of the indices linked to the linguistic manifestation. This
amounts to the establishment of the categories or semic codes,
the determination of the isotopies and the segmentation of

the text into segments corresponding to the discursive elements.

The existence of parallelisms which are maintained when
a shift in the language of the manifestation occurs justifies
to a certain extent the practice of working upon a translated
text. It is correct to add that if reference to the original
text only permits us to develop the information linked to the
system of surface indices to the maximum, it does not permit
us however to avoid entirely the problem of the "translation."
Even if we decide to make use of the original text, in our
case the Greek text, we would not be able not to think nor to
speak it in our own language with our own cultural code.
Historical studies and philological work continue to be indispensable even if they are insufficient for dealing with a
story lacking as they do a narrative theory and a meta-language which assures the passage from one language or code to
another. If our purpose is to give an account of the signifying organization of a pericope taken from written literature, we cannot avoid taking the Greek text into consideration. Strictly speaking, when taking into account the selected analytical approach, original and translated text are at
first sight two distinct texts; we do not know if the nature
of our object of study is preserved from one text to the
other.

ELEMENTS OF A DESCRIPTION

The Segmentation

The question of the segmentation of a text is subordinate to that of its closure. The segmentation of the
pericope of the "Abundant Catch" makes sense only if we
suppose that this fragment was correctly separated out and

that it functions as a kind of micro-text within the Gospel of Luke. All along we have assumed this to be the case.

When segmenting a text, we know hypothetically that a correct segmentation must assure the application of the reading rule according to which the segments which are identified must correspond to discursive elements, in other words that it must permit the establishment of equivalence and transformation relations.

In practice we can proceed by repeated trial and error. For lack of obvious demarcative signs, we will adopt as a first approximation and under the caution of verification that segmentation which sets up figurative parallelisms. If an initial segmentation produces a distribution of elements in the form of $a \ / \ bab \ / \ ab$, we will look to see if the segmentation determining a regular articulation of $ab \ / \ ab \ / \ ab$ is not more satisfactory in all respects.

The mere fact of repetition in the unfolding of a text of whatever series seems to ground the equivalent of a norm governing the reader's expectation. Every variation with regard to this norm consequently represents information which can produce a meaning effect. Thus, it functions well, for example, in a series such as $ab \ / \ ab \ / \ ba$ which contains a parallelism in chiastic form, or $ab \ / \ ab \ / \ a\emptyset$ where the absence of the manifestation of b in the third segment is interpreted as a zero-sign. The form $ab \ / \ ab \ / \ \emptyset a$ would combine the possibilities of the preceding variations.

The existence of a system of regularity at the level of manifestation offers a possible form of the text's organization; it does not correspond either to a constant or to a discursive constraint. With regard to the principle of equivalence, there is nothing which prohibits, for example, two different elements of the content from being manifested in a syncretistic manner at the same point in the sequence.

We shall encounter some actualizations of the type ab / $\frac{a}{b}$ / ab which do not make use of parallel series and which do not establish a textual norm.

THE THREE STATES OF THE RELATION OF THE TWO PROCESSES

Let us try to show that the segmentation of our text into three segments (vv. 1-2), (3-7) and (8-11), corresponding to the articulation of the discourse into three units, A, B and C respectively, satisfies the conditions laid down above. Each element makes reference to the two processes (yet to be constructed) of PREACHING (P1) and FISHING (F2) whose operators or operating subjects are Jesus (A1) and a group of fishermen (A2) respectively. The organization of the text into three elements has as an initial effect that of cutting up the chronological *continuum*--the story of the Abundant Catch appears as the description of an uninterrupted sequence of situations and actions--into three phases that we could designate as the initial situation, the mishap and the final situation (the consequence of the event or mishap).

Already in an intuitive way it appears that that which changes when passing from one segment to another is first of all the kind of relation linking P1 and F2 and the relation of conjunction and disjunction which unites A1 and A2.

The spatial relation between the operating subjects (A1, A2) is expressed in terms of conjunction and disjunction. It is not to be interpreted apart from the type of contact be it visual, "He saw two boats" (A) or verbal (B and C). It is possible to imagine for this text the existence of a demarcating system which causes the passage from one discursive element to another to coincide with a change in sign--whether virtual or realized--of the spatial relation

between A1 and A2. In a system which has two positions
(conjunction/disjunction) the second passage (from *B* to *C*)
must annul the effects of the first (from *A* to *B*). Indeed,
the rule of inversion is respected when we arrive at *C* even
though the initial situation is not reestablished. The introductory statement of *C* indeed has to do with a process
of spatial separation but in an imperatival form (a type of
statement about which one cannot say if it is true or false).
In order for nothing to have happened between the first and
last elements, it would be necessary for Jesus, by keeping
to the letter of Simon's injunction, "Depart from me, Lord,
for I am a sinful man," to agree to do so.

If we were to attempt to describe in detail the nature
of the relation P1 - F2 which forms a basis for the isotopy
of the story, we would realize that the text develops the
following three states:

A : P1 and F2 are two independent processes. The simultaneous presence of A1 and A2 on the shore (the operating
subjects in the two processes) is transformed in the encounter through Jesus' gaze. It is presented as a contingent
fact dependent upon a pure, non-signifying spatio-temporal
contiguity;

B : The processes are interdependent. Jesus is conjoined spatially with the fishermen. After being separated
from the crowd which pressed upon him, in order for Jesus
to climb into one of the boats, he performs the function of
the factitive subject (in the sense that he asks Simon to
put out a ways from the shore and, on a second occasion,
asks him to fish). Being situated in a common place—the
boat—the two processes (P1 and F2) no longer appear to be
simultaneous and independent of one another; the textual
succession reveals now a chronological succession. The
fact that both the ordering of relations may be interpreted

themselves as a relation of subordination accounts for
the hierarchical relation which unites the factitive subject (Al) to the operating subject (A2).

Jesus accomplishes Pl away from the shore in the boat
in the figurative position of a fisherman. We will read
this bit of information given in the text as a figurative
comparison all the more readily since the similarity between
both processes is indicated through the repetition of the
verb ἐπαναγεῖν, "to put out a ways," which introduces a movement of the boat as a necessary first step toward the accomplishment of Pl as well as for F2.

C : Finally, in the last element the relation of similarity between the two processes set forth in *B* makes possible an operation of substitution on behalf of Pl. The linguistic manifestation of Pl is seen in the metaphorical· use
of ζωγρῶν, "catching alive."

It is necessary to recall that the metaphorical relation of similarity is an oriented relation. Everything that
is said about FISHING may be interpreted on the isotopy of
PREACHING, but not vice-versa: preaching from the boat may
pass as the figurative expression of "fishing for men" without the fishing meaning "preaching to fish"! The "compared"
is to the "comparer" as the signified is to the signifier:
Pl is the topical process of our story (the compared) and
F2 the correlated process (the comparer).

The orientation of the metaphorical relation is on
equal footing with the subordination--marked in figurative
and textual terms--of fishing to preaching. Pl and F2 appear in this order in *A* and in *B*: in *A* the boat and the
fishermen appear as the focal point of Jesus' gaze; in *B*
F2 is dependent upon Jesus' initiative, the one who is the
operating subject of Pl.

The examination of the Greek text appears to confirm

Discursive Elements	P1/F2	Stage in the Process and Result	A1-A2 Contact	Topographical Relationship of A1-A2*
A (vv. 1-2) initial situation	Independent and simultaneous order: P1 + F2	P1: positive end result F2: negative end result**	visual A1 oriented toward A2	Simultaneous presence in a neutral space with regard to P1 and F2 disjunction
B (vv. 3-7) mishap	Independent and successive F2 subordinated to the initiative of the operating subject order: P1 + F2	complete realization of P1 and F2 superlatively positive result of F2; result of P1 not made explicit	linguistic in the order A1 + A2	Simultaneous presence in a marked space: the boat conjunction
C (vv. 8-11) final situation	Irreversible substitution of P1 for F2 order: F2 + P1	inchoative with regard to A2 who becomes operating subject of P1	linguistic in the order A2 + A1	Non-disjunction followed by a lasting conjunction independent of places and times

*The interpretation of the topographical relation in terms of conjunction or disjunction is in function of a type of contact. We will admit that linguistic contact is opposed to visual contact in the same way that *conjunction* is opposed to *disjunction*.
**The nature of the result is made explicit only in *B*. We will refer in *A* only to the absence of reference to the object of fishing, the fish.

the pertinence of the segmentation effected in function of
the demarcating signs already recognizable through the translation. In the Greek text, segments *B* and *C* begin with the
same type of syntagm: ἐμβὰς δέ, "now climbing into ..." and
ἰδῶν δέ, "but when he saw ..." We encounter another form of
the aorist followed by δέ in *B:* καθίσας δὲ, "then he sat
down ..." The latter is distinguished, however, from the
other occurrences in that it takes up again the subject previously described in *A*. (See graph insert previous page.)

PROCESSES AND ACTORS

The Syntactic Invariant

In linguistics a distinction is made between verbs which
have either one, two or three "places" (to die, to strike, to
give). We propose to interpret these "places" as the location of the manifestation of positions defined with regard
to a structure made up of five posts belonging to the functional or syntactic component of the content and conditioning
the representation of any process.

Such a structure is not linked univocally to a linguistic
statement of a given size; it may just as easily be manifested
by a word, a sentential or suprasentential statement or by
non-linguistic behavior expressed linguistically.

The substantive "gift," the verbal syntagm, "Pierre gives
a rose to Marie," or the story of the transferal of the bou-
quet from Pierre's hand to that of Marie would imply the same
schema, GIFT, which interrelates the positions of object,
source, target and operator (or operating subject) which is
characterized by the syncretism of the positions of operator
and source. In the statement, "Pierre gives a rose to Marie,"
the place of the grammatical subject occupied by Pierre

manifests in a syncretistic manner the positions of source and operator.

In addition to the positions specified up to this point, and without seeking to give justification for this decision here, we will add a fifth post which corresponds to an anthropomorphic level of representation which we could call the *wanting*. The paraphrase of the statement, "Pierre gives a rose to Marie," would then be "Pierre wants that Pierre who has a rose cause Marie to have a rose," which we will conveniently note in the form:

Pierre: Pierre   (Pierre , Marie   ; rose)

Wanting: operator   (source , target ; object)

or, if A1 is Pierre, A2 Marie and A3 the rose:

A1   :   A1   (A1, A2; A3)

Except for any indication to the contrary provided expressly at the level of the manifestation, the position Wanting, that is of the wanting subject, is occupied by the same actor who functions as the operating subject (operator).

In the context of this analysis we will call factitive subject the actor who as distinct from the operating subject causes the operating subject to act in accordance with his wanting. For convenience sake, we will note this in the form:

A4   :   A1   (A1, A2; A3)

without distinguishing a virtual process (what is wanted) from a realized process (the result of doing or of a causing to do). This causing to do may take many different forms such as that of a contract, a physical compulsion or a threat.

The existence of this five-post structure conditions our description of the process of which it represents the invariant syntax. The introduction of internal constraints bearing upon the manner in which these posts are invested by the actors enables us to specify the classes of processes (for example, those of GIFT or of KIDNAPPING). The elements of these classes, that is the particular processes, will be specified and distinguished in an extrinsic way in function of the semantic component of the content. We will see below how FISHING and PREACHING presented as isomorphes within the analyzed text are to be distinguished in proportion to the semic investment of the actor-object: fish *vs.* men.

The Figurative Trajectory

When considered with the aid of a stable structure which makes up its invariant syntax, every process may be described as a series of an indefinite number of operations called a figurative trajectory. A figurative trajectory appears as an algorithm of operations--the paradigm would be the cooking recipe. Each recipe may be interpreted with the aid of a five position schema and represented as a figurative trajectory.

In the second part of our text the process of FISHING is represented with the help of a succession of simple operations (of which certain ones may remain implicit) which is projected upon the chronological order thus taking the form of a symmetrical series of the type

$$a, \; b, \; c \; / \; \ldots \; / \; c^*, \; b^*, \; a^*$$

where a and a^* form a pair of complementary and inverse terms:

to climb into the boat, to put away from shore,
to lower the nets

/ ... /

to retrieve the nets, to return to shore,
to climb down from the boat

Topical Process and Correlated Process

With a view toward constructing P1 and F2 (the two processes of our text) we will direct our attention to the metaphor located in C: a local and particular manifestation of
the relation which is foundational for the text's isotopy,
PREACHING and FISHING. We will admit that this metaphor sets
up the structural isomorphism of the topical and correlated
processes. We note for P1 and F2 the common form TO CAUSE TO
HAVE FOR ONESELF, or more precisely, TO CAUSE TO BE THERE
WHERE ONE IS, with the target post being occupied in that
case by a *locus* which is linked hypotaxically to the operating subject. This locative and non-attributive process
appears to us to conform to the semantism of ζωγρῶν, "catching alive," and the manner in which the text while neglecting
to make reference to the final receiver of the object (men
or fish) places a stress upon the excessive contiguity of
Jesus and the crowd; the boat and the fish: "pressed by the
crowd"; "the two boats were filled to the point that they
began to sink."

The Construction of the Actors

Once the nature and form of Pl and F2 are determined, we must turn our attention to the construction of the actors who occupy the posts and the system of their relations in Pl and F2. The initial relation of spatio-temporal contiguity between the two processes (the topical-correlated relation being marked by a focalizing procedure), their interrelation in B where the fishermen bring about the realization of the boat's displacement in Pl's trajectory and where Jesus functions as factitive subject of F2 as well as the ultimate conversion of Simon and his companions to a situation of preaching, will appear as the figurative expression of relations which are grasped on a higher plane of abstraction.

When confronting a narrative text we are in principle capable of drawing up an inventory of the characters. We know how to distinguish them from one another and to perceive their identity through the mishaps of the story. In order to comprehend the discursive transformations of the text, we must do more. We must construct the system of actors. Toward this end it is necessary to understand the relation which links these entities (actors and characters) of different sorts.

Along the line of A. J. Greimas' research, we will define the actors as the place where the functional and semic components of the content are invested. It is frequently the case that an actor occupies in a syncretistic way several posts simultaneously within the same program (a complex process made up of the concatenation and/or the subordination of several simple processes).

The identity of the character is established in and through the narrative text. In the traditional narrative at

least, this identity rests upon the stability of the appellations (or of certain figurative characteristics) and the use
of anaphors.

The constructed identity of the actor will be noted by
us with the aid of a numerical indice added to the capital
letter "A". This identity is not subordinated to the invari-
ance of semantic investments which can change throughout the
course of the story when passing from one discursive element
to another. On the contrary, it conditions the perception
of changes which are interpreted within the discourse in terms
of transformations. We can imagine distinguishing two principal classes of actors within a given narrative according to
whether their semic/functional investment is or is not subject
to variations through the course of the story. Of these two
types of actors the second serves in some way to pose the contents while the other has the function of transforming them.
This kind of distinction covers up to a certain extent what
the reader does intuitively when distinguishing between secondary and principal characters.

In general, we call characters those figurative, anthropomorphic elements of which the reader is in principle capable
of providing an inventory on the basis of an examination of
the text. The actor belongs to the figurative level built up
by the text. As is the case with each figure, he appears as
a signified with respect to the verbal statements which manifest him. And he functions as a signifier with respect to the
signification of the discourse. We cannot give any details
about the actor without constructing the process in which he
functions. A word for word correspondence between the actors
and the characters does not usually occur though the possibility of it happening cannot be ruled out. We do not pass from
one group of actors to another by a simple transposition.

In the reading of the first segment of the "Abundant
Catch" we will stay with the following three characters as
a consequence of our reading habits: the crowd, Jesus and
the fishermen. We will separate the figurative elements
lacking an animate feature or an anthropomorphic character
such as the shore or the boat; also we will be reluctant
to record God who does not belong explicitly to the "diege-
tic" space: God does not intervene directly and his name
appears in the text only in the grammatically subordinate
form of the noun complement.

All of the characters which are retained do not have
the same status: Jesus is an individual character; the
crowd and the fishermen are collective characters. It is
true that the fishermen are represented in the rest of the
text by differentiated figures: Simon, those in the first
boat, those in the second boat, and then from among those
in the first boat, James and John. The progressive indi-
vidualization of the actors is determined by the concommi-
tant transformation of the semic and functional investment
of the collective actor to whom they refer.

If we were to imagine distributing these characters
into two groups according to whether they belong to PREACH-
ING space (P1) or FISHING space (F2), we would note that in
one of the spaces we are dealing with only a single character. The single actor that we can make out of the fishermen is not enough for establishing a process. Therefore,
we must acknowledge the implicit existence of a figurative
element corresponding at least to an actor who is able to
occupy one or more posts within F2.

Without the metaphorical correspondence of P1 and F2
which is imposed by the discursive organization, we might
have interpreted PREACHING in terms of the representation
of PREACHING which is most familiar to us: communication

of the Word of God in conformity, moreover, with the initial
indication according to which Jesus was "pressed by the crowd
which heard the Word of God." From such a perspective the
crowd would be the receiver in a process of COMMUNICATION
which has as its object the Word of God and as its operator
Jesus. Such an interpretation creates a difficulty within
the framework of our analysis because it produces a P1 which
is non-isomorphic with F2. If the fish should appear as the
equivalent to the Word of God (and not the crowd) we could
not see very easily on the basis of which elements in our
text how it is that we might fill the posts of source and
target for FISHING, which would correspond to those that
God and crowd would occupy with respect to PREACHING.

Until shown to the contrary, the way we have written
P1 and F2 above remains preferable. Therefore, we are bound
to relegate the act of communicating or transmitting the
Word of God to the crowd (with respect to the limited context
under study) to the rank of a stage in the PREACHING figurative trajectory, just as we do for the lowering of lines, for
example, with regard to FISHING.

Let us point out that the reading of the first segment
in and of itself does not enable us to construct the processes
designated in a figurative way; it does belong to the whole
of this micro-story to impose a way of constructing Jesus'
preaching and of giving it meaning. This is not necessarily
all of the meaning that it has within the Gospel of Luke considered in its entirety.

Let us designate the actors of P1 with an uneven number
and those of F2 with an even one: A1 (Jesus), A3 (crowd),
A2 (fishermen), A4 (fish). We may write P1 and F2 without
specifying at this point in our analysis how the positions
of wanting and location are to be filled:

P1	Am : Al	(location a,	location b ; A3)
F2	An : A2	(location c,	location d ; A4)

Let us take the occasion offered us here to underscore the difference which separates the sentential analysis from the discursive analysis by pointing out that neither the function nor the relative importance of the actors can be deduced from a mere summary of the grammatical functions of the syntagms which manifest them. The crowd as well as Jesus are the grammatical and topical subjects in each of the four equivalent propositions in which they are manifested. We may not decide beforehand the actantial function of God on the basis·of the position of noun complement to the direct object governed by ἀκούειν, "to hear." The linguistic manifestation does not directly permit the determination of the contents of the actors without having to go through the construction of the discursive elements which assure the construction and selection of the processes.

THE THREE SEGMENTS AS REALIZATION OF THE ELEMENTS A, B, C

The Particular Role of the First Element

The study of different discourses (in both prose and verse) shows us that the figurative parallelisms which are particularly abundant in the beginning are rare and less evident at the end of a text. More precisely, parallelisms in the rhetorical sense of the term are more numerous in the first segment where they have to do with relatively short syntagms and occur less often toward the end where they serve to correlate the statements whose dimensions may coincide with a segment of the text in its entirety.

An initial concentration of figurative parallelisms of this sort is due primarily to the fact that the first segment is responsible for providing the conditions and indicators needed by the reader in order to deal with the textual information. The simplest means for coding and signaling them as such consists in their repetition controlled through the parallelism process.

The Lukan text appears to conform at this point to the general rule. Of the five statements making up the first segment, the first four are grouped into two sets of pairs which are distinct in terms of their syntactic nature and their grammatical subject but homologable from a semantic point of view. The infinitives *(a, b)* as much as the independent statements *(c, d)* realize the series /situational statement and perceptual statement/: the crowd presses upon Jesus and hears the Word of God; Jesus stands on the shore of Lake Gennesareth and sees two boats.

a	situation	}	topical and grammatical subject:
b	auditory perception		the crowd
c	situation	}	topical and grammatical subject:
d	visual perception		Jesus

The spatial situation of the four following figures (crowd, fishermen, Jesus and boats) is very clearly defined. The scene takes place on the shore of Lake Gennesareth. But this position is indicated in the text in an oblique manner for the first two figures (they are situated with respect to Jesus and the boats) and in a direct manner for the last two. By paraphrasing the text we could say that the location of the crowd and the fishermen on the shore (the end-result of two opposite trajectories: land-to-

water and water-to-land) is a function of the co-presence
of Jesus and the boats in this place.

In the form of a chart and by respecting the order
of appearance in the different statements we obtain:

position of:	*defined with respect to:*	*statement*
crowd	Jesus (defined obliquely)	*a*
Jesus	shore (defined directly)	*c*
shore	shore (defined directly)	*d*
fishermen	boats (defined obliquely)	*e*

In the two contiguous statements within a segment organized by the procedure of parallelism, the repetition of the
same syntagm (παρὰ τὴν λίμνην, "by the lake") in effect establishes a connection between Jesus and the boats even
though the semantic interpretation of this connection is
not obvious. We may consider this connection to be a reading marker whose natural place is at the beginning of the
narrative and which is concerned with the correlation of
places and actors and with the positing of the kind of relation to be established between places and persons and, at
another level, between topological and ontological codes.

According to our chart Jesus and the boats belong to
the same paradigm as the shore: if Jesus is not a place
(in the figurative sense of the word) he can function nonetheless as a *locus*. Jesus and the boats are mobile reference points in relation to the different processes in which
they are implicated. In the same way that the boat corresponds to the *here* for fishing, Jesus can designate the *here*
for preaching. But if the fishermen and the boats are linked
to a geographically determined space, it is not so for Jesus
who as *locus* may coincide with any place whatsoever. It is
his displacement which permits the simultaneous presence in

the same space of two *loci* or, in this instance, of two processes. Having already presented our analysis of the two
processes, we can say that the *here* of Pl and F2 corresponds
to the place where the operator (fishermen, Jesus) and target (boat, Jesus) are found.

The pertinence of the Jesus-boat connection appears to
be marked in a redundant way by the semantic correlation of
proximity versus *distance* which accompanies the passage of
the initial statement *a* to its opposite, the terminal statement *d*: the crowd presses Jesus (excessive conjunction),
the fishermen wash their nets some distance from their boats
(relative disjunction).

The relation between Jesus and the boats is one of repeated figurative contents that we could have referred to
above as evidence for the relation of equivalence between
the identified discursive unities carried on. When we pass
on to *B* the coinciding of the specific *loci* of Pl and F2
(Jesus climbs into the boat) gives rise to what we have
called here a figurative comparison: Jesus preaches while
being in the position of a fisherman. By contrast, Jesus
and the boats will be in *C* in a relation of exclusion at
the exact moment when F2, having become syntactically similar to Pl, may be substituted for Pl. Simon and his companions cannot choose to follow Jesus without deciding to
abandon their boats on the shore. When the fishermen renounce their fishing, the boats are no longer their place
of reference; they go away and quit the shore definitively.

From the first element onward Jesus appears as the
principal character. Manifested linguistically in *a*, *c*
and *d*, implied in *b* as the bearer of the Word of God and
as the one who gazes in *e*, Jesus is present in each of
the statements in *A*. It is he who now in a figurative
way establishes the link between Pl and F2. The second

process is not designated in an explicit way until the final statement of the first segment which contains the second major statement of the text. In d, the boats, as the object of Jesus' gaze, introduce unexpected information with regard to the usual figurative trajectory for FISHING; this is why καὶ εἶδεν δύο πλοῖα, "and he saw two boats," may be felt to be an "event" proper to A. For that matter, the boats do not refer in a univocal manner to the FISHING figurative trajectory. They could just as easily designate metonymically a process of movement over the water.

The Analysis of the Second Element

The succession of statements, moreover of text segments (as we have already stated), appears as a chronological succession. In his response to Jesus (v. 5), the place of which within the text respects the temporal order, Simon supplies information which could have already appeared in A since it concerns the situation of the story at its beginning: the night has passed in vain; the fishermen have caught nothing.

To be precise, B perhaps only formulates explicitly what is already in part readable for someone who would have shared the same cultural code as the author and his receivers: if normal fishing must take place at night and if its final stage is the cleaning of the nets, the moment of A that the author has considered best not to indicate explicitly could only be the end of the night or the beginning of the day; this is a moment on the temporal order which mirrors the boundary location, that is the shore where the scene unfolds.

The information relative to the unsuccessful fishing located in B has the effect of reinforcing the contrast between normal and abnormal fishing (fishing performed during the day and under quite clearly unfavorable circumstances) and could retroactively give iconic value to the absence as in A of any lexicalized reference to the object-value of fishing--the fish.

The contrast between a null catch and an overabundant catch becomes significant if we refer to the concomitant transformation which affects the distribution of functions within F2 when passing from the first to the second element. Nocturnal fishing is distinguished from diurnal fishing by the fact that the latter takes place at the instigation of Jesus and not solely by the desire of Simon, the owner of the boat.

The contrast between the negative result and the superlatively positive result of F2 will therefore be interpreted as the consequence of the opposition between an autonomous doing (normal) and a doing under contract (abnormal). We admit that the effectiveness of Jesus' wanting is due to the fact that he himself is, as it were, under contract with respect to God. Indeed, Jesus is not a master fisherman; moreover he himself does not function as operator of F2. Furthermore, he is not comparable to a hero of μῆτις ("personified Force") or κράτος ("personified Wisdom"). Could it be that Jesus disposes of a magical power which assures his mastery over nature, over the elements and living creatures? In considering the consequences of the doing, more precisely the causing to do on Jesus' part (having recognized his divinity the fishermen renounce an apparently lucrative activity), we see clearly that fishing be it from the hand of a magician, has value only in relation to the preaching that it signifies.

The analysis of the second discursive element is a function of that which has already been made of A although it complements the former by permitting us to specify, complete, readjust or correct the construction of the content of the initial discursive element. So, it is by virtue of the syntactic isomorphism of the two processes--marked in vv. 3 and 4 by a linguistic-figurative parallelism--that we can propose the hypothesis that the function of Jesus in *B* with regard to F2 is equivalent to that of God in *A* with respect to P1. At the same time, F2 is reformulated in *B* and the reader is in a position even to infer the correct and permanent form of P1 which has up until now escaped him.

Examination of the Greek text discloses the existence of a parallelism in *B* which is analogous to the one encountered in *A*. It consists of the repetition of the verb ἐπανάγαγειν, "put out a ways," followed by a complement designating in the first instance departure, ἀπὸ τῆς γῆς, "from the land," and in the second the point of arrival, εἰς τὸ βάθος, "into the deep water."

Whether it is a matter of putting out from the land or of moving out further to deep water, Jesus' injunction in both cases has as its aim to establish the right distance between Jesus and the crowd, on the one hand, and to go where the fish are to be found on the other. With regard to the processes themselves (whose isomorphism is again underscored by this parallelism), the requested movement may represent in terms of spatial disjunction the semic distance implied by the nature of the process which must separate the operating subject and the target subordinate to it from the actor in the position of object. In the final element when Simon says to Jesus, "Depart from me, Lord ...," it is indeed the difference in the semic investment that is expressly referred to by the sudden need felt for maintaining or establishing a spatial distance.

The series of statements from vv. 4-6 in itself forms a complete sequence, for it manifests a complete and ordered series of simple processes which coincide with an element of content. The brief dialogue on the part of Jesus and Simon corresponds to a mandate (v. 4) followed by an acceptance (v. 5) which may be interpreted as a contract; v. 6 represents the actualization of the fishing process upon which the contract and its positive result bear. Thus, the process of fishing appears reformulated not so much on the plane of practical doing as upon the most abstract plane of the actor's positions. The wanting-to-do is no longer the fishermen's; more specifically, their wanting is subordinated to the acceptance of a mandate. Jesus functions as a factitive subject, that is to say, in this case, as the actor who through the intermediary of a contractual relation (mandate and acceptance) causes a second actor to function as operating subject of a given process.

Conforming to the convention already stated, we will write the complex program which establishes the relation of factitive and operating subjects in the form of a single process. The factitive subject will be noted in the place normally occupied by the subject of the wanting-to-do.

Having become functionally comparable at every point at the end of the second discursive element (realizing at the level of the syntax of the content the relation of metaphorical similarity that the text establishes between them), PREACHING and FISHING correspond to the same formula:

$$A_k : A_l \quad (A_m : \text{locus of } A_o , A_n : \text{locus of } A_l ; A_o);$$

for P1:

God : Jesus (land, Jesus ; crowd)

and for F2:

Jesus : sinners (deep water, boat ; fish)

Without turning to a direct discourse style and without making reference to a factitive subject of PREACHING, v. 3 (which we have not yet accounted for) manifests the same canonic sequence as vv. 4-6 in an elliptical form.

The first contract exchanged between Jesus and Simon concerns, however, only one (unstated) phase of the figurative trajectory of P1 (Jesus puts out from the shore in order to preach) and not the process itself. Here there is no reference in direct discourse style to Jesus' words and Simon's response remains implicit. That perhaps has the result of underscoring the hypotaxic character of the doing with which the mandate is concerned.

The call for help may be interpreted as the figurative manifestation of the superlative. We know that in certain languages, for example Italian, the repetition of a qualification may serve as an indicator of the superlative. It functions in the same way here by taking up once again the figure of the boat filled to the sinking point with fish. The meaning effect is linked to the repetition which follows immediately and not to the nature of what is repeated. It makes no difference whether it is the word or the figurative trajectory that is repeated.

The Analysis of the Final Element

By means of the inversion of the order of speech, C formally contains a replica of the dialogue between Jesus and Simon found in B. However, from the semantic point of view, there is no reciprocity in the connection between these two verbal exchanges.

V. 8 appears as the consequence of the successful catch which runs counter to all expectations. Simon speaks first not in order to offer himself in turn as factitive subject

of either process Pl or F2 but in order to express the sense
of amazement that seizes him (even as it is shown by the commentary which separates Simon's statement from Jesus's statement) and to affirm a relation of dominance between Jesus and
himself which links the Lord to the sinner. Hereafter, Jesus
is recognized. The injunction concerning the spatial distance
(unrealizable) corresponds in a quasi-stereotypic form to an
assertion. The content of this assertion is the qualification
of Jesus as an actor who belongs to another "space," the divine
sphere.

Simon's injunction does not correspond to a mandate about
one of the processes in operation. It is situated at a figurative level where the spatial distance is charged with manifesting, as we have said above, the semic distinction between
actors.

In an analogous way, Jesus' affirmation, "henceforth you
will be catching men," is an injunctive assertion that we will
define as a mandate in which the enunciator can conceive of
no other consequence than that it be accepted. Jesus does not
deny the assertion implied in Simon's injunction and responds
to his proposal with a counter-proposal. Instead of departing
he will enlist the fishermen within his own semantic space,
the one that the activity of preaching defines. The momentous
and accidental encounter with which our text begins is thus
changed into a durable and functional relation. It is appropriate to look for the meaning of this miracle story within
this final transformation. Jesus maintains a relation of syntactic subordination between Simon, James, John and Simon's
companions established in B, but transposing it from F2 to Pl.
This entails, we presume, a change of semic investment of Al
and A2. An analysis of the semic component of this story's
content should enable us to account for it.

The conversion of Simon and his companions into disciple-

preachers occurs in three stages in the entire narrative.
It is worth taking the time to recall those steps. In the
first phase Jesus learns from Simon that he is fulfilling
a role with respect to one phase of Pl's figurative trajectory (v. 3). Jesus then occupies the position of factitive
subject of F2 whose preceding negative result is then reversed in a superlatively positive result (vv. 4-7). Consequently, Pl and F2 are at every stage--in both syntactic
scheme and practical result--homologable. Finally, an implicit contrast assures the transposition in the PREACHING
isotopy of the syntactic relation established in the FISH-
ING isotopy. In this way the closure of the pericope of
the Abundant Catch is truly verified.

We have dealt with the group of fishermen as a collective actor defined by a precise functional and semic investment. It would be tempting to say now that the story comes
to an end with the constitution of a new collective actor,
thus effecting the synthesis of Al and A2. We prefer another hypothesis over this one which more clearly conforms
to the description that we have already worked out. We will
consider that in C we continue to have two processes, one
synonymous with the other, and this not withstanding, in a
hierarchical relationship to one another. God and Jesus
and Jesus and the disciples would appear then as the factitive and operating subjects respectively of Pla and Plb.
Such a construction does not run counter to an intuitive
reading; it accounts for the fact that nothing in the text
indicates that the initial process of Jesus' preaching has
changed with respect to the actors who fulfil the functions.

In the figurative form which is characteristic of the
story, the pericope of the Abundant Catch could offer an
abstract representation made up of an ordered series--in
practical terms it is open ended even if the Lukan text

goes no further than to introduce Plb--the PREACHING process such that the operating subject of Plq functions as factitive subject of Plr immediately subordinate to it.

Before concluding, let us sum up in essence our analysis in the form of two charts:

Chart I: Distribution of the functions of operating subject and factitive subject in the three discursive elements and the nature of the practical results of the processes.

Discursive Elements	Operating Subject		Factitive Subject		Practical Result	
	P1	F2	P1	F2	P1	F2
A	A1	A2	A5		1	0
B	A1	A2	A5	A1	1	1
C	(a) A1		(a) A5		1*	—
	(b) A2		(b) A1		1*	—

*The result is not made explicit

Chart II: Relations of the actors with respect to the positions of factitive subject, operating subject and object.

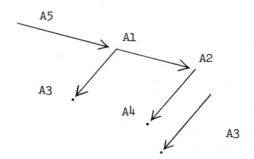

The distinction between the two processes is marked by the univocal correspondence which connects objects A3 and A4 to Pl and F2, respectively. An arrow directed to the left indicates the relation connecting the operating subject and object; an arrow to the right indicates the relation of factitive subject and operating subject.

Two arrows stem from Jesus (Al), the principal character: one to the left and one to the right. We will say that Jesus plays the role of a mediating character (this being understood in the very technical sense that Jesus alternately occupies in two successive and similar statements one of a pair of functions that the text places in a relation of complementarity).

Similarly, two arrows stem from A2, but both are oriented to the left: Simon and his companions fulfill the same function within the successful fishing and preaching programs (the former prefigures the latter).

This second chart tends to establish the idea that the set of figures occupying positions with regard to Pl and F2 now form a system. The former would be understandable only in relation to the construction of a semic code; these figures would then realize different actorial positions of the code. But we will not go into such a construction at this time.

CONCLUSION IN THE FORM OF A BEGINNING

It is possible to generalize the weight of the point that our limited study has advanced and argued: namely, that "miracle stories" exploit the correlation established between two isotopies and that the miraculous performance (most often explicitly marked as such by phrases like "seized with amazement") belongs to the correlated content which may vary from miracle to miracle and not to the topical content which is truly stable throughout the Gospel. The miracle would not therefore represent within the Gospel discourse Jesus' topical doing: it would be the signifier of a message whose meaning is located elsewhere. The qualification of Jesus as a guardian of superhuman or supernatural powers manifested in marvels could in no way exhaust the meaning of the miracle. It would derive from a presupposition by virtue of which the nature of the doing (in this case superhuman or divine doing) implies a corresponding qualification of the operating subject.

If the miracle story is based upon the correlation of two isotopies, it is similar to the parable with which it would have in common the creation of an interpretative doing (faire interprétatif). Miracle stories and parables appear as enigmatic discourses to the extent that in order to understand them it is necessary to perform an isotopic conversion. And in order for this to happen, it is necessary to know or to discover the axis which guarantees their semantic correlation. This common characteristic of both miracles and parables is oftentimes made explicit within the heart of the statement. Jesus himself provides the group limited to his disciples with commentary upon the parable. The latter consists in a word for word translation of the figurative elements of the correlated isotopy (properly speaking, the parable) within the topical isotopy. In the case of the miracle, disciples and apostles are left to themselves as if they had to overcome a test with regard to their knowledge as to how to interpret. In two instances in the Gospel of Mark the necessity for the disciples to have understood the multiplication of bread is noted (Mk. 14: 51-52; 16: 17-21).

Once we have established the semantic correlation

of the spaces in P1 and F2, we are aided by the presence of
the metaphor in v. 10. The existence of a metaphor--in a
strictly metaphorical sense--is, however, neither necessary
nor sufficient for characterizing the miracle story. We can
imagine other procedures capable of providing the information
which is indispensable for the reading: the latter may be
coded in an earlier pericope in the Gospel text, whether miracle story or parable. It is a relation of this kind which
seems to link the parable of the Sower to the narrative of
the Feeding of the Five Thousand, for example.

Before offering any explanatory commentary, the parable
of the Sower, even in the conformity of figurative details
with everyday experience, for example, appears as a message
which makes sense only if the manifested isotopy is the signified instead of being the signifier of Jesus' speech. It
points to the proverbial type of discourse rather than to
everyday speech in accordance with the distinction recently
made by A. J. Greimas.[6] The sense of the parable, the principle of its coherence, can only appear by means of an isotopic transfer. This takes place in the remark, "The sower
sows the word" (Mk. 4: 14); "The seed is the Word of God"
(Lk. 8: 11). The same correlation of isotopies--*food* versus
word--insures a form of intelligibility in the Feeding of
the Five Thousand. The miraculous character of this distribution of the five loaves and the two fish to a crowd
numbering more than five thousand persons rests, linguistically speaking, in the fact that within the space of the
communication of food Jesus accomplishes what is normally
realized in the space of the communication of the word.
Contrary to the topical object of the word, food does not
belong to the class of objects (e.g., enlightenment, knowledge, message, information) which lends itself to a *participatory communication*. This concept is taken from A. J.

Greimas who writes:

> The transfers of this kind are not limited
> to the modalities alone: the Feeding of the Five
> Thousand in the Gospels is explained only by the
> inexhaustible nature of the receiver's possessions.
> The Lithuanian divinities called *kaukai* do not di-
> rectly provide riches for those for whom they care;
> they only make the goods inexhaustible, and their
> consumation does not diminish the quantity of it.
> (*Langages* 31, pp. 33-34)

At the moment when Luke's reader encounters the Feeding
of the Five Thousand, he is not taken by surprise; he already
has cognizance of the Abundant Catch which indicates the operation to be done in order to put two actions into a metaphorical correspondence, and of the parable of the Sower which
makes explicit the existence of a category *food* versus *word,*
thereby grounding the transformation of the isotopies.

By virtue of the isomorphism postulated between the
topical and correlated processes, however, the Feeding of the
Five Thousand compels us to think of preaching as a statement
of *participatory communication* and no longer as a process in
the form of a CAUSING TO HAVE FOR ONESELF (LOCATIVE) UNDER
CONTRACT. The two ways of construing PREACHING linked to the
Abundant Catch on the one hand and to the Feeding of the Five
Thousand on the other complement each other without being
contradictory. Each of the two miracles contributes to the
analysis of the Gospel notion of preaching.

NOTES

1. A. J. Greimas, *Du Sens* (Paris: Seuil, 1970), p. 158.

2. *Ibid.*, p. 191.

3. C. Lévi-Strauss, *Anthropologie structurale* (Paris: Plon, 1958), p. 230.

4. *Du Sens*, p. 158.

5. *Anthropologie structurale*, p. 232.

6. *Du Sens*, pp. 309-314.

V.

Miracles and Parables
in the Gospel Narrative

The needs of the analysis called for the extraction from
the overall narrative of four micro-narratives--two miracle
stories and two parables. We are familiar with these designations: exegetical works devoted to these forms of expression abound to the point that the title: "Miracles and Parables" seems almost to suggest the comparison of two sets of
pericopes or, at the very least, of samples taken from these
two sets. Structural analysis cannot be content with these
classifications which are established outside of its own procedures. From the semiotic point of view the distinction between these literary genres, which is in large part a cultural
one, is not so obvious. Though it has not raised this issue
up until now, structural analysis does not prejudge the grounds
for this classification but, on the contrary, leads to the
testing of its pertinence. Structural research must *justify*
this classification; this is the task that we shall take up
in this particular study.

One series of questions calls for examination. The horizon of these questions is, in the first instance, the meaning
of the overall narrative against the backdrop of which the
miracles and parables stand out. No interpretation of the
whole is as yet available to us. Without claiming to fill this
void we will propose as a general hypothesis that the overall
narrative is not a succession of episodes lacking organic connection, but rather that it is structured from within by means

223

of a controlling narrative program whose principal object
could be identified with the values represented by the metaphor "Kingdom of God." We shall call the manifestation of
this program the *primary narrative*. This manifestation can
be understood either as the *attribution* of the "Kingdom" or
as the authentic and certain *communication* of the "Good News"
which is a condition for entering into the "Kingdom."

A second hypothesis which remains to be verified is that
miracle stories and parables constitute special enclaves within the primary narrative. This is what justifies their comparison with one another, for we can compare only that which
is comparable. To this end we will group miracles and parables under the common notion of *work*. By contrast to the *action* which is displayed within the primary narrative and *poses*
the values of the "Kingdom," miracles and parables *ex-pose*
the two dimensions of this action as distinct from the principal program: that of the "doing" in these *works of power*
(the miracles) and that of the "saying" in these *works of
speech* (the parables). As a first step we will identify the
formal markers which differentiate them from the primary narrative under the opposing category of /work/ *vs.* /action/,
and which distinguish them from one another under the category of /doing/ *vs.* /saying/.

Next, we will investigate the *function* of these "works"
within the overall narrative. For that reason we shall gath-
er them all together under the common notion of *call for interpretation* by taking the terms *call for* in the sense of "demand." Miracles and parables for different reasons are calls
for interpretation for which the primary narrative proposes
resolution: an active or *practical* resolution (in the sense
in which an artist is said to interpret a piece of music) in
the case of parables; a significative or *cognitive* resolution
(in the sense in which an observer is said to interpret an

event) in the case of miracles.[1] Thus, our second step will
be to establish the structures of these calls for interpretation by following the work already begun in the preceding
chapters, but which needs now to be filled out and generalized.

Finally, our third step will be to examine the *operation*
of these functions within the main flow of the narrative, that
is to say their concrete function in terms of the diversity of
\actors and situations. In this return to the primary narrative a sort of indirect verification of the general hypothesis
presented at the beginning will be sketched out, of at the
very least, certain elements which must be taken into account
will be examined in greater detail.

1.   THE FORMAL ASPECT OF THE SECONDARY NARRATIVES

The same operator, Jesus, is the source of these works
(the miracles and parables)--works which are either done or
spoken and clearly delimited as to their beginning and end,
thereby completed and closed off. This is what gives them a
common character. They are no less different with respect to
the values that they produce.

1.1 *The Parables*

a. *Parables and Primary Narrative*[2]

Apparently there is nothing that distinguishes parabolic
narratives from other narrative forms. The same narrative and
semantic procedures may be applied in both cases. Consequently the parables may be drawn from out of their contexts and
considered separately. They belong to the genre of narrative.
The criterion of plausibility is not sufficient either as a
means for characterizing them. The parables admit of neither

the marvelous nor the stupendous. Leaving aside their paradoxical and unsettling character, we would have less difficulty in accepting their plausibility than we would that of
the miracle stories. And yet as a result of the interplay
of a distanciated enunciation which makes them into stories
recounted by a storyteller, the parables appear to be *ficti-
tive* narratives whereas the rest of the Gospel narratives,
including the miracle stories, appear to be *historic*al narratives. Our use of the term *historic* neither posits nor denies
any necessary reference to the "reality of the facts," that
is to the extra-linguistic order in whatever might be the way
in which this "reality" is understood. *Fictive* or *historic*
are used here as strictly *correlative notions which have va-
lidity within the narrative*. It is the statement of this opposition within the narrative which concerns us. It calls,
therefore, for a definition in semiotic terms. In the first
place, it signifies the correlation between a primary stating
(énonçant) narrative and a secondary stated (énoncé) narrative.
Whereas the primary narrative conceals its narrator, the parable is stated as a told narrative produced by a particular
actor, Jesus, and intended for other actors all of whom are
found within the text. Thus, it is a narrative within a narrative. For that reason the primary narrative provides the
parable with its *referential context*. Moreover, whereas the
primary narrative ever produces "the referential illusion"
through its naming of persons, times and places, the parables
are narratives which unfold within an indefinite time and
place with anonymous characters reduced to their thematic
roles in contrast with other secondary narratives such as the
story of the death of John the Baptist.[3]

However, while we could place them in the genre of fable
or tale, the parables do not refer to a *world other than* the
world of the primary narrative. They are not myths which

recount the origin of the world nor utopias which describe
the organization of the world to come. Even when they an-
nounce the end of time, the possibility is conjured up by the
situations of crisis which belong to the hearers' experience.
In a general way they are entirely concerned with the coming
of the "Kingdom of God" that the primary narrative describes.
Thus, the world projected by the parables is in some way in
an isotopic relation to the world of the primary narrative.
Not only do the parables have their anchoring point in the
primary narrative due to the fact that they find their author
and listeners within the latter, but also by the fact that
their content--the told tale--rather than merely being "acted
out" could be "lived" by its listeners without their having
to modify greatly their ordinary surroundings. They have
nothing to do with the marvelous or fantastic or ghost-like
but only with the exceptional, with situations which are
pushed to the limit. Clearly the parables are *fictions* but
these *fictions* represent on a closely related stage what is
at stake in everyday life. They provide a type of exegesis
of the actions and controversies on the part of the actors in
the primary narrative. In short, they are "show and tell"
lessons. As the series of three parables in Luke 15 shows,
the transition from primary narrative (the controversy between
Jesus and the pharisees concerning the proper conduct vis-à-
vis sinners) to the *fictive* narrative (the Prodigal Son) is
made gradually and progressively by means of two comparisons
which directly and then indirectly involve the narrator ("I
say to you") and his listeners ("Which of you," "Who is the
woman who ..."). Both comparisons establish the continuity
between the historic scene and the parabolic scene. At the
conclusion of this transition, the listeners see the actions
that they themselves could *manifest played out* by other actors.

Therefore, from this point of view, the parables are

contemporaneous with the primary narrative even though they
are some distance removed from it. They directly translate
the primary narrative into an internal time. We will have to
analyze even more closely the relationship between the primary
and secondary narratives. But we can now observe the difference which divides the *historic* from the *fictive*: *though
there is a syntagmatic break between these narrative forms,
there is nonetheless a semantic continuity.*

b. Parables and Miracles

The parables open up a space of pure knowledge. This
feature will allow us to distinguish them from miracle stories
in a more precise way. In fact, the *practical* transformations
which are reported at their own narrative level have as their
sole consequence for the hearers that of bringing about a
transformation of *knowledge*. What the hearers of the Gospel
narrative are left with is an acquired knowledge. The parable
is a communication of knowledge, or more precisely, the apprenticeship for an interpretative competence on the order of
a know-how-to-do. This know-how-to-do does not eliminate the
distance between *fiction* and *reality*; the distance remains in
the interplay between the two. It is precisely in the parabolic interplay, i. e., at the semantic level, that the hearers find the solution to the problem. Therefore, they are not
qualified automatically to be operators at the level of the
primary narrative. The parabolic narrative is a poetic creation. Its goal is neither to give information about the historic elements which are necessary for the comprehension of
the primary narrative nor to persuade, advise, prescribe or
legislate. In and of itself it is an action of language upon
language, or if we may, a pure creation of language, *the creation of a model of values by means of speech.* In the final

analysis, it is by making use of the possibilities of language
that the narrator can hope to modify the situation presented
by the primary narrative. Thus, set in relief against the
primary narrative, the parable makes us perceive the message
as message. In Jakobson's terms, it illustrates the *poetic
function* of language. It constitutes a discursive type which
we could call the *interpretation,* properly speaking, of the
events reported by the primary narrative. The latter provides
the contextual interpretation of the parable, that is its historic application, but with this qualification: far from representing the only possible application, the Gospel context
realizes but *one* of the possible interpretations. Perhaps we
could refer at this point to what A. J. Greimas says about
literary and religious discourse with regard to their cultural
contexts: "It is not that these discourses—religious and
literary—are defined by cultural contexts, but on the contrary that the cultural contexts are defined by the connota-
tive interpretations of the discourses."[4] In short, within
the Gospel narrative the parables introduce a *hermeneutical
structure* by establishing a text-to-context relation *in such
a way that the parable is to its context what the meaning is
to its application.* It is in this way through the application
(or non-application) of the proposed meaning, that the context
"interprets" the parable. It does so by providing the parable
with one of its referents.

1.2 *Miracle Stories*

    a. Miracles and Primary Narrative

    Whereas parables interpolate a pure speech process in
which the accent is placed upon the discourse as such within
the Gospel narrative, miracle stories belong exclusively to

the *historic* thread of the narrative. In this way they
belong to the *reality* of the primary narrative and not to
the *fiction* in the same way as do the teaching or didactic
discourses and the accounts of conflicts, actions, processes
and events in the rest of the Gospel. However, as we are
going to demonstrate, miracle stories constitute special
enclaves which have their own autonomy within the primary
narrative. This gives them the character of deed as distinct from the principal program. They introduce a diversion within the syntagmatic continuity.

The simplest way to account for this phenomenon of divergence is to observe how miracle stories are inserted into
the interaction between characters. It may be taken for
granted that the main Gospel narrative is the narrative of
relations (their establishment and transformation) between
Jesus and three permanent groups of characters: the disciples, the opponents and the crowd. This last group represents a type of collective, anonymous and witnessing character, a more or less diversified group which provides the
first two categories with its members. It is noteworthy
that Jesus never performs miracles on his own behalf (cf.
the Temptation and Passion episodes), nor for his opponents
(to whom he refuses to give "signs") nor for his disciples
(an exception is made for the nature miracles which would
require special treatment). The miracle is usually performed for the benefit of an unknown person, most often the
sick, who one moment emerges from the crowd and the next
disappears back into it never again to return to the principal stage except where in a few instances he joins the
group of disciples. This sheds light on one point: in the
sphere of ordinary relations between Jesus and his partners
and on the trajectory of the hero's principal mission, that
is his basic program (which is characterized by a teaching

activity initiated by Jesus and whose goal is the formation
of a community), the possibility of the miracle arises through
the intervention of "the other," of his needs and demands and
thus comes from an outside source. In the domain of the communication of the values of the "Kingdom," of acceptance and
resistance that they encounter on the part of the ordinary
listeners, the miracle is the object of a double outside request: by the very fact that it originates with an unusual
actor (one thinks of the intrusion of the paralytic through
the roof of the house!) and because the object pleaded for
is not immediately included within the values proposed by the
Gospel message. When the miracle story is included within
the flow of the primary narrative, its orientation is directed
toward other goals. The *contract established* between the one
who requests the miracle and Jesus signals this divergence.
It plays the role held by the enunciation in the production
of the parable. A divergence is created. It makes the miracle a work which is set apart. This work has its own cohe-
siveness in and of itself. Indeed, the blind man sees, the
man possessed is freed, the paralytic walks. These transformations are meaningful in and of themselves. But the values
accorded them are no less different from the values proper to
the "Kingdom." The former do not share a necessary relationship with the latter. It is not enough to be healed in order
to be saved; it is not necessary to be a paralytic in order
to be pardoned. The contract, therefore, deflects the initial program toward a secondary performance: the values
which are sought after in the first case and in the second
are *semantically* different. There is no doubt that they are
not totally heterogenous; they imply or presuppose one another. We could even establish a metaphorical relation between
the performance of the miracle and the action of the "Kingdom": a metaphorical relationship between life and faith,

healing and forgiveness, sick and sinner, raising up and
resurrection, fishing and preaching, bread and word. And
yet for all of that the results provided by the miracle and
those attributed at the end of the principal program differ
from one another. Their contents are not overlapping. The
relation between them is one of *correlated content* (related
to the miracle) to *topical content* (related to the primary
narrative). This relation gives the miracles a particular
position in relation to the parables. Both of these narrative forms represent within the overall narrative the group
of "works" performed by Jesus and this feature separates
them from the primary narrative. But whereas the parables
are disconnected from the primary narrative from the narrative point of view, *miracle stories by contrast are in a
syntagmatic continuity but are disconnected semantically
from the primary narrative.*

b. *Miracles and Parables*

The most obvious distinction between the two has to do
with the transformations brought about in the somatic or cosmic domain for the miracles and in the domain of knowledge for
the parables. However, we cannot leave it at that. The miracles, like the parables, raise the question of their interpretation. Undoubtedly the initial meaning of the miracle is
too obvious to be questioned. There is no need for it to be
explained. On occasion it is even the subject of an extremely
careful and objective verification: the royal official can
ask about the hour at which his son is healed and note its
precise coincidence with the moment when the word is uttered
by the miracle worker (John 4: 51-54). For that reason, the
miracle appears as an object of incontestable knowledge; it is
an astonishing object, an object of amazement, but also as a

consequence, and taking into account its exceptional character, it is an object of query. The question of the correlation between the correlated content and the topical content
cannot be avoided. If the initial meaning of the miracle
goes without question, its secondary meaning, that is to say
its relation to the principal program, remains ambiguous:
"They had not understood about the bread," it is said of the
disciples. If the full comprehension of the miracle requires
not only the authentication of its effectiveness but also the
recognition of its presuppositions--namely the identification
of its author, Jesus, of his mission and of the values motivating him--then recognition is the product of an interpretation.
The articulation established by the operation of the miracle
between the initial (correlated) meaning and the secondary
(topical) meaning constitutes the object itself of the interpretation. As is the case with the parable, the miracle therefore introduces a call for interpretation. However, this
"call" leads to appreciably different results. The parable
places a particular knowledge at the disposition of the listener. This knowledge may require explanation but usually the
parable's *meaning* is easily accessible and of a public or popular nature. On the contrary, in those instances where there
is difficulty in the interpretation, it is in the application
to the referential context. For if the parable is a practical
lesson, it introduces a "know-how-to-do." But the question
is how to apply this knowledge in a concrete way in ever new
situations, how to provide it with a *referential praxis*. It
is not a matter of discovering a new *meaning* but of *referring*
it correctly to a new situation. The miracle presents a different problem. As a somatic transformation, the narrative
states it as an unquestionable fact. But its *meaning* in the
domain of the "Kingdom" remains to be understood. The articulation of this meaning in the principal program is indeed

the interpretative task which is accomplished through an
act of belief, namely through a knowledge whose truth is
assumed. *It is no longer a matter of imagining a practical reference as in the case of the parable, but on the
basis of this referential fact (the miracle) of imagining
a meaning which conforms to the "Kingdom of God."*

1.3 *Conclusion*

What the parables and miracle stories have in common
is that they are *works* attributable to one and the same actor, Jesus, who is the operating subject of the principal
program. These works are arranged about the primary narrative as if in a mirror; they ex-pose the meaning and the
doing of the primary narrative. Whereas the parables are
actions of language, miracles are symbolic actions. The
former point to a cognitive doing, the latter to a pragmatic doing. The parables establish an interpretative call
within the narrative; they are *fictions* but lack reference.
Directed towards themselves they represent the working of
discourse upon itself and it is through this accomplishment
of the word that they open up an interpretative field. The
interpretation consists precisely in providing this discourse with its reference and its application to the plane
of the primary narrative within the context (a context
which is always problematic and, consequently, dramatic)
of the "Kingdom" which comes in the midst of controversies.
The performance of language is always successful, but the
interpretative performance is not necessarily so. Normally
it should lead to the manifestation of a knowing-how-to-do.
Miracles, in turn, establish a call for interpretation but
with a different structure. Their foundation is factual
(somatic), but as a result of their insertion into the

primary narrative, they take on an additional significance.
As event and no longer as discourse, as *realities* and no
longer as *fictions,* miracles take as given the performance
of faith which discovers their properly religious significance. The somatic performance is always successful, but
the act of faith is not. The latter would have to arise
out of the recognition (in the broadest sense of the word)
of their author with respect to his being and his vocation
and, consequently, his authority. This recognition represents the end-product of an interpretation which lays hold
of the values proposed and manifested by Jesus. It is in-
augurated by belief, that is to say through the acceptance
of a competence and then an authority, a guarantee of true
knowledge. This belief ultimately establishes the disciple
as a participating subject in the establishment of the
"Kingdom." It remains for us now to develop both of these
interpretative structures--the one directed towards the
reference, the other towards the *meaning*--through a closer
study of the functions of parables and miracles within the
primary narrative.

2. FUNCTION OF THE PARABLES AND MIRACLES

2.1 *Function of the Parable*

The function of the parable derives from the link which
exists between the primary and secondary narratives. This
link is the hermeneutical structure. The production, comprehension and interpretation of the parable by the actors in
the primary narrative *simulates* the hermeneutical process
that a linguistic group manifests with respect to its cultural tradition within the Gospel narrative. We may, therefore, apply three general hermeneutical laws taking into

account the fact that what we have is a simulated, intra-
textual process. In order to analyze this process we shall
refer to P. Ricoeur's understanding of hermeneutic which we
shall adopt as our frame of reference. We may distinguish
three moments in the general hermeneutical process: distanciation, ex-position, interpretation. We shall take up each
of these steps in turn.

a. Distanciation

The parable inserts a narrative into a narrative, a text
into its context. This is a closed series of events which
from the *narrative* point of view is not in continuity with the
story. Personages appear without any syntactic relation to
the personages in the primary narrative. Actions are produced
which are unconnected to preceding actions. In this regard we
can say that the parables are distanciated from the primary
narrative. They lay down the conditions for a hermeneutic by
ex-posing themselves as a "text." In fact, we should not expect to treat them as a simple extension of the dialogical
situation which serves as their framework. They are not the
speaker's direct expressions: parabolic narratives are written in the third person; the enunciator disappears before the
characters on stage; the listeners are not directly addressed;
the story seems to recount itself simply out of the pleasure
of being told. The parable is therefore neither question nor
response. It can give rise to one or the other, but in itself
it represents a completed and closed text. It stands on its
own. In spite of its brevity, it is a *complete work*. And
just as with any work, it is in fact autonomous, a work of art,
a created thing, which points more to a "poetic" than to a
"communicative praxis." It is autonomous in a three-fold way:
with regard to the author's intention; with regard to the cul-

tural situation; and with regard to the original receivers.[5]
The parable does not express the author's sentiment nor are
the reactions that it provokes important for what it *says*.
It does not relate a situation; on the contrary it deviates
from one. Between interlocutors in the initial situation
is interposed *the mediation of an objective text* whose importance goes precisely beyond this situation. Other interlocutors in other situations could make use of them as a
text of reference. Thus, the parable as "work" creates a
separation, a *distance* by which it assumes the status of
an object. One of its fundamental properties will be to
be "decontextualized" from the primary narrative as much
from a cultural as from a psychological point of view, and
to be able to be "recontextualized" in a different way.
It is in proportion to this distance with respect to the
context that the parabolic text can play the role of a
critical and novel call vis-à-vis the milieu in which it
is heard.

b. *Ex - position*

The parabolic text as a completed work appears therefore as an objective structure calling for deciphering.
It objectively results from the neutralization of its references to the immediate context. This suspension of references follows a strategy. This is the necessary condition in order for the *fiction* to be able to pose and organize a new semantic universe apart from its context. The
fiction is not connected through the redescription of the
cultural world which produces it. Rather, it is separated
solely in order to produce, along with the help of language
resources alone a completely different *fictive* world. It
cuts out the references to the ordinary world only in order

to exhibit another image of the world. In this regard, it
is the substitute for experience: it is the experience not
of the real but of the possible. This is the role that Aris-
totle attributed to the tale: namely, to be *creator* of new
possibilities for being-in-the-world.

But at the same time, the tale does not pose another
world. It stands as a model which is *to be imitated* by the
characters of the primary narrative. It therefore provides
as a sort of rereading, a redescription of the contextual,
but in the imaginative mode of the possible. It enacts the
possibility of new relations among the hearers involved.
This is done by proceeding with a redistribution of roles
and values. Thus the difference between the "one who sins"
and the "one who repents" takes precedence over the difference between the "one who sins" and the "one who is righteous." The opposition between "sin" and "righteousness"
will be seen to be relativized and ultimately subsumed
under the radical opposition between "affliction-poverty"
and "joy-overabundance." By means of this ex-position of
a system of new values, the parabolic *fiction* offers an
alternative: it both anticipates a world to come and it
implies the critique of the present world. This creative
aspect also involves a subversive aspect. Yet once again
it does this in the form of a "play/game." The "play/game"
seems to be the closest comparison that we can make to the
parable. In the hearing of the parable, *something is being
played* just as a theatrical or symphonic piece is played
and the listeners are caught up in it. With the help of
the communication of this parabolic knowledge, the listeners are drawn away from their ordinary preoccupations with
daily concerns, from staid behavior in order to enter into
a new world where anything is possible and where they experience a new way of being and acting. At the end of the

"play/game" there is no certainty that the listener has
automatically changed his behavior; the "play/game" does
not take the place of a choice. But neither does it
simply provide new information. From this point of view
the parable is a simulator of problems which are to be
resolved in the concrete life. This is the function that
the parable of the Good Samaritan fills: the scribe finds
the solution of the "play/game." The "play/game" has
therefore both a cognitive and pragmatic quality about it.
In the end the scribe obtains a competence: the "play/game"
confers a magic power-to-do upon him. The parable is not
only something *which* is played, but also something *in which*
one plays; it is an instigator of action.

c. *Interpretation*

The hearing of the parable requires a "play/game"
competence (both narrative and semantic) on the part of
the listener which is necessary in order for him to hear
the parable. The act of hearing normally succeeds if the
act is reduced to the mere comprehension of the parable.
The primary narrative notes itself that the parable as a
cultural object presents a public and open character.
Being open to all it is in principle comprehensible to all.
Let us agree to call "explanation" the result of this performance which consists in grasping the internal meaning
of the parables. Yet explanation is not enough. The parable is not a simple "play/game." It is necessarily produced within a context. As we have seen, this position
gives it a critical and subversive character. Between
text and context emerge comparisons, relations of opposition or similarity, of compatibility or incompatibility.
We shall call these comparisons between text and context

"interpretation." The interpretation entails two elements:
the one cognitive and the other practical, a consequence of
the two-fold nature of the "play/game" as we have already
observed. To put it another way, the parable requires that
it be understood and then applied with respect to a context.

Such is the task of interpretation which, on the basis
of the objective distanciation of the parable, brings about
a return to the context. On the cognitive plane the interpretation could point either to a semantic displacement between the two universes of text and context (thus the horizon of "compassion" is substituted for the horizon of "righteousness" in Luke 15) or to reversals in the syntactic positions of the actors (thus in Luke 10 when the scribe asks,
"Who is the neighbor?" his question leaves us to assume that
one has to choose between the partners; the parable permits
the problem to be reversed: "Who showed himself to be neighbor?" by asking him to choose between different actors in
the parable). The return to the context therefore enables
us in principle to apply the meaning of the parable to the
actors in their own situation in the primary narrative. The
world opened up by the *fiction* brings them to a new comprehension of themselves. They are judged by the objective
shift that they have been led to make. If the subjectivity
of this knowledge is defined in relation to the known object,
according to the general law of the relation $S \rightarrow O$, let us
say that the parable (A) by proposing a *fictive* world first
of all virtualizes the relation of the hearer to his everyday world (B) and conjoins it with a new model of knowledge.
The hearer therefore gains a new dimension of his subjectivity
in the parable.

However, this actualization of the cognitive subject is
not necessarily accompanied by a change in praxis and, above
all, by a submission of the *deontic* moral judgment concerning

what must be done. In the system of values developed by the
parable, the hearers are invited to choose either the positive table of values or the negative table of values. They
have to retrace the interpretative path that the narrator of
the parable, Jesus, had himself followed by way of a reverse
process. Indeed, *prior to* the production of this work (the
parable), the narrator had to yield himself to an interpretation of his own behavior just as his interlocutor did in
order then to be able to transpose them into a *fictive* story.
After the enunciation of the parable the hearers must effect
a reverse transposition, that is to interpret, to translate
the proposed model into praxis. But in fact their concrete
reaction is seldom mentioned in the context. In any event,
the thrust of the *fictive* narrative is directed beyond the
closure of the primary narrative.

2.2 *Function of the Miracle Stories*

In contrast to the parable which establishes the *fiction*
(the *text*) the miracle is inserted within the flow of the narrative (the *context*). However, as we have already stated, it
forms an enclave within the context. It is an enclosed narrative. And at the heart of the narrative we find a physical
transformation--either a healing or an exorcism. The miracle
as a *factual reality* represents a performance which is not
cognitive in nature like the parable but is rather of a concrete type. For this reason it takes on the material form of
a *work*. The mechanism which will make out of the miracle a
call for interpretation is organized around this work where
the salvific program of the Kingdom is ex-posed.
The miracle's autonomy is not total. While it is real
in its coherence as a complete work, it is relative in its
antecedent and consequent connections. The miracle is a

narrative structure integrated within the primary narrative. It is linked in this case to what precedes and what follows afterwards: to what precedes by the strategy of the *request* (or anti-request); to what follows afterwards by the instance of *recognition* (or of non-recognition). What request and recognition have in common is that both postulate performances which fall under the category of knowledge and of want though on two different planes: the one on the plane of the correlated content and the other on the plane of the topical content. The complexity of the analysis springs from this. For in between the two planes there exists a relation of presupposition which establishes an interpretative structure in the narrative. It is now a matter of discovering the meaning of the miracle on the plane of values proposed by the Kingdom. Request and recognition in turn contribute to the setting in place of the mechanism of interpretation. This is what we are now going to show in greater detail.[6]

a. *Accomplishment*

The miracle is the irruption of power. It effects a transformation: domination over the sick and the powerless; attribution of health and liberty. The miracle has a tangible effect. Its intrinsic value is no less evident. Putting aside the extraordinary "difficult" nature of the performance with regard to its end result, the miraculous deed is reduced to something quite ordinary. "Who among you does not pull his ass up out of a pit on the sabbath?" The miracle therefore manifests nothing extraordinary or marvelous. No pot of figs is changed into a pot of coins. It engages in the extraordinary only in order to restore the ordinary to life. As the result of Jesus' compassion, the miracle reintroduces the excluded into the area of the common life. But

if the miracle's effect appears normal, it is so with respect
to its effectiveness. The miracle always surprises and sometimes frightens. On occasion, the power which is exhibited
in the miracle is discharged in an anonymous and uncontrolled
way. The case of the woman with a hemorrhage is an example
(Mk. 5: 25-34): At the woman's touch an uncontrolled force
leaves Jesus. An irrational power is at work which avoids
interaction with human beings. And yet, if it is a well-
attested fact, it is so because the miracle is grasped completely within a dialogical context. Whereas the parable
momentarily breaks the interpersonal relationship by producing
a discourse in the third person, the miracle is completely
immersed within the dialogical situation. The miracle, which
is most often the object of prayer or the result of a command,
mediates in a concrete way the relations between an "I" and a
"you," that is in an interchangeable position the relations
between Jesus and the sick. The case of the woman with the
hemorrhage is not an exception to the rule. Along with the
blessing secretly stolen, there follows as well the reestab-
lishment of the intersubjective relation in the confession of
the truth and the recognition of faith. The miracle is therefore inseparable from the intersubject conditions in which it
appears. It plays a part in a program and does not constitute a program in and of itself. Its objective meaning is
not, as it is the case with parables, independent of the attitudes and intentions of the questioners. For that reason,
it is distinguished from ritual which is also a praxis that
has "something to do" with sacred powers. For the ritual is
a codified process, organized, repetitive, informed by a mythical discourse and with predictable results. By contrast,
the miracle is included within the dialogue; there is nothing
codified about it in advance. It is not organized, for it
participates in ever new situations. As a singular event, it

is not repeatable; as an intersubjective action, its result
is not certain. In short, this is a negotiated action: the
miracle forms the object of a contract.

b. *Request*

The strategy of the request is stretched out over an
ordered series of operations. It is first of all a matter
for the one who asks *to persuade* the operating subject, Jesus,
so that he might bring about the attribution of the requested
values whether it be healing or the expulsion of demons. However, since these values are not immediately recorded on the
trajectory leading to the establishment of the "Kingdom," it
is a matter then of *motivating* him to establish them. The
harmonizing of the wants as postulated by the contract therefore calls for understanding on a double plane: the one of
correlated values, the other of topical values. This is what
is manifested in turn by the task of persuasion and then of
motivation.

1. *Persuasion*

The request is not always orally expressed. It may be
dressed in a variety of ways: either it may be implied si-
lently in a movement (this is most often the case: someone
approaches Jesus; the sick are brought to him, the paralytic
is lowered from the roof) or formulated in a prayer, entreaty
or silent cry. In any event, the request calls for the *expectation* of a program which will be carried out: namely,
the liquidation of the lack and the obtaining of the hoped-
for blessing. In turn, this expectation requires on the part
of the one who makes the request the discerning of a competence, of a power proper for the execution of the request.

The task to be undertaken is correctly sensed to be an exceptionally difficult one. Ordinarily, this power is not questioned either by the one who benefits from it or by Jesus' opponents. It is normally presupposed. However, it is not obvious as the disciples' hesitation and the doubt of the father with a possessed child illustrate: "If you *can* do anything, come help me" (Mk. 4: 22). "If you can!" ... "All things are possible for the one who believes," Jesus responds. We see that the persuasion is not a one way street; the one who makes the request implores, but Jesus strengthens his trust. In order for the request to be authentic, it presupposes faith in the existence of Jesus' power-to-do. We can detail here the double transformation brought about by faith: in objective terms the *impossibility* of the requested healing becomes a *possibility;* in subjective terms *improbability* becomes *probability*. This is the primary aspect of faith.

But this convention concerning Jesus' inherent power is still not sufficient for making a request out of the inquiry. Jesus' power is not questioned by the demons. It is so certain that it is rejected by an anti-request (to keep Jesus from acting: Mk. 1: 24; 5: 7). On the contrary, it is a matter of persuading Jesus with the request; this is the task of persuasion which consists in causing-the-subject-to-want: "If you want ..." would be the introductory formula to the request. This is the heart of the request. Let us note here that the request is the transitive form of a process which can on occasion take a reflexive form in the "compassion" felt by Christ. Jesus is moved to "compassion." He "comes-to-want," and this fact clearly shows that the request implies an agreement among partners with respect to the want: it is a contract. It is at this point that the miracle will be formed into a call for interpretation.

2. *Motivation*

The proposed contract introduces a diversion in Jesus'
initial program, namely the establishment of the Kingdom.
It implies a shift in orientation.   Indeed, the values which
are negotiated by the contract are not equivalent to the values of the Kingdom.   It is not enough to *persuade* the subject
to *perform* the miracle; he must also be *motivated* by appealing
to the topical values which totally control his *action*.   Conversely, the one making the request must in turn be motivated
by the same values.   The contrast rightfully presupposes that
the correlation between topical values and correlated values
be recognized and accepted by both parties to the contract.

This correlation exists within Jesus' mind.   He manifests
it very clearly in the episode of the paralytic: the forgiveness of sins is linked to his healing.   This correlation also
accounts for his compassion and the initiative that he oftentimes takes with regard to the miracles.   We sense that Jesus
is compelled by a "having-to-do" which secretly inspires his
actions.   However, it appears that Jesus does not consider the
scope of this having-to-do as is shown by the interpretative
performances in which he is led by the argument of the Syro-
phonecian woman (Mk. 7: 28).

By contrast, the correlation between both orders of values does not necessarily exist in the mind of the one who
makes the request.   Its secret character makes it the object
of a necessary *interpretation*.   Actually, the one who makes
the request must rise up to the level of the Kingdom's goals.
His desire for a blessing must be articulated by his desire
for superior values and he must first of all take hold of them.
Thus, there is a mutual motivation on the part of both partners to the contract.

However, the interpretative performance which is required for the success of the miracle is not easily accomplished. Jesus expressly solicits it but is often met with disappointment: "faithless generation; how long must I suffer you?" (Mk. 9: 19). Without actually perceiving it the questioner through his request has set into motion a mechanism which should lead him straightway to the knowledge of a program which has heretofore escaped him: *what is at stake for the miracle presupposes what is at stake for the Kingdom.* But this connection is not always made in the questioner's mind. We must at least be suspicious of the existence and acceptance of trust. This is why the contract takes the form of a *fiduciary contract.* Between the manifestation hoped for of a visual sort and the secret manifestation of the "Kingdom" there stands a fiduciary relationship. *Interpretation blends with belief for the one who makes a request.* We can appeal here to what A. J. Greimas says about the interpretative doing: it is the inference concerning the plane of /being/ based upon the plane of /appearing/, not by a necessary logical implication, but by the establishment of a *fiduciary relation* under the sole responsibility of the knowing subject.[7]

In summary, the want and the competence that Jesus sets into operation in his response to the request flow out of the particular performance of the miracle. The latter is enclosed within a more comprehensive program whose goal is to establish the "Kingdom." As a consequence, the request requires of the one who makes it the establishment of a contract in the double form of persuasion and motivation so that the second englobes the first. The fiduciary contract consists of the articulation of both of these operations. It is faith in the values of the "Kingdom" which makes the miracle possible, and not the reverse. For this reason, the request postulates an *interpre-*

tation which bears precisely upon the correlation between the two orders of values. Faith *motivates* the one who makes the request along the axis of the "Kingdom." It makes him an actualized although unrealized subject of wanting. Within this accession to the universe of the "Kingdom" we must therefore situate *the main test* of the "miracle" on the part of the one who benefits from it. As a consequence of this test, the persuasion forms instead a secondary and difficult task ("Lord, help my unbelief"), and the success of this performance at the level of the realized miracle represents in everyone's eyes the "mark" of the hero as expressed by faith. The miracle is the glorification of belief: "Your faith has saved you."

Thus, we can see that with the miracle story, the focus changes with regard to the common notion that it comes about as the result of power: the main test plays a role in the movement to belief which is a certain knowledge, although in a secretive mode (/being/ and /non-appearing/). The miracle as a somatic performance is the figurative manifestation of /appearing/ which is added to being in order to form what is true (/being/ and /appearing/). It therefore gives rise to *belief* as true knowledge, that is *recognition.*

c. Recognition

The strategy for recognition which comes after the performance is no less complex than that of the request. At the level of factual execution the miracle calls first of all for *approval.* This is the verification of the proper execution of the contract and is expressed in the form of recognition and of glorification directed toward the benefactor. But the movement toward recognition does not stop here; it should normally lead to the *ratification* of the system of values which are the motivating power behind the want of the operating

subject. Correspondingly, we can see that approval comes
with respect to the performance and the ratification with
respect to the motivation.

1. *Approval*

Approval takes the form of recognition. If recognition
is equivalent to "identification through memory," following
the definition found in *Petit Robert*,[8] approval is the recognition of a prior cognition: it is the anticipatory cognition which characterizes the moment of expectation. The
factual manifestation of the miracle offers us material for
reexamination. We have already seen the latter at work in
the sort of exacting "inquiry" carried out by the royal official regarding the circumstances surrounding the healing.
The recognition of this fact leads in other words to the
recognition of the power inherent in the benefactor. This
is an extraordinary power whose manifestation provokes ad-
miration, praise and consequently the *fame* enjoyed by Jesus
which spreads throughout the land. But actually does the
mistrust evidenced by Jesus in the face of this kind of fame
not show that the recognition is not complete when it remains at this level? This is not what he expects. As a result, he gives the order to remain silent (a repeated prohibition which is very poorly observed) concerning the publi-
cizing of the miracles. For the recognition remains incomplete as long as it does not rise to the level of the system
of values adopted by the Master. Actually it is accomplished
only at the level where the Kingdom is established.

2. *Ratification*

Ratification has to do with the conformity of the

completed work to the values which secretly animate the subject. However, this ratification is not so obvious. Take,
for example, the scribe's murmuring at the healing of the man
with a withered hand on the Sabbath (Mk. 3: 1-6), or the controversy concerning the power to forgive sins in connection
with the power to heal (Mk. 2: 1-12). As for the beneficiaries of the miracles, they are not always the best qualified
to perform this ratification: the nine lepers who have "forgotten" to come and witness to their recognition are good examples of this (Lk. 17: 12-19). But the ratification oftentimes does succeed. It consists in an *evaluation* of the subject's operation but on the basis of the system of values
where the subject is felt to stand. Thus the fiduciary contract is verified. Belief or certain knowledge become true
knowledge. Next it is a matter not only of accepting this
system of values (which is the case after the moment of motivation) but also of entering into an *active obedience* to the
recognized authority of Jesus. Therefore, we will see something more in the ratification than an *assertion* of knowledge
concerning the existence of certain values; we will see the
initiation of a wanting-to-do in the bringing of the sanc-
tioned values to life. This is what several miracle stories
manifest when they report that the one who has experienced
the miracle, such as Blind Bartimaus (Mk. 10: 51; cf. also
Mk. 5: 18-20; Lk. 8: 1-2), begins to "follow Jesus." *The
fully completed ratification makes a disciple out of the
believer in so far as his want is concerned.* The beneficiary
or witness as subject of a wanting-to-manifest is then associated with Jesus' narrative program. He achieves the level
of actor in the primary narrative whose existence was already
postulated. It is by means of this ratification that the
reintegration of the miraculous episode into the primary narrative is carried out and the gap between work and action is

reduced. At the conclusion of the miracle performance,
understood here in the broadest sense, the one who makes
the request not only views his physical state as transformed, but is also conjoined by his want to the values
of the Kingdom. He has grasped the *meaning* of the Kingdom in his request; he has ratified it at that moment in
his wanting-to-do. Consequently he has entered into the
manifestation of the program of salvation.

We may summarize the miracle schema in the following
chart:

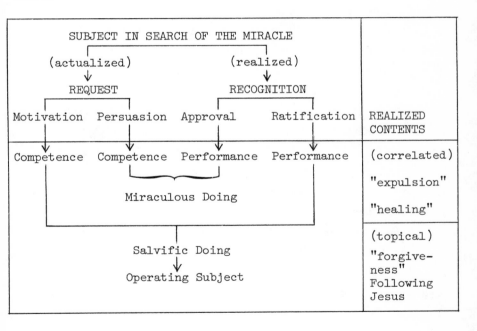

Remarks: The "Nature Miracles"

It would remain for us to show that the structure of the
miracle such as we have established it is applicable as well
to the "nature miracles": the Multiplication of Bread, the
Calming of the Storm, the Wedding at Cana, the Miraculous
Catch of Fish, the Walk on Water, etc. Without being able to

give an accounting of all of the necessary justifications, it seems that we can confirm this. Far from being pure manifestations of power, nature miracles possess both at their beginning and end the double process of request and recognition. But we must note the following differences: (1) the nature miracles are concerned in a special way with a select group destined to become apostles. Most often the crowd ignores the miraculous deed as such even if it happens to be the beneficiary of the miracle (with the exception of the Multiplication of Bread in John 6). (2) Most often the miracle is provoked by Jesus himself. The disciples are content to indicate the lack ("we have not caught a thing"; "They have nothing at all to eat") and Jesus seeks to provoke them into performance. (3) It all takes place as if Jesus through the initiation of the miracle wanted to bring his disciples to the recognition that they have or will have at their disposal a competence which is analogous to his own in terms of *saying* (teaching) and of *doing* (miracles). The organization of the nature miracles would lead therefore to the constitution of a *collective actor* who is called upon to acquire the competence proper to the actant Jesus in function of the preaching of repentance first (Mk. 6: 12-13) and then of announcing the Gospel (Mk. 16: 15). We will have to await Jesus' resurrection in order for this recognition which is a long time in coming before it is fully acquired. It will therefore be linked to the comprehension of Christ's death and resurrection.

2.3 *Conclusion*

Thus, little by little the functions that the parable and miracle story perform within the primary narrative are spelled out. Both parable and miracle call for interpretation with each possessing its own structure. Parables lead to *specific practices;* miracles stimulate the search for *meaning.* A curious criss-crossing in the nature of their operations and the results of the interpretation occurs. The parables are *verbal* operations which call for a *practical* interpretation; miracles are *somatic* operations which call for a *cognitive* interpretation (it is true that the latter is the basis for a voluntary commitment). It is not impossible to set up an order for these two groups of calls for interpretation. It is clear that in the algorithm of the primary narrative the miracle precedes the parable as the establishing of want on the plane of the Kingdom; it precedes its determination in the form of a specific kind of behavior. For the one who is not "converted" by the "miracle," it is difficult for him to allow himself to be instructed by the parable, that is to hear with a mind that is actively obedient. Conversely, for the one who does not hear the parable, it is difficult if not impossible for him to give a specific content to his voluntary commitment. However, the precedence of the miracle over the parable, though it be demanded in the linking together of narrative statements, is not necessary for each actor. It is not necessary to have experienced a miracle in order to be called, for the primary narrative provides other mechanisms for following after Jesus into the perspective of the "Kingdom." We have already said that even if the miracle "presupposes" the salvific plan, the latter does not necessarily imply the miracle. This is what gives the interpretation of the miracle its *fiduciary* character. We can even anticipate that when belief is ultimately founded in commitment that the usefulness of miracles will disappear. This would explain the cessation of miracles near the end of the Gospel.

Thus, we have two *models* that can be constructed from

parables and miracles. They are abstract models. The building of these models rests upon the *a priori* hypothesis that the group of miracles and parables altogether submit to the law of a unitary structure. But it is obvious that the different elements of this structure are not always *manifested* in each of the micro-narratives related by the Gospel text.

3. PARABLES AND MIRACLES IN THE STRATEGY OF ACTORS

It is obvious that the parables and miracles play a specific role in the strategy of their author, Jesus, as much with respect to his disciples as to his opponents and, more generally, the crowd. In remaining faithful to our initial proposal, we will attempt to show that parables and miracles correspond to strategically different positions.

3.1 *Parabolic Narratives*

a. *The Narrative Plane*

The consideration of strategy forces us to take the process of enunciation into account. The parables are speech acts. They are enunciated in different contexts: of teaching, warning, persuading, power conflicts, promising, prophetic pronouncements. Thus, the parables are in support of speech or performative acts;[9] they make explicit their propositional content. This performative force englobes them in every way. Moreover, if we consider the behavior of the hearers, we can observe that they produce contrasting reactions: either that of eagerness to know or aversion; either that of comprehension or the lack of comprehension; either that of acceptance or refusal. Therefore, there is an obvious articulation on the part of the parables in their context. They belong to the

global action that Jesus has upon his listeners. But we must
not mislead ourselves concerning the meaning of this articulation. Even though it is surrounded by a series of narrative
statements, it is not this sequence which illumines the parables *but on the contrary the parables which cast light upon
the narrative statements*. We have seen that the parables in
and of themselves are indifferent with respect to the context.
Whatever the attitudes of the speaker or his listeners may be,
their propositional content does not change. They project out
upon their situations. They do not transform the context by
their statement alone; rather they *duplicate* this context by
transposing it onto the plane of a higher knowledge. Take,
for example, a parable spoken in a conflict situation. This
conflict is ex-posed by the parable in the form of a displaced
narrative which is reducible to an ordered transformational
model: the parable is no longer what is at stake in the conflict; it *states* what is at stake in this conflict. The parable becomes the judge of this conflict. It is the structure
itself of the parable which is conflictual in nature. It
substitutes a fictive conflict for the lived one. All of
Jesus' artistry is present at this moment: the momentary interpretation of an intricate struggle where the passions are
in confrontation with each other, where the motivations com-
pete secretly, through the insertion of a strange story with
actors in the third person wherein the ordered organization
of the conflict and its ultimate resolution will be exposed.
The speaker's performativity will be exercised before ("lis-
ten") or after ("Let him who has ears to hear, hear," "Do
likewise") the parable, but there is no performativity in the
narration itself *of* the parable. Certainly there is performativity *within* the parable, but it is a performativity which
is *described* and not *carried out* by the narrator.

It suffices for an understanding of this point to compare,

for example, the parable of the Vineyard Keepers with the accusations leveled against the pharisees by Jesus: "You seek to kill me" (Jn. 8: 37). The propositional content of the statements is virtually the same, but in so far as the enunciation is concerned, it is, on the one hand, the word which presents the murderous action in a figurative way and it is, on the other hand, the word which paralyzes the opponent in his criminal intent. The one narrates; the other judges.

For all of that the parable is not reassuring. In the face of the crowd which presses close to hear, Jesus identifies ideally four classes of listeners in the parable of the Sower of which only one will be recognized as faithful to his listening. Whether the performing word acquits or condemns, the parable is disquieting: it questions the hearing itself.

This is the fundamental strategy: to depersonalize the dialogue whether it be peaceful or conflictual in order to make possible a free repersonalization. By definition we could say that the narrator sets aside his own personality in order to have heard a voice other than his own, that is unless he causes the voice which bestows meaning to be heard rightly by disappearing within it while his listeners lose themselves in the "naked" hearing. *The parable is that moment in which the word belongs to no one.*

It is not that the parable hardens into an abstract discourse. Quite to the contrary! As a creator of clearly typed characters, of defined actions within the framework of specific situations, *the parable offers itself as an ordered interplay of predicates of action.* Thus, Luke's parables present repeatedly the predicate of action "pity." These predicates of action are set off in a pure form, as it were, by causing the figurative roles to vary. The

listeners are not invited to slip into the role of a father
of a family or of a samaritan, but to invest themselves despite the disparity in their social roles with the predicates
of action which are made *available* by the parabolic discourse.
The parables are not merely norms but rather simulated actions
being both game rules as well as a regulated game, law as well
as invention, i. e., story in which the dominating figure shows
the choice to be made. Any performative word may emerge from
them by slipping imperceptibly from the example to advice or
injunction just as eventual concrete applications may emerge
from them. With regard to the parable's fictional polemic, it
is to be located properly with the actors. However, let us
say once again that even if the parable indirectly imitates
the actors in the primary narrative by means of the interven-
ing scenario, that is not its goal. It is neither approving
nor condemning, persuading nor consenting. The reason for this
is that *the parable does not denote*. It refers to no one. It
is the appearance of meaning in the midst of power. It creates
the illusion of freedom within the narrative. As a model of
worthy actions, the actors by investing themselves with the
proposed predicates identify themselves as the *referents* of the
the parable. Whatever may be the part they play, they will
never be able to do anything other than verify the ordered interaction of statements. The only way to contradict a parable
would be to propose another one. For in fact the parable evi-
dences a power; there is a constraint exerted, namely that of
an alternative and preferred choice. Ideally one could propose
another alternative within another model. It does not seem
that Jesus' opponents ever show themselves to be capable of
this. The author of the Gospel narrative does not allow it to
happen. As a result the parables play the role of *truth operators*. This is their function. Although incorporated within
the narrative, they do not intervene directly in the network

of transformations; they translate it. From the point of view
of the speaker, they provide the game rules. Therefore, parables function more as a reflecting mirror than as a narrative
mechanism. With regard to the actors introduced within the
narrative, they are condensations of truth: by varying the
figurative roles, they effect a *noetic reduction* of the roles
to a single predicate of action, whether positive or negative,
which transcends the difference in social roles. They therefore display an intentionality wherein the truth of the want
is recorded.

b. *The Semantic Plane*

In abstract terms, it can be said that the parables make
possible a passage from the *possibilities* offered by a model
to the *selection* of one of these possibilities. From this
angle the group of parables makes up a sort of second Gospel,
a combination of values and desires, of actions and counter-
actions, as well as their ultimate restriction to a fixed
choice--an unreal, atemporal, discontinuous, reductive but
axiologically oriented Gospel of which the primary narrative
would be the ambiguous, concrete, factual application. Under
these conditions, the relation of the world of the parables
to its context will necessarily appear indirect, slanted and
peculiar: a relation between a world of "truth" and "secret,"
a relation between the certitude of "knowledge" and the per-
plexity of "decision." As true as it is to say that the enunciation of the parable is inserted within a given context, it
is just as true to say that the parabolic statement encompasses its context as one of its anticipated manifestations.
There is a kind of mutual englobing of "text" and "context."
In semiotic terms the parabolic world *envelops* the whole of
the Gospel narrative. It reveals its decisive risks from the

sending of the Son to the final judgment, passing by way of the communication of the word (the introduction of the model of behavior for the disciples), to say nothing of the drama of the Passion and death of the narrator. *The parables therefore are a story of the story.* As such, they represent a discourse of reference. Such a discourse is not to be taken, of course, in the sense of a discourse about method. It does not recount the process of the Scripture's historical formation nor does it reveal the model for constructing a reading of the Gospels. It narrates the narration itself; it hears the hearing, but upon a higher plane. It does not situate the process of understanding either in the empirical subjectivity of the speaker or in the psychological perception of the listeners, but in the delivery of a meta-narrative word which is capable of building a semantic structure which serves as a reading code for the comprehension of the primary narrative. It is in this power of reflection upon itself that in our opinion the divine origin of the word is to be found (see below on the parable of the Sower).

This is why the parables do not draw their "truth" from their reference to the actors, much less draw their *meaning* from the actions which manifest them at the contextual level. Paradoxically, by means of a kind of folding back upon the operation itself of the story, they teach the teaching and the non-teaching, its success and its failure, and how the hearing either creates or does not create the hearing, that is how it produces the life and death of the teacher. The story of the story is located within a narration which is prior to the speaker himself as well as to his listeners. In short, the parables "break apart" the narrative relationship between the speaker and his listeners to the extent of breaking apart the meta-narrative relation of parabolic "speaking" and "understanding." They cause both the speaker and his listener to

enter into a meta-linguistic story which from that moment on
is no longer exchanged merely between the interlocutors of the
primary story (the latter are no more than the historic variables) but between a knack of speaking and of understanding
which is in some fashion universal.

c. Two Examples

What we are trying to communicate will perhaps be more
clearly perceived if we take as our starting point the effect
produced by two parables, one from the beginning of the text
(the parable of the Sower) and one from the end (the parable
of the Vineyard Keepers).[10]

1. The Parable of the Sower

The "parable" of the Sower and its "explanation" constitute an entire unit. Without the explanation, the parable of
the Sower would be reduced to the framework of a discourse on
agriculture. It is the explanation which develops it into a
parable by orienting it toward the figure of the "Kingdom."
The explanation does not "decode" the parable; rather it trans-
lates it into a metaphor of the "Kingdom." Where the primary
narrative had distinguished four types of ground (path, rocky
ground, thorny places, good earth), the explanation names four
categories of listeners: those who hear the word and have it
stolen from them; those who hear the word but lack any roots;
those who hear the word but allow it to suffocate like a
branch without fruit; and finally those who hear it and bear
fruit. In the movement from parable to explanation, Jesus
provides an "interpretation" which puts aside completely the
notion of sowing and situates itself entirely upon a cognitive
plane. This interpretation makes a distinction between those

who hear the parable and do not understand; those who do not hear and do not understand; those who desired to understand but did not hear (the past prophets); and finally those who hear and understand. *Refusal* on the one hand and *desire* to understand on the other enable us to reduce the first category to the second and the third to the fourth. Hearing is subordinated to understanding as the latter is to conversion.

Having said that, what is the impact of the parable upon the context? An initial remark: we must not confuse this *naming* of classes with the *designation* of categories or hearers. It would be wrong, as it is frequently the case, to refer to the crowd as the class of hearers who do not understand and to the disciples as those hearers who understand. Among the hearers in the crowd we find candidates for conversion, while the disciples will constantly be reproached (especially in Mark) even after the resurrection for not understanding and for having a hardened heart. This means that the fact of being the ones privileged to hear the explanation and cognitive interpretation does not confer upon anyone the right to be grouped among "those who understand." The parable does not have this *referential* function. That this is true can be verified by the fact that the interpretation which is given of it on the cognitive plane does not refer merely to the presence of actual hearers. The desire of the Elders was able to make up in some way for the hearing which was lacking. To put it in other words, the parable suggests an order from the actual *hearing* to the *understanding*. It is not the hearing which accounts for the understanding. On the contrary, the man hears because he understands: "Let him who has ears to hear, hear." Understanding may be defined only by its own reduplication. One either does or does not understand. As for the one who has not lost it up until the moment of hearing, "Someone will take away from him even what he already has." We only know

what must be done in order to be able to understand. But
the understanding does not permit us to derive any explanation; it is attested by its fruit, namely conversion.

A second remark. This is the reason why the *meaning*
itself of the "parable" is not directed toward the "explanation." Even less is the latter measurable by the intelligence
of the listeners. It is up to intelligence to enter into the
explanation which is aimed directly toward the parable of the
seed. The growth of the seed along with its metamorphosis is
the image of the growth of the Kingdom. It is not just a parable about parabolic communication. It carries within its sym-
bolism all the forms of teaching: discourse and parables,
warnings and persuasions, commands and prayers, but also re-
fusals or conversions and the behavior which flows from that.
All of this is encompassed in its representation. There is
nothing prior to the word which is characterized as divine.
There is no explanatory action which does not find its origin
in it. It sets in motion all human action. Its growth is
surrounded by silence like the seed which grows without anyone
knowing how. It is like poetry: "It explains nothing, but
makes everything explainable." What the parable requires is
that the hearing be in agreement with the understanding and
the understanding with the conversion. But neither the speaker nor the listeners have control over the operation of the
word. Therefore, the parable is not a pedagogical "trick"
nor a psychological strategy. It states the priority of the
speaking over what is said, of understanding over the hearing.
In short, every noetic explanation of the word which begins
with either the speaker or the hearer comes to an abrupt end
if it does not return to the germination of the seed. The
parable of the Sower is a story of the *self-referential* action
of the divine word: "story" and thus the word's work; "self-
referential" and thus a narrative generated totally by the

word and returning to it after having given rise to the
hearing. Therefore, within the story it is the image of
this category of word in its divine state. It is in relation to this word that the speaker's knack (his contribution as translator) is defined: as either the sterility
or fertility of different listening contexts.

2. *The Parable of the Vineyard Workers*

Evidently this is the most personified of all parables.
Jesus appears to be describing himself here with the reference to the Beloved Son. The polemical context leads us na-
turally to see in the vineyard workers those adversaries who
bring loss upon themselves even though they clearly understand this. Therefore it is by means of the actual murder
that the persecutors prove and "fulfil" the prophecy. Paradoxically, by destroying the narrator, they confirm the truth
of his word. And yet, the parable does not function as an
accusation, even less is it a provocation to murder. The
parable does not have a performative effect in this sense,
first of all because it presents a metaphorical character
and is enunciated as a story in the third person. It remains a fiction open to everyone to recognize himself in it.
Properly speaking, the parable does not denote. It is not
even, for Jesus, a way of allowing us to see that he had
foretold the murderous intentions of his opponents. This
possibility is in some way presupposed. Therefore, it is
not the present or future situation upon which the parable
draws its truth. What is its function then if it is not
foremost an accusation or warning? It is to provide this
murder with a meaning. The pharisees believe that they
honor God by doing away with the blasphemer. But the parable locates this murder in another story and by inserting

it within another schema gives it a totally opposite meaning. It makes this murder appear to be an attempt at taking over the inheritance, that is of the religious power, by the pharisees. It is for the purpose of remaining the masters in the interpretation of the law that they want to do away with Jesus and not in order to honor God. On the contrary, they dishonor his messengers. Thus the parable does not point to the murder which is to come; the intention to carry out this murder has in any case been known for a long time. What we have here is a *struggle for meaning*. It is fully at this level that the context surrounding the parable is situated. It is devoted entirely to the verbal polemic between Jesus and his opponents. Within this polemic Jesus' opponents prove themselves powerless to explain their attitude vis-à-vis John the Baptist, just as they are incapable of making Jesus stumble over various controversial questions (taxes to Caesar, the resurrection of the dead, the first commandment, the relationship of David to the Messiah). We are witnesses to Jesus' triumph in this combat in order to determine who holds the authority of the word: "It is literally a matter of having the last word, that is of triumphing in the verbal exchange."[11] It is upon this verbal supremacy that the meaning-effect of Jesus' death is dependent. This is the meaning: the pharisees have not understood a thing even though they perfectly well understood the referential allusion to murder. The parable does not draw its truth from the reality of this deed, but on the contrary the deed is verified by the meaning which ultimately dominates the parable. The parable therefore plays the role of a truth operator. It is capable of playing this role because it is capable of engendering a story about the story.

d. *Remarks on the Meaning of Narrative as Narrative*

We must raise the question of the meaning that the
parable derives from its general form as a narrative. What
does the properly narrative character of the narrative bring
to the meaning? It may be useful in this regard to compare
the *parable* to the formulation of the *Law,* that is to say
to that which is differentiated the most within a common
semantic field. Both the parable and the law in fact have
to do with action in its relationship to meaning and, to
be more specific, to the *norm*. We intuitively sense that
the effect produced by the story of *an action manifesting
a norm* is not the same as that produced by *the statement
of a norm*. The prescription of "compassion," for example,
does not have the same impact as the story of the Good
Samaritan on the same theme. Certainly the semantic content of the term "compassion" surfaces in both cases. But
in the prescription--"one must have compassion"--the term
is grasped in an action. In the parable we are no longer
concerned with interpreting a concept but with an action.
The concept offers an idea to be realized but the realization adds in no way to its intelligibility. It may even
bog down the meaning in the particularity of one situation.
It only provides us with an *illustration* of the meaning
and it will always be possible to oppose to a similar example a situation in which the application remains in
doubt ("Who is my neighbor?"). The clarity of the concept
is deceiving. Owing to the fact that it disguises its
origin in praxis, it remains an unspecified semantic sub-
stance. It is opposed to nothing. By contrast, within
the parabolic story the meaning is not given for the sake
of contemplation but is produced in action; it is the

regulating rule. And as the action is necessarily a transformation from one situation to another (for example, the
passage from the man who is wounded and abandoned to a man
who is sheltered and cared for), the meaning results from
the process itself which, in order to create its effect,
must begin by doing away with its contrary. The meaning
then appears in an action which mediates between two states.
In essence this is *conversion*. Whereas prescription imposes
the application of a norm which is always indeterminate with
regard to the situation, the story creates this norm in the
description of a process. Consequently the norm appears as
the regulating rule of a praxis. It is disclosed on the basis
of what the man does and not what he thinks. To this it can
be added that the norm--an essential condition for the action--
appears in the course of the narrative in an ordered sequence
of conditions. As soon as the praxis comes to the foreground,
consideration of the transforming subject necessarily enters
in in terms of his knowledge, power and want. The norm is not
separated from the subject who carries it out by way of his
competence and intentions as well as by the situation that he
occupies. At the opposite end of the chain, consideration for
the transformed subject of state likewise enters in and, along
with it, an entire series of elements which are indispensable
for the comprehension of the action. The parable brings the
norm immediately to bear upon the intersubjective relation.

Allowing the meaning to be grasped in a regulated behavi-
or produces a particular effect upon the hearer: the parable
no longer provides material for verbal discussion but introduces a differentiation in praxis. The hearer is invited to
reflect upon his own praxis: the norm is no longer *before* him
as an object of his uncertainty. Either the rule or its contrary now regulates his actions, so establishing it *from within*. The hearer then discovers it on the basis of what he does.

He does not gain access merely to the knowledge of what he must do; he passes from one kind of praxis whose significance remained obscured to a reflexive praxis. For the hearer is never outside of a situation and the parable is not concerned with an abstract subject. It questions the subject as to his want. How? By *distancing* the subject, by presenting his want to him in other thematic roles, in other types of conduct and contrasting attitudes. It then permits the reduction of the spontaneous attitude to its *meaning content*. If the parable is eminently speakable whereas the conflicting life situations are not, it is precisely for this reason that a differentiation is produced. A grasp in meaning is brought about. Thus the distinction between *fiction* and the *real* is strengthened. Interpretation has reduced it to the distinction in the same act between understood meaning and implicitly lived meaning (and not to the simple difference between the idea and the real). This is why the parable eventually makes repentence and conversion possible. Thus, prescription and parable both create suspense, but the response that prescription calls for is one of agreement upon principles; the response that the parable calls for is a change in praxis. The one stimulates obedience, the other conversion.

3.2 *The Miracle Stories*

In contrast to the parable, the miracle story is not indifferent to the context. Whereas the context takes its meaning from the parable, the miracle story receives its meaning from the context. The miracle story is not, however, entirely homogenous with the primary narrative. It introduces a diversion into the course of the narrative. As we have seen, it introduces a subordinate program whose execution is quickly brought about before the entire program of the Gospel can

continue. Miracles are distributed precisely along the narrative chain in the form of loops which take us away from the
context only in order to return us to it.

a. Divergence and the Reduction of the Divergence

We shall not return to the phenomenon of divergence which
is provoked by the miracle pericope. Let us simply recall that
the miracle is the object of a request which comes from an actor who is an outsider to the group of Jesus' usual associates.
Being divergent with respect to the proper object of Jesus'
mission and immediately a visible success, the miracle has as
its raison d'être the establishment of the beneficiary as well
as the spectators of the miracle as attentive hearers of the
Word of God. From this point of view the miracle is a *sign*.
The miracle represents a message, an object of knowledge, which
returns us to the definitive value of the principal program.
So, the reduction of the divergence may be understood by means
of an interpretative doing which links the "difficulty" of the
performance to the "difficult" task of the Kingdom.

On the one hand this hypothesis assumes that the miracle,
as a reality brought about, is not totally homogenous with the
values of the Kingdom, and on the other hand that it is reducible to them along the narrow path of an interpretation in so
far as the interpretation associates the miraculous work with
the manifestation of salvation on the basis of a metaphorical
relation between the blessings accorded both sides. There is
in fact no necessary relation between healing and salvation as
has been said. The miracle does not remove the formidable
question raised by sickness or death. Healing is not a guarantee against adversity. Moreover, Jesus expressly forewarns
his disciples that they will be confronted as he is with suf-
fering and persecution. The problem of evil will only come to

light on the night of the passion. What is so astonishing
about the miracle therefore is not the restoration of health
but the fleeting intervention of a sacred power. The event
produces a *sign*. It raises the question about the religious
system. How are we to understand it? At this point the
miracle can become the stakes for a conflict of interpretation.
The problem is to know whether the miracle finds its meaning
in the semantic framework of the Kingdom *or* in the framework
of traditional religion. In his choices of time and, similarly, of beneficiaries (primarily the lowly, the unclean, the
sinners from every station in life), Jesus provokes a conflict.
He does not condemn his opponents for their inability to perform miracles (their sons moreover do have the power to cast
out demons); rather he condemns them for being unable to admit
to the miraculous sign within the ritual context of their religion. On the other hand, this admission is possible from
the perspective of the "Kingdom." Jesus' strategy is quite
clear: he deliberately provokes confrontation. One of the
few times in Mark that Jesus takes the initiative in performing a miracle and even deliberately falls into a trap set by
the pharisees is for the purpose of provoking a scandal by
healing on the Sabbath (the episode of the man with a withered
hand, Mark 3: 1-6). In so doing he refuses to see any contradiction between the daily needs of life and the strictures of
religious observance. In short, he performs the miracle under
such circumstances that he forces a revision of properly religious meanings. Both the doing and the results of the miracle
are compatible with the values supported by Jesus and not with
those defended by the scribes. Its powerful character derives
from an unknown force; however, this force can be understood
as *divine* only in the upsetting of traditional values. Any
perspective outside that of the Kingdom excludes the use of
this amazing power. To put it in other words, in order for

there to be a true interpretation, the "difficult" nature
of the miraculous doing must be homogenous with the values
of the Kingdom.

b. *The Classification of the Miracles in Function of the Context*

If our hypothesis is correct, two consequences are
entailed.

(1) First of all, no miracles are possible in a program which would not lead to the manifestation of the values
proposed by Jesus. The model that we have built must indeed
take into account the impossibility as well as the possibility of the miracle. It must explain, for example, the refusal
to perform a miracle at the moment of temptation. It is too
obvious that it may not be put to the use of the Tempter's
goals. This hypothesis likewise justifies the "impossibility"
of the miracle in the face of the disbelief on the part of
Jesus' companions in his own homeland. The source for the
absence of faith, indeed the doubt about the competence of
the subject ("a prophet is without honor only in his country,"
Mark 6: 4), hinders the establishment of the fiduciary contract. The same reason would lie behind the refusal to respond to the request for a "sign from heaven," which is demanded by the pharisees (Mark 8: 11-13). Such a sign would
have produced a reversal of the interpretative structure; the
miracle would no longer presuppose faith, it would imply it.
It would no longer be the difficult task which is asked for
and obtained by the believer as the "mark" of his faith. It
would become the principal, factual test for which faith would
be only the empirical recognition. It would be changed only
for the empirical recognition. It would be changed into a
test (and moreover a quite degrading one); it would no longer

be a call for interpretation. But Jesus did not accept this.

(2) The miracle will therefore occur only given the hypothesis of an integration within the primary narrative and within the perspective offered by the Kingdom. As we have seen, the articulation occurs at two moments: both prior to the performance in the *request* and afterwards in the *recognition*. At the center of this organization stands the object itself of this request and recognition: the carrying out of the healing. The latter poses the case or "motif" of interpretation. Indeed, this structure is rarely manifested in its entirety. There is, however, one miracle which brings together all of the elements of the structure and which has functioned as a model for us: the healing of Blind Bartemaus (Mark 10: 46-53). But most often the same miracle *motif* will contribute to the manifestation of this or that element of the structure. The different "images" of the same motif enable us from this point of view to differentiate and to classify the miracles. There is a single structure; however, its applications differ. Let us give a few examples of this in summary form.

--In a general way the "summaries" of Jesus' activity and the mass healings are grounds enough for asserting the link between the topical content and the correlated content. A relation is asserted between "preaching" and the "performing of many miracles" without it being defined (Mark 1: 32-35, 3: 7-12, 6: 12-13, 54-56).

--At the phase of the *request*, persuasion and fear develop the miracle-working competence of Jesus, whether this power be appealed to (Mark 1: 40, 5: 28, 7: 28, 8: 22), fought against (by demons: Mark 1: 24, 5: 7) or questioned (Mark 5: 36, 9: 23-24). As for Jesus' salvific competence on the level of the Kingdom, it is

illustrated either by the affirmation by Jesus himself
when he sets up the correlation between the power to
forgive sins and that of healing (Mark 2: 10) or by the
faith of the one who requests the miracle (Mark 2: 5,
5: 34, 7:26-29, 10: 47-48), or by the narrator (Mark 6:
34), or conversely when contested by his opponents
(Mark 2: 7, 3: 2-6). This competence gives rise therefore either to trust or mistrust.

--At the phase of *recognition*, a number of miracles
have the motif of manifesting Jesus' fame (Mark 1: 28,
45, 7: 36), fame that Jesus most often rejects (Mark 1:
44, 7: 36, 8: 26). We know the reason for this reser-
vation: Jesus demands a *ratification* which is worthy
of a commitment to follow him (Mark 5: 18-20, 10: 52).

In closing, let us stress one major function of the miracles: that of providing grounds for the recognition of the
operating subject. We know that Jesus ordinarily rejects any
publicity about his miracles. It is all the more interesting
to see the way in which he himself sets forward the interpretation of his miracle-working power both in the discussion of
Beelzebul (Mark 3: 22-30) and the healing of the paralytic
(Mark 2: 1-12). We can make the following points from this
double self-affirmation: (1) his power could not come, without contradiction, from the Prince of Demons; his power comes
from God; (2) there is a conjunction in the same actor of the
power to heal and the power to forgive sins and, indeed, the
power to preach. The first power includes the second as the
greater power incorporates the lesser. Jesus stresses therefore a quasi-unique authority, a common competence. The "difficulty" of the task is very much the same for the forgiveness
of sins, for preaching or for the performance of the miracles.
But there is one difference: the performance of a miracle

gives rise to a work, a visible, manifested, noticeable-because-it-is-exact, result, whereas the task of the word and of salvation remain underground, secret, mysterious, the fruits of which are always slow in coming. The miracles show the invincibility of the salvific doing. As the parables produced a clarification of lived experience by reducing it to clear and speakable aims, the miracles produce at certain precise moments a reduction of the salvific doing to its *visible instrumentality* by calling attention to a competence which is beyond comparison. In both cases this reduction is obtained in a passage by way of a *fiction*. There is a kind of fiction which is produced by the doing and a fiction produced by a saying. "Fiction" is used here in the specific sense of a molding or shaping of a plastic figure. The fiction provides interpretation with the occasion for reducing the salvific doing in its entirety to this all-powerful instrumentality. But whereas the parables cast light upon a common *action* (the same performance in a variety of thematic roles), the miracles point to a common *competence* at work in the different kinds of performances: word, praxis, miracles. All three demand the intervention of an actor who has an exceptional power at his disposal. This very competence is thus at the source of the know-how-to-do, of a salvific doing or a miraculous doing, or rather the same divine nature of the competence. The miracle thus manifests the "difficult" character of the salvific act in its entirety. This is why the final miracle (that of the Cursing of the Fig Tree, Mark 11: 20-26; also cf. 9: 29) happens "to motivate" the need for prayer. This return to the divine sender indicates the source from which the salvific action springs and draws its strength.

3.3 *Conclusion*

The Gospel narrative, as is the case with every story, is the story of human actions, in this case the action of a principal subject: Jesus. But every action is the result of the conjunction of the saying with the doing. On the one hand the human doing necessarily puts human relations into play even to the point of its most material productions; and these human relations necessarily unfold in a world which always is and already has been interpreted. On the other hand, the word which anticipates the interpretation is itself through its natural performativity at the root of human relations. Thus, human action occurs in the coming together of speaking and doing. But the saying as well as the doing may at certain times be intensified to the point of appearing "to isolate themselves" from the action in which they are rooted. Parables and miracles as such represent within the Gospel story extrapolations of speaking as such and of doing as such. The saying and doing radiate from them, as it were, as if in a pure way. The one produces a singularly intelligible object; the other a tangible object. Both then create a *fiction* or a *work* which in some fashion or other stand alongside the action. They are complete creations in their own right. But both bring us back to the principal narrative which is hierarchically superior to them. Or rather, the action itself seizes them up again in its own dynamism. It is nourished by their contribution. Indeed, even though they are speaking effects, the parables are a discourse about better behavior: the action makes them the instruments of its correctness. As for the miracles, even though they are effects of power, they present an interpretative call which can find its resolution only in the designs of the "Kingdom." Thus, parables

and miracles are micro-narratives which recast the primary
narrative: the parables provide the primary narrative with
its meaning while receiving their performativity from the
latter; the miracles provide the primary narrative with its
instrumentality while receiving their meaning from it. Thus,
by making their way through these works (the parables and
miracles) the actors all at once become aware of the risks
and resources of their actions.

NOTES

1. Miracle stories and parables are therefore works
which call for interpretation. The primary narrative is
that which interprets. There are two kinds of interpretation: *cognitive* on the part of the miracles; *practical*
on the part of the parables.

2. In order to simplify the comparison, we shall limit
the study to the type of parable that we call "parabolic
stories," in contrast to the parables which are simple comparisons or examples or which come close to the genre of prov-
erbs and sayings.

3. In order to mark the semantic use that we will make
of the series of terms *historic* (or *real*) versus *fictive*, as
an opposition within the narrative, we will always italicize
them.

4. "Le contrat de véridiction," mimeographed text, pp.
4-5.

5. P. Ricoeur, "Herméneutique et critique des idéolo-
gies," in *Démythisation et idéologie* (Collective Work, Paris:
Aubier, 1973), p. 52.

6. We shall take virtually all of our examples from the
Gospel of Mark.

7. *Maupassant. La Sémiotique du texte: exercices pratiques* (Paris: Seuil, 1976), pp. 107-108, 121, 187-188. The
knowledge of a knowing subject may be modalized by doubt, sup-
position, plausibility, probability, conviction and certitude.

These modalities of knowledge form the set of values which are given the name *fiduciary values*. For this reason, we label the relation which is established by our interpretative doing between /appearing/ and /being/ a *fiduciary relation*. For the knowing subject, this relation is necessarily influenced by one of these modalities since it is neither an immediate fact nor a logically necessary conclusion.

8. Quoted by A. J. Greimas, *Ibid.*, p. 41.

9. *Performativity* is attributed to linguistic acts which are not content merely to assert what is the case but to say what they do and do it in the process of the saying: for example, in the act of saying, "I promise," *I in fact do promise* given the right situation.

10. For a more detailed study, we refer to a work by C. Chabrol and L. Marin, *Le Récit évangélique* (Paris: Aubier, 1974), Part II, pp. 93–164.

11. A. J. J. Cohen, "Réflexions sur le spectacle du sens dans le récit parabolique chez Matthieu," in *Le Récit évangélique*, edited by C. Chabrol and L. Marin, p. 142.

EPILOGUE

Toward a New Approach
to the Gospel Text

Where does the path that we have just taken lead us?
Why bother with a semiotic analysis of the Gospels? Questions of this sort have often been asked of us at the conclusions of our work sessions and bear witness to an unful-
filled desire: one would like to end up with a list of the
acquired and usable "results." One is accustomed to other
agendas, to other readings which are held to be of more
value. Rather than respond and risk placing the wrong accent upon our objectives, it is better to go back over the
steps that we have already taken. What is it that we have
accomplished?

1. ANOTHER ROUTE

Many of us have been trained in and have made application of historico-critical exegesis. It lies at the root
of an unquestionable renewal in the reading and study of the
Bible. It is honored by the widely accepted results which
are now disseminated in books, dictionaries and even in the
notes of recent translations of the Bible. Texts are set
once again in their literary and cultural contexts and echo
for us the questions and needs, the certitudes and hopes of
men who seem at one and the same time to be similar to and
different from us. The cultural difference which separates

them from us, a difference which is acknowledged by the historical perspective dominant in this research, makes the following hermeneutical problem unavoidable: can the "original" meaning of the texts become meaning for us today, and if so, how? Regardless of what one might think of Bultmann's program of demythologization, the debate over this question has drawn attention to the question of language, interpretation and meaning.

Similarly, in other areas of knowledge, human language has become the specific object of investigation. Linguistics has constructed models and offered them to other disciplines, and the study of language has led to the study of what it produces (discourse and text) from a perspective in which the problems of signification were posed in and for themselves. There should be nothing astonishing about the fact that exegetes have themselves begun to take an interest in a semiotic analysis of discourse. The discipline in which they are trained, philology, does not distinguish between the study of language and that of its literary works. What would our understanding of Hebrew or biblical Greek be without the knowledge of the writings of the Old and New Testaments? And even if the words and phrases of the text were not enough to consider, biblical scholars are beginning to concern themselves with the meaning of texts taken in their entirety. This concern had to be ventured one day or another following the route of discourse analysis. The temptation has overcome us in the form of Greimasian semiotics which has proved itself to be the most demanding practice and to have made the fewest concessions to our previous practices. We were forced to look for the roots of the meaning in the text.

In the Text

Throughout our analysis we have given up as a means
for understanding texts the asking of those questions that
bring us to know their author, time and original milieu.
We are not questioning their value or usefulness for any
investigation into meaning. But by placing parentheses
around this knowledge for the purpose of attempting an *immanent* analysis, we were forced to define a problematic
and to hold on to it. In wanting to make several methods
agree with one another too hastily, we run the risk of
forgetting that point of view which governs each method and
marks the boundaries of its application; we are kept from
testing the extent of its possibilities. It is clear that
the author, the time, the history and the world to which
the text refers present other problems and call for procedures outside of the text itself and the *textual* function
of the meaning.

The choice of an immanent analysis does not render
superfluous that exegetical work which is devoted to the
literary and cultural milieu of the text. On the basis of
their discursive configurations the text's literary and
cultural milieu point to a "language" that the encyclope-
dias or lexicons of biblical theology have explored and
detailed precisely on the basis of texts. Thus, the appearance of the robbers, a priest, a levite, a samaritan or
an innkeeper in the narrative scene situated somewhere between Jerusalem and Jericho points to a previously organized cultural code. The text breaks apart the order of
this organization and distributes the semantic values in
another way in the forms taken by these characters. By
being opposed to the language, the text marks the beginning

of another language: the contrast between priest or levite
and samaritan will in addition say something different from
the original language.

On the other hand, if we allow ourselves to be engrossed
in the socio-cultural world to which the text belongs or to
which it makes reference, we run the risk of overlooking the
interaction of elements which compose the textual *simulacrum*
of this world and determine the meaning. For example, a geo-
graphical knowledge of the "Sea of Galilee" and the surrounding area leads us to raise a certain kind of question in Mark
6, such as: how is it possible to go from one point to another more quickly by foot than by boat? We can sidestep the
question by appealing to the narrator's freedom or his lack
of knowledge about such places. Only an immanent analysis of
the topographical data in the text, which is treated as the
representation of semantic values which are to be identified,
enables us to cast light on the signifying function of the
land and the sea, the river and the mountain. Likewise, a
critical interest in the milieux where the fixed traditions
are shaped by the text is undeniable. But the meaning-effect
that is produced by placing Mark 6 in the context of a euchar-
istic celebration in the first century may conceal the semantic problem raised by the bread *and the fish* in this text.

To the Roots of Meaning

In addition to its being immanent, the semiotics that we
have adopted is also structural. Every oral or written discourse presupposes a structured system of relations which bestows a form upon these elements and makes the meaning possible. The elements are significant and may be described as
such only through the relations that exist between them. This
is a basic postulate. The discourse does not manifest its

structures; they must be exposed through a process of abstraction and with the aid of a theory. But this postulate enables us to describe and to explain what experience believes it receives as an immediate given, namely the meaning.[1]

The *form* about which we speak (must it be specified?) is not opposed to the "depth" or the "content" as in certain literary or exegetical discussions. In the latter instance, "form" is understood to mean a means of expression or a fixed cultural type of text (the "literary form") or the manner in which the means of expression are organized in view of a certain effect (and so one speaks of "literary structure"). By distinguishing between two planes, that of the *expression* (or signifier) and that of the *content* (or signified), we are admitting that both must be analyzed with the goal of making both of their forms appear. And we have already distinguished on the plane of the content itself several levels of formal articulation: the narrative, discursive and logico-semantic levels. The semiotic square has helped us to represent both the paradigmatic relations between the semic values represented at the discursive level and the logical operations which correspond to the transformations at the narrative level. We have tried to show as well from what deep organization the meaning of the analyzed texts emerged.[2]

This procedure has enabled us to discover a subtle architecture. The parable of the Good Samaritan and the parable of the Prodigal Son turn upon the debate which sets Jesus off against a lawyer, i. e., Jesus against the pharisees. We will no longer speak simply of an artificial or "secondary" connection between the episode of the Feeding of the Five Thousand and Jesus' Walk upon Water that can be attributed to Mark as if that were enough to account for it. The story of the meal and the lack of rest which introduce these pericopaes goes beyond the concern to provide an introduction which is called for by the necessity of having Jesus, the disciples and the crowd meet one another in the context of a desert forecast by a traditional story. Whatever the circumstances of the constitution of the text or the intentions of the redactor may be, its coherence arises most fundamentally from within. Similarly, the literary deconstruction that we are permitted to practice upon Luke 5: 1-11 in order to refer these elements back to their different sources and authors[3] shifts the attention away from the textual organization that, by contrast, places a value upon the relations of equivalence and transformation between the three segments as J. Geninasca has analyzed them.

A similar procedure would prove itself fruitful so as to appreciate the differences (and their semantic stake) among the variants of the biblical or Gospel text offered by the manuscript tradition, or even yet among the different readings that the Greek text and particularly the unpointed Hebrew text support and about which philology remains uncertain. The doublets and parallel versions of similar pericopaes which are to be found in the Gospels and in the entire Bible call for a similar treatment and invite us to compare their deep models.

The texts grouped together under a common "literary form" raise a noticeably different problem. With respect to the parables and miracle stories, we have seen that this type of collection does not necessarily provide a good point of departure for a semiotic study. The criteria which are used to compare them are not the same as those which would permit us to describe them semiotically. Semiotics forces us to reexamine the structures which are more elementary than that which we call the literary form. Research into these structures and the interest in their procedures of meaning production enable us to compare and to characterize these texts in a new way with respect to their basic differences, texts that common sense would tend to oppose to one another. The same attention could be paid to the biblical texts gathered together in collections under a common literary form in many recent works (oracles, laments, "mashals," judicial proceedings, etc.).

Finally, the commentaries that the Gospels and the Bible constantly generate offer semiotics a privileged terrain for analyzing and defining interpretative discourse. They no longer give the impression of being an indistinct mass or a forest given over to the caprice of nature when they are considered on the basis of their code, as compared to that of the text commented upon. It is the case that a deep model which is held in common governs both the text and its commentaries; no text ever exhausts the resources of the model.[4] We find here something which goes beyond the restrictive limits of the research into sources or literary influences and whose criteria frequently lack precision.

2. ANOTHER RELATION TO THE TEXT

After the Text

The Gospels, indeed the whole Bible, are frequently read as the traces of their authors' intentions. It happens that along with the genesis of the written work is introduced the communication of meaning from the time of the wanting-to-say of the author to his original readers. This original communication is oftentimes given as an example, indeed as a "norm," for the appropriation of meaning by today's readers.

Rather than retrace what went on before the text, semiotic analysis defines its position with respect to what comes after. We are the ones who are performing the analysis and the task before us does not lend support to the claim that meaning is imposed as a fact to be received nor that the worker leaves his tools in the shade.

The Process of Reading and Semiotics

The position of the reader and his activity before the
text are largely acknowledged today in "new approaches" taken
toward the Bible. In contrast to historical exegesis which
is accused of mummifying the meaning, and in contrast to those
interpretations which are based upon an incorporation of the
original receivers and the present readers of the Scriptures,
we claim that there is a difference between past and present
and that we make the text work in different "ways."[5] Is meaning not multiple in nature and is the interpretation not relative to the place from which one speaks?

How do we situate semiotics within the variety of readings and analyses possible? It begins by withdrawing itself.
Reading *performances* are multiplied ad infinitum in that they
are repeated and they open up new pathways. This fact could
give rise to a psychology, a sociology and a phenomenology of
reading. To opt for the semiotic point of view is to ask oneself about the power-to-read: the story of the Abundant Catch
can be read as a comedy which is about a fisherman who unfortunately caught too many fish; the parable of the Prodigal Son
as the abortive murder of the father; the dividing up of the
bread and fish among 5,000 men as the refusal to accept money
which affects the products having an exchange value and the
restoration of their use value.[6] Every reading is the product
of a discourse which starts from a text. However, this operation is the exercise of a *competence,* and this is what is of
interest to semiotics. Semiotics asks itself what are the
codes of this discourse and what relations exist between them
and the codes at work in the text. In the examples which were
just given it appears that the models which control the reading manifest a selective organization of the text. The latter

offers a surplus for other readings.

We must not expect semiotics to define the best possible reading. Each reading defines its own criteria for determining what is good and bad, true and false, with all of the nuances of what is certain, probable and plausible. Philology has its own criteria just as interpretative readings (theological, philosophical, Marxist, etc.) have theirs. These criteria both point to an organization of values and authorize truth operations. Semiotics does not have to provide a value judgment for them; it simply exposes them and compares them to those values and truth operations of the read text.

However, is the semiotician himself not first and foremost a reader? It is true that he reads and rereads the text which he analyzes many times in order to formulate and to verify his hypotheses. He is characterized by his concern for comprehensiveness which guides his readings in the investigation of an organization which articulates the whole text. Above all, he does not open up a new path towards the interpretation so much as he tests the reading itself by questioning the power-to-read of the text under examination concerning its power-to-speak. "New" readings stimulate the semiotician in his questioning. But he is concerned with describing the text for the text's sake; it is the text's signifying work that he is concerned to describe.

These theoretical definitions do not function as a model for reading. The latter demands of them the capacity to represent the signifying text as such. Thus, by addressing the text on the basis of a theory of text which is either to be validated or invalidated, semiotic analysis is endowed with a competence which is sufficient enough to give it its distinctiveness. The properly interpretative readings avail themselves of another competence which has also to be constructed and asserted. But their concern for the "real" or the "true" which the language either reveals or conceals must take into account along with it the real that is original, fascinating and difficult to grasp--the order of language. By placing the text at a distance from its readings so as to evaluate the semantic transformations between the text and its readings, semiotics exposes the process of reading and learns to keep a close watch over the discourse which it inspires.

The Semiotic "Doing"

By distinguishing between a semiotic and an interpretative reading in their relationship to the text, we do not claim any special privilege for our analysis. Being subject to criticism even within the semiotic that we authorize for ourselves, our analyses themselves also represent a work of the text and indicate an apprenticeship. There is nothing mechanical about this process. It is worthwhile to insist upon this point, for perhaps one will find a mechanical atmosphere about our models which lack any spirit and which constrain the reading and disregard the intuition, the creativity of the reader. On the contrary, the semiotic doing requires imagination. Theoretical concepts force us to look carefully. The relations out of which the text is woven and the pertinent semantic categories do not offer themselves up to the analyst. In order to discern them he must oftentimes introduce a variant: that is, he must imagine a counter-text. But intuition is not appealed to as the miraculous source of an original reading or an impressive commentary. It merely suggests a hypothesis--to expose the text in the form of a model and then verify it by returning to the text.

This procedure is both deductive and inductive. With the semiotic square, for instance, it is not a matter of forcing the text into a logical schema which is defined in purely a priori terms. The relations are defined in advance within the square, but the text decides which terms are to be recorded and ultimately remains the master of the business of selecting from among the possibilities presented by this organization. It would be a mistake to think that semiotics as a method moves from the particular--this text--to the general or "universal" (the structures of any story, the abstract categories). It aims for a deductive theory of discourse, but its analyses are practiced only upon specific discourses. These latter constitute the "reality" which is infinitely complex and varied in its manifestations, that semiotics explores. It can advance only by taking into account the plane of the manifestation and its work has meaning only if it enables us to render an account of it.[7]

Experience shows that the task is never complete. It also shows its pedagogical value. Far from being reserved for a few initiates, a study with a semiotic orientation lends itself readily to group research and favors the activity of the participants. Another relation is established between expert and beginner, for no one holds the keys to the text. It becomes impossible to rely upon memory of it and to apply to the passage under study what was otherwise learned about the author (his theology or the preoccupations of his time). The analytical tools do not give us any answers; they help us only if we make use of them by putting them to work in the text. Narrative programs, roles and isotopies are to be built. And in principle, every person is able to do this since he knows how to tell stories and to engage in discourse, and since he carries within him this logic of language which enables him to read and write.

At the outset, experimentation with the models leads to certain problems. There is a great temptation to use them as schemas which are to be found in the texts. We progressively

discover their nature as instruments for constructing our
relationship to the text. Meanwhile, and before even having
tasted success, restrictive views of the meaning have been
abandoned. This text segment has begun to speak in relation
to other texts and the field of reading is enlarged. Victory
has been won over what lures us into racing through the text
without giving it time to resist.

3. OPEN QUESTIONS

Along the way our analyses have succeeded in raising
questions to which we have not been able (or have not wanted)
to respond. We would have been too hasty or too pretentious
within the limits of this work. These questions still remain.
Either semiotics enables us to see them in a new light or they
appear at its borders with other domains.

Enunciation

For example, we have not sufficiently examined the enunciation in the texts we have studied. If we appeared to downplay the issue of their authors or original readers, it could
be understood that this was done in order to avoid investing
the analysis with data taken from other discourses. For it
is clear especially in the case of our texts that the author
about whom we speak is a character constructed out of and on
the basis of procedures which are not those of semiotics. On
the other hand, the written work is distinguished from oral
discourse, among other reasons, by the way in which it is
separated from the communication between sender and receiver.
The author disappears and is removed for the sake of what he
writes in the absence of the reader and the text becomes accessible to every competent reader. He offers a "world" of

meaning, at a distance from the "real world" and disconnected from its original context. By his very presence he signals the moment of production and the moment of reading and interpretation which makes the communication possible.

On occasion we have indicated that the structure of a text presupposes a moment of structuration. It penetrates the levels of the text that we have distinguished: through the actualization of the models, the distribution of positive and negative values, the orientation of the transformations of content, the construction of figures and the organization of the plane of the manifestation. This moment builds the competence which is necessary for reading and understanding. It is in this way that we have inquired in Luke 10 as to how the narrative defines its receiver by delineating a post which is assumed by the reader.

There is much to be investigated on this topic by way of an immanent analysis. Pointing to the "enunciative markers" is not enough. The relationship between statements and the enunciating subject may be sharpened with the aid of the notions of *débrayage* and *embrayage* ("shifters") proposed by A. J. Greimas.[8] This investigative track that he opens up could also be of benefit for the biblical text where interpolation and persuasion are practiced in a thousand not-so-obvious ways.

The operational value of the notion of *intertextuality* would also have to be tested as well as the relationships of transformation that can exist between the texts. We would have to go into detail as to the conditions of a discourse upon the social enunciation of texts, which are not to be identified with the social (economic, political, ideological) conditions of their production. The extent of the questions justifies in a certain way that we limit the research in order to advance cautiously where control is possible.

History

One should not try to oppose to our immanent analysis
the importance of the history to which the texts refer, a
history upon which they depend and within which they intervene. This importance is underscored in a vigorous way when
we come to the Gospels or to the rest of the Bible: is the
faith that they express not a witness to and interpretation
of the "foundational" facts? The development of another
textual dimension does not imply that this question be ignored. By referring to an exceptional past event and by
having clothed it with a meaning that the historians have
restored, these writings are not any the less readable and
meaningful for the present; for texts are separated from
their source and continue to provoke readings and interpretations. The demand for interpretation and the competence
to do this inscribed within the text open up the future.
Far from threatening the historical condition of the written
work, the immanent analysis, which brings to view the demand
for interpretation and competence, respects the historical
condition. An immanent analysis does not reflect history,
it produces it.

As for the referential dimension of the text, to be
specific about the problematic involved, it would not be
superfluous to analyze this within the philological and
historical discourse to which the Gospels give rise. This
would be a good example of the way in which semiotics views
the problematic.[9]

Hermeneutics

Hermeneutics is sometimes understood in too vague a fashion as the act of "translating" or "actualizing" in the present the message of past texts. For the Gospels, the historical point of view which keeps them temporarily at a distance favored "taking up" the meaning again through an existential interpretation of human experience. More commonly, we seek to bridge that temporal and cultural distance by playing upon the analogies of the situations: "It is very much the same thing, at base, that we live when ..."

Semiotics analysis today removes the text from its readings. The power-to-read that it gives back corresponds to the faculty which the texts possess in giving rise to speech, by virtue of the models that no discourse can ever exhaust. It is here that the interpretative inventiveness which discovers new variations in these models is rooted.

On the other hand, hermeneutical reflection develops the original "world" that the written work opens up before it.[10] This world of meaning calls for interpretation. A hermeneutic takes place when a semantic universe is interpreted within a context, whether it be contemporaneous or not with the work itself. Historical discourse about the texts poses the same hermeneutical problem as does their "actualization." By circumscribing the interpretative moment within the text, semiotics mediates the interpretation in a more radical way than does any historical reading.

Exegesis

As is the case with the exegesis of classical texts, biblical exegesis usually operates at the intersection of several disciplines (textual criticism, philology, source criticism, historical criticism, etc.). Occasionally, it believes itself to be threatened by semiotics, but it is the case that semiotics is invited to collaborate by taking its place within the plurality of methods.

If it is true that semiotic analysis opens up the text and makes reading possible, it could not but have repercussions for exegesis. But it would be a misunderstanding of the semiotic task to expect that it would help clarify one or the other specific feature of the text. On the one hand, it is concerned with the meaning on the basis of that which makes it possible and would not be able to take the place of the exegetical procedures. The connecting link between the semiotic doing and the exegetical procedures is worth examining if we wish to avoid confusing their domains and competencies. On the other hand, semiotics is introduced in order to investigate exegetical discourse itself. In this way, and without pretending to supply it with something to say, semiotics helps us to see what exegetical discourse does when it speaks. If the pressing need is to establish "an exegesis resting upon a renewed problematic" and to test a theory of reading,[11] then semiotics is already making its contribution.

Not in Conclusion

Many questions remain to be answered.[12] In a sense they bear witness to the interest in the semiotic task. It is not only the route which is changing; the scenery is replaced even in the most frequented and familiar regions. Semiotics opens up new points of view.

The illustrations that we have given of a particular semiotic doing would not be satisfactory if it were a matter simply of tallying up our research or of deciding upon what semiotics is capable of bringing to the study of the Gospels. What was important was to travel down the road and to advance to the point where once having overcome the initial difficulties, other difficulties present themselves, thus justifying the set of tools which was borrowed at the beginning without yet clearly knowing what was to be done with them.

In closing, if it were necessary to recall the elements in the study which particularly captured our attention, we would have to think of the resistance that we have met in the texts themselves. Their narrative organization is more subtle than we expected of texts which are said to be popular in nature. The cognitive dimension constantly interferes here with the link between events and somatic behavior. It duplicates the action by means of an interpretative doing which follows them or installs within the story a fictional scene within the narration in which other actions take place. The problems of competence and the manipulations of the modalities (want, power, know-how) appear particularly insistant whereas the object of value in the global program dissolves into the form of various figures which at first are difficult to define. As for the isotopies, the variety of figures (actors, doings on different planes, places, times) make the identification of isotopies a sensitive if not problematic task. The axiological valorization appears more clearly but it can give rise to subtle transformations by the interplay of the different points of view of different actors (as for instance, in Luke 15).

The effect of the contrast, which we could easily expand into a commentary, between the parabolic narratives and the miracle stories, quite clearly illustrates the complexity of the Gospel text. It escapes any simplified schemas. But after all sorts of readings, the Gospel text remains open.

NOTES

1. "What is perceived as meaning may be described as form": Ivan Almeida, *L'opérativité sémantique des récits-parables. Sémiotique narrative et textuel. Herméneutique du discours religieux* (Unpublished Ph. D. dissertation; Louvain: Institute Superieur de Philosophie, 1976).

2. J. Geninasca names and orders the levels that he distinguishes in another way. Upon the textual continuum he superimposes a *discursive level* articulated in very discrete units. The observable parallelisms (linguistic and/or thematic) serve to assure the correct establishment of the relation of semantic equivalences which hold, hypothetically, between the different discursive units. The narrativity is a function of the oriented semantic differences (called transformations) which affect the contents when we pass from one discursive unit to another. In order to analyze these transformations, Geninasca conceives of a *figurative level* of processes and actors of which he distinguishes two representations: the *thematic representation* that the text provides (in terms of actions and precise qualifications, characters, etc.) and the *semantic representation* which is built in accordance with its *functional* and *semic* components.

3. Cf. J. Delorme, "Luk 5, 1-11: Analyse structurale et histoire de la rédaction," *New Testament Studies* 18 (1972), 331-350.

4. Cf. L. Panier, *Récit et commentaire de la Tentation de Jésus au désert. Approche sémiotique des discours interprétatifs* (Unpublished Ph. D. dissertation; Paris: Écoles des Hautes Études en Sciences Sociales, 1976).

5. Cf. F. Refoule, "L'exégèse en question," *Le Supplément* 111 (1974), 391-423.

6. Cf. F. Belo, *Lecture matérialiste de l'évangile de Marc* (Paris: Cerf, 1974), p. 331.

7. Cf. A. J. Greimas, *Sémiotique et sciences sociales* (Paris: Seuil, 1976), p. 15 (with regard to the linguist).

8. See the use that Greimas makes of this and the distinction that he introduces in *Maupassant* (references are

given in the Index to the word "débrayage").

9. See Greimas, *Sémiotique et sciences sociales*, especially pp. 22-23.

10. Cf. P. Ricoeur in *Exegesis. Problèmes de méthode et exercices de lecture*, edited by F. Bovon and G. Rouiller (Delachaux, 1975), pp. 179-228.

11. P. Beauchamp, "État et méthodes de l'exégèse," *Esprit* (April, 1973), 843-858 (especially pp. 853-and 857).

12. Is it necessary still to conjure up the problem of the historical situation of semiotics and semioticians? The relation of semiotics with ideology? Its relation with the believer's interpretation of religious texts?

POSTFACE

by A. J. GREIMAS

An encounter as unexpected as that taking place between
semiotics which proclaims its scientific vocation and a text,
the Gospels, which itself refers in one way or another to the
moment of faith! How are we in fact to explain their mutual
and long-lasting interest in one another, of semiotics for
biblical studies and biblical studies for semiotics?

The fact is that semiotics, at least as we conceive it,
is first and foremost a state of mind before it is a method.
It is an ethic which expresses the demand for rigor both with
respect to itself and to others; this is a condition of the
effectiveness both for its own doing and for the transmissi-
bility of knowledge that it enables us to acquire. It is
these underlying features that the semiotician recognizes on
the part of the Gospel readers. They account for the marriage
of convenience (in the loftiest sense of the term) which was
entered into right away in the earliest days of semiotics.
They account as well for the exceptional contribution that
religious semiotics is making to discursive semiotics as a
whole.

Since it is a matter of mutual agreement, we obviously
can ask ourselves what both parties gain--or hope to gain--
from this collaboration with one another. It is to this
question, indeed much more as a beneficiary than as a contri-
butor, that we will attempt to respond by referring back frequently to the collection of studies we have just read.

First of all, semiotics offers the biblical scholar a meta-language which has a neutral value, that is a way of speaking about the text while being removed from it. Semiotics gives the appearance of being an empty jargon; but it is quite easily learned and is especially unavoidable. It enables this discourse about discourse to be distinguished from its textual object. In addition, it makes it possible to maintain the univocal nature of its terminology and the verifiable coherence of its discourse. This neutrality enables us to avoid the metaphorical transpositions and changes which continually make appeal to the reader by rendering apparent his own ideological positions adorned to suit the tastes of the day before even taking into consideration the potential richness of the text. In other words, the proper use of the semiotic metalanguage affords the possibility for making the text speak by suppressing to as great an extent as possible the parasitic mediation which attempts to worm its way in between the message and its receiver.

Contrary to certain present tendencies, the semiotic approach does not pretend to offer a singular nor especially a definitive reading. Imperfect as it is with respect to the tools it seeks to perfect, it admits from the start to the principle of the plurality of possible readings, not so much for the reason that the text is ambiguous, but that it is capable of saying several things at once. While merely asking to make use of what has been gained from philological and historical investigation, semiotics refuses to consider them the *ultima ratio* for its own activities. Making the text speak consists, in the first instance, in avoiding an explanation which refers to something other than the text. Before taking up the historical question, for example, it would be worthwhile to make certain that history itself is explained.

In the final analysis what is a method of reading if it does not teach us to read, to locate behind the letters which blacken the paper this other thing that we call the meaning? A method must not teach *what* must be read but *how* it must be read in order to be prepared at any moment to face the unknown and unexpected. Semiotic reading, which is rigorous with respect to this "how," states that it is not responsible for the read content (the "what"). This does not mean that everyone is permitted to make his own way within the text, to find within the text his obsessions, presuppositions and habits. By taking itself as a heuristic device, semiotics states the game rules which supposedly guarantee the real presence of the text and enable the reader not to be reflected in it but rather to recreate it.

The semiotician's interest in a work such as this is two-fold: it bears at once upon the text and the meta-text which analyzes it. The Gospels possess the peculiar feature of manifesting within the apparent simplicity of daily life stories (textual organizations which semiotics is supposed to be the best equipped to handle) a constant underlying concern for the question of the necessary conditions for a certain and assured transmission of the "Good News," a fundamental and by no means resolved problem for any theory of language. Every factual and pragmatic sequence thus appears subject to a second reading which is situated in the cognitive sphere, and the most ordinary description of the stories requires the creation of an otherwise complex mechanism for its reading. The immediate impression of mastery over the text through an accumulated know-how-to-do gives way quickly to an unquenchable curiosity that makes it one of the privileged places of present-day research.

Consequently, we can see that the analyses which are brought together here are not to be considered as applications of semiotic methods upon a particular domain, but as research which is representative of semiotics as it is being practiced. As a result, what we will have to say concerns both semiotic theory and practice.

Among the difficulties inherent in the rapid development of this approach and in the strategy of this newly emerging research which had to be adjusted to fit it (e. g., the necessity for constructing a theory which is hypothetico-deductive in nature and which has had to undergo a partial development and verification), we must single out the problem of the connection between what some persons call the macro- and the micro-structures of a text. Our understanding of narrativity enables us to project upon a large enough text the global narrative schema which supposedly accounts for its essential articulations. However, this general model remains largely hypothetical as long as it is not validated by rooting these constructs in the manifested text at each one of its steps. While semiotic praxis "knows how to do" a syntactic analysis as well as a semantic analysis of mini-narratives or autonomous sequences, a methodological gap is immediately apparent between both types of textual organizations on account of these very same advances.

One of the purposes shared by several chapters in this collection is to bridge this gap. This can be seen quite clearly: if the ultimate objective remains the reading of the entire text in all of its articulations and at all of the pertinent levels, tactical procedure requires that we proceed in a step-by-step fashion while seeking to establish beyond the micro-narratives and the dialogue scenes the intermediary discursive units that are larger than the macro-sequences. This is a promising methodological innovation.

The obstacle to be overcome when wanting to identify and establish these unities comes first of all from the diversity of discursive organizations to be found at the surface, the juxtapositions and dove-tailing of segments traditionally known as "stories," "dialogues" and "descriptions" through which the discursive unit that we seek to mark off appears, for example, either as a dialogue which is prolonged in a story or a story in turn developed into dialogue, etc. These surface discursive mechanisms, which obviously constitute a distinct object of study, must be exposed in order to allow for the deepest structural relations guaranteeing the permanence of the text to appear. It is for this reason that the dialogue situation which puts Jesus in opposition to the pharisees and which at first appears to be a referential and "primary" situation consequently loses this privileged status and appears within the discursive units ultimately constituted as one figurative isotopy among others, readable in the same way as the pastoral isotopy (the Lost Sheep) or the familial isotopy (the Prodigal Son). Similarly, Walking on Water is to be read in one of its functional significations as an oblique response, albeit implicitly a negative one, with regard to the Apostles' returning from their mission.

As we know, the consequences of the procedures leading to the establishment of textual macro-sequences are not un-important. If their unity is based only upon the coherence of the signification beyond the variations at the discursive levels it is of little import then that the enunciator by seeking to produce the signification constructs stories about events (feasts, miracles) or stories of words (parables): it is of little import that he will make use of somatic or verbal language, respectively, as a *modus significandi*. Both types of stories must be read in the first instance as meaningful,

textual organizations. This does not mean that the problem
of veridiction does not arise in the course of the reading;
rather, it presents itself elsewhere than at the level of the
discursive surface. As a result of the penetration of one
discursive level into another, the more or less full "truth"
of a segment is dependent upon its position in relation to
the other segments. Each hierarchically superior level has
the effect of "referentializing" the lower level (the dialogue which is inserted into the narrative referentializes
the latter; the "fictive" story which is developed on the
basis of the dialogue renders the dialogue situation "real").
The signification of a text and its truth constitute two
separate problems.

Enlarging the discursive units has repercussions at a
deeper level, namely that of the narrative syntax. If the
technique for constructing narrative programs and elaborating
more complex programs by integrating what we call the secondary programs appears to be easily in hand, then an entire
inter-programmatic, relational network makes its appearance
and calls for a methodological treatment which is far from
being established. Upon learning of Jesus' and his disciples'
movement by boat, the crowd (a knowing subject) is transformed
into a subject with a wanting-to-do and runs ahead on foot.
Here, then, is the crowd's autonomous narrative program. When
Jesus (a knowing subject) becomes aware of this program, he is
"filled with compassion" and reacts to it by transforming this
subject which was only a virtual intentionality into a realized subject of state through his instruction. Here is a very
clear example of the clash of narrative programs and we could
cite many other instances of the same phenomenon. How naive
are those persons who think that the simple amplification of
the inventory of proppian functions, or a limited number of
these functions, exhausts the problematic of the discourse's

narrative organization. The analyses offered here, on the contrary, show that it is at the level of the manipulation of programs, of their connection with one another, of their derivation and overlapping, that the real problems of the narrativity appear and so reflect the complexity of inter-human relationships.

The disruptions undergone by the narrative programs necessarily affect the reading of the significations that they articulate. An independent reading of the parable of the Prodigal Son, for example, is in part weakened and superseded by its insertion into a much larger context. The recognition of this larger context implies a total rereading. We can distinguish roughly between two sorts of pre-texts for these readings. One type of pre-text is syntagmatic in nature. Walking upon Water may be read as an expected and almost necessary consequence of the pericope of the Feeding of the Five Thousand which as a performance by Jesus is intended as a glorifying syntagm. The recognition of Jesus who remains alone on top of the mountain takes place in a secretive way. We can anticipate that he will be proclaimed on the level of appearance. That would be the role of the miracle story (either a miracle which he refuses to perform or which is misunderstood due to the incompetence of the subject-receiver). Other re-readings are solicited for paradigmatic reasons. This is the case with those discursive units which are developed as a succession of parables, as variations upon the same theme, which we can superimpose one upon another and which yield consequently to a single reading.

Furthermore, the Gospel text appears as the strategically privileged place of methodological reflection upon the ways in which pluri-isotopic discourse functions. The advantage that the mechanism which produces the parables in a syntagmatic succession offers as over against, for example, a symbolist poet who fuses together several isotopies into a single textual manifestation, is that of simplicity, or rather let us say of progressive complexity. It is as if in the presence of the comparable parabolic narrative, it was sufficient to effect a blurred application of one discursive configuration upon another in order to obtain a more precise complementary application of the latter parable. Thus, the story of the Abundant Catch examined by J. Geninasca may be considered as a discursive expansion of the process of "catching fish" that can be applied to another process of a similar sort, namely "catching men," so that the sub-articulations of the expanded process can be explained within the framework of a condensed process. A closer examination of the overlapping of the process of "teaching" and "feeding" in the narrative of the Feeding of the Five Thousand shows however, that the establishment of the appropriated actantial structure provides the starting point for just such an application. It is the presence in both parallel narrative programs of an object of value transmitted by the sender to the receiver and the partial semic identity of the two values (the nourishment being interpreted axiologically as "that which is badly needed") which constitutes the mechanism for connecting both isotopies and authorizes the passage from one to the other.

The situation becomes more complex when it is no longer simply a matter of two superimposing isotopies (where the one isotopy located upon the cognitive dimension and for this reason considered to be hierarchically superior to the pragmatic isotopy may be said to be fundamental and to receive supplemental information provided by the other), but instead when we have multiple isotopies which have a similar discursive expansion and whose hierarchic relations are not obvious. This is particularly the case with the parabolic block capped by the story of the Prodigal Son. The five isotopies--socio-religious (the publicans and sinners), pastoral (the sheep), monetary (the coin), familial (the prodigal son) and heavenly (the sinners and angels)--which are spread throughout the text and partially dove-tailed (with the "feast" playing the role of connector) must be reduced in principle to a single reading as a consequence of a back and forth reading between isotopies and a reading back into the text.

The procedure for applying one discursive configuration to another (to which we have paid only slight attention) encounters an initial difficulty due to the fact that all of the reading isotopies are pragmatic and figurative. How then are we to choose a basic isotopy upon which all of the others are founded? For instance, once having performed the "reflexive transformation"

/X has lost the sheep/ => /the sheep becomes lost/

this story about the sheep may be read in terms of the isotopy of the prodigal son, but the reverse is equally possible. The famine and false sender of the lost son may be translated in terms of the hunger which the sheep suffers and bad grass which attracts him. A new difficulty is added by the fact that the transformation at issue cannot be applied semantically to the lost coin. Not only do the different configurations possess different narrative dimensions, they also operate from opposite points of view (the story of the Lost Coin deals with a searching subject and not the lost object, whereas the story of the Prodigal Son in its expanded form focuses on the problematic of the alienated subject). It is as if in order to account for the ensemble of discursive configurations, a new, abstract isotopy has to be constructed which while being based upon an underlying actantial structure would enable us to display all of the configurations involved by laying them out in the form of a cluster whose leaves are of unequal dimensions. The actantial structure which would accept all of the investments contained in diverse configurations could, for example, be that of the communication which brings the subject whose goal is conjunction face to face with the subject who submits to disjunction. This is a structure which is to be seen in the axiological organization of the content and is characterized by the oppositions of the schemas /affinity/ *vs.* /distinctiveness/ which thus renders comparable sequences as different from one another as the miracle of the Feeding of the Five Thousand and the parable of the Prodigal Son precisely because they are situated along the same isotopy.

The difficulties that this complex problem raises for a proper reading of the parables and pluri-isotopic texts in general only goes to illustrate the as yet uncertain state of our knowledge with respect to the organization of the semantic component of the discourse in its totality. The analysis by J. Geninasca provides an interesting attempt to fill the lacunae of a discursive analysis *stricto-senso* by introducing the procedures of the text's temporalization (that is where the figurative trajectories under consideration as processes are analyzed in terms of temporal series owing to the use of aspectual categories) and in those of its spatialization. He seeks to build in a somewhat less convincing way the network of formal relations between the different positions or *loci* of the text. There is no longer any doubt that the spatial mechanism which is put to the service of the textual organization plays an important role as has been shown in many in-depth studies, particularly in the area of biblical texts. At present in the current stage of research, overall solutions are unfortunately still difficult to catch sight of.

It is much more interesting to note a new approach to this problem in the analysis of the sequence containing the Walk upon Water. Here, different types of movements (by boat, on foot) are considered as metonyms for the places (sea, land) where they occur. They point ultimately to the elementary figurative structure of the universe by showing Jesus' movements to be the denial of the /distinctiveness/ of the elements constitutive of nature and the assertion of their /affinity/. Spatial articulation thereby becomes an independent figurative language which is homologous with the semiotic square that organizes the deep structures of the content.

Though it appears secondary, one consequence emerges from such an interpretation of spatiality: within the framework so constituted the Walk upon Water ceases to be an accidental manifestation selected in a haphazard way by some supernatural power-to-do. Rather, its purpose is to enter into the logic of the discourse itself in a half-foreseeable manner. In order to bring about separation, aquatic space is selected as the place of disjunction. By taking the terrestrial route and passing the test, the crowd negates the domination of the sea with its feature of /distinctiveness/. Therefore, Jesus' terrestrial movement upon aquatic space appears as the assertion of universal /affinity/. Be that as it may, we have here an example of a convincing procedure that semiotics can propose to the reader.

A new problem arises and is brought out into the open when we examine the relation existing between the thematic roles and thematic trajectories which, in principle, should only be that of a syntagmatic expansion. The Gospel text is populated with characters who in the fashion of popular stories are pure thematic roles: publicans and samaritans, fathers and sons, shepherds and sheep are individuals only to the extent that they are given thematic roles in terms of which

they are named and from whom a certain kind of behavior is
expected (their figurative trajectories), behavior which
conforms to their semantic nature and which is fixed once
and for all. But in contrast to what takes place in the
proppian story, Gospel characters often act in a way which
is counter to their presumed thematic "being." It is as
if this "being" were only an "appearance" and the action
much more than their being revelatory of their true nature.
Consequently, if the Gospel establishes a taxonomy of characters with each being responsible to his own role, in the
final analysis it is only for the purpose of producing thematic trajectories which do not conform to what is anticipated. On the basis of these trajectories the reader easily
recreates the new role which characterizes them. The text
has "worked" as we would say today. It is this type of work
which is described in this collection and defined as the
recategorization of thematic roles.

Different analyses contained within this collection
bring to light another characteristic of the Gospel text.
Contrary to what takes place in the proppian tales and in
simple stories such as, for example, Maupassant's *Deux Amis*,
the narrative programs which are developed here and which
are taken up by the subjects in apparent opposition to one
another, are for the most part not contradictory. Jesus,
for it is with him that we are concerned, as subject refuses
to regard his opponents as an anti-subject and to consider
the program that the latter intends to establish as contradictory to his own. Both of the given narrative programs
are parallel and incompatible but not contradictory with one
another. The example of loving the neighbor will make our
comments more concrete. Jesus is not opposed to the program
of "loving the neighbor" as prescribed by the Law; he only
says that this is not the point here. It is not a matter of

the choice as to who the object "neighbor" is, but rather
of the competence of the "loving" subject. In a general
way we can say that Jesus' response always remains oblique;
it falls outside of the anticipated taxonomic framework.
The place from which Jesus speaks is an elsewhere which is
not to be identified with the space where the old values
are ordered.

When we wish as a next step to put together an abstract
representation of these shifting narrative programs by placing them (after they have been translated) onto the semiotic
square and thereby providing an account of the structure of
signification governing the text, we can give them the form
of two criss-crossed schemas taking the form of /adapted/ *vs.*
/overadapted/ or /determined/ *vs.* /overdetermined/. However,
we see very clearly that when considered in and of themselves,
these oppositions are not contradictories, but like the thematic roles that the discourse recategorizes, they become contradictories only as a result of the textual process which
organizes them through the unfolding of its own proper logic.

An organization of the structures of signification such
as this enables us to place the Gospel text (from a formal
point of view apart from any consideration being given to the
invested content) in the class of innovative discourse. Con-
servative discourse, as represented, for example, by the marvelous Russian folktale, supports a semantic micro-universe
and articulates it by means of a series of logical operations
which are located within the semiotic square in such a way
that the trajectory created by the text aims at returning to
the initial *deixis* and reestablishing beyond the axiological
disorder the former values. Mythical discourse as defined by
C. Lévi-Strauss selects for itself its own axis of contraries
somewhat in the manner of our text. However, the narrativiza-
tion of its elementary structures leads only to an overcoming

of the contradictions and hints only at the possible co-
existence of contraries (of one or several contraries, for
example) by means of the double assertion of a complex category. To the extent that we can evaluate it on the basis of
the first two chapters of this work, Gospel discourse invests
the schemas of the semiotic square with two incompatible categories not for the purpose of dissolving their antimony, but
rather in order to bring about the passage which enables us
to found a new axiological *deixis*. Thus, to take up once
again the example we have used, the negation of /distinctive-
ness/ permits as a result of the appearance of the term /non-
distinctiveness/ the projection of a new trajectory which will
find /affinity/ as its complementary term and so establish the
deixis upon which the new Gospel values are located and recategorized.

Though our formulation may appear pedantic by dint of our
desire to be precise, it ought not to hide the stakes involved
in making such a claim. We sought to explain in an admittedly
allusive way what the analyses in this collection suggest:
namely, a new hypothesis, a way of reading the doing and the
saying of Jesus. Even a superficial reading of the Gospel
brings to light the existence of two worlds and the communication between the two appears all but impossible not so much
because they are squarely opposed to one another as that they
do not speak the same language. The task of making another
discourse understood and of establishing an actualized communication seems to be the "formal" concern which governs the
production of the Gospel texts considered here.

SYMBOLS AND NOTATIONS

≃   :   equivalence

∧   :   conjunction

∨   :   disjunction

vs.   :   versus,
           opposed to

=> :   transformative
        doing

—> :   direction of
        an operation
        of transformation

// :   setting forth of a
       semantic value; cf.
       p. 57 n. 14.

INDEX OF TERMS AND IDEAS